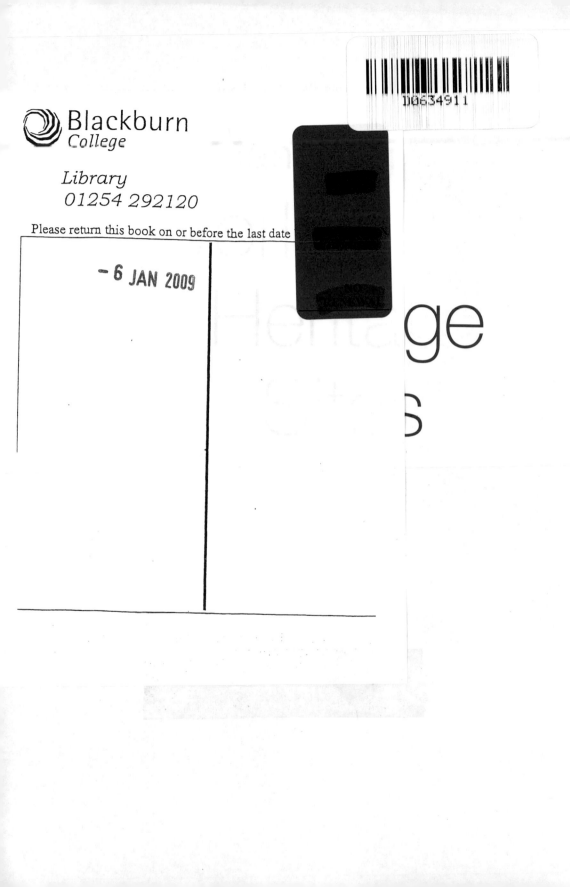

Blackburn
College

Library
01254 292120

Please return this book on or before the last date

- 6 JAN 2009

ge

s

For Mum and Dad (Anna Leask)

For Alix and Elliot (Alan Fyall)

Managing World Heritage Sites

Edited by

**Anna Leask
and
Alan Fyall**

ELSEVIER

AMSTERDAM • BOSTON • HEIDELBERG • LONDON • NEW YORK • OXFORD
PARIS • SAN DIEGO • SAN FRANCISCO • SINGAPORE • SYDNEY • TOKYO
Butterworth-Heinemann is an imprint of Elsevier

Butterworth-Heinemann is an imprint of Elsevier
Linacre House, Jordan Hill, Oxford OX2 8DP
30 Corporate Drive, Suite 400, Burlington, MA 01803, USA

First edition 2006

BLACK. EGE
L.

Acc. No. BB 11377
HSC 790.069
Class No. 790.069
Date 18 10 9 09 LEF

Copyright © 2006 Elsevier Ltd. All rights reserved

No part of this publication may be reproduced, stored in a retrieval system
or transmitted in any form or by any means electronic, mechanical,
photocopying, recording or otherwise without the prior written
permission of the publisher

Permissions may be sought directly from Elsevier's Science &
Technology Rights Department in Oxford, UK: phone (+44) (0) 1865 843830;
fax (+44) (0) 1865 853333; email: permissions@elsevier.com. Alternatively
you can submit your request online by visiting the Elsevier web site at
http://elsevier.com/locate/permissions, and selecting *Obtaining
permission to use Elsevier material*

British Library Cataloguing in Publication Data
A catalogue record for this book is available from the British Library

Library of Congress Cataloguing in Publication Data
A catalogue record for this book is available from the Library of Congress

ISBN-13: 978-0-7506-6546-9
ISBN-10: 0-7506-6546-7

For information on all Butterworth-Heinemann publications
visit our web site at http://books.elsevier.com

Typeset by Charon Tec Ltd, Chennai, India
www.charontec.com
Printed and bound in The Netherlands

06 07 08 09 10   10 9 8 7 6 5 4 3 2 1

Working together to grow
libraries in developing countries

www.elsevier.com | www.bookaid.org | www.sabre.org

ELSEVIER   BOOK AID International   Sabre Foundation

Contents

Contents

Figures

Tables

About the Editors

Anna Leask

Anna is Senior Lecturer in Tourism at Napier University, Edinburgh, UK. Her teaching and research interests combine and lie principally in the areas of heritage visitor attraction management, visitor attraction pricing and general conference management. She has also co-edited *Managing Visitor Attractions: New Directions* (2003) with Alan Fyall and Brian Garrod and *Heritage Visitor Attractions: An Operations Management Perspective* (1999) with Ian Yeoman. Anna has presented and published extensively in the field of visitor attraction management in both UK and international contexts. She is currently leading research in the School of Marketing & Tourism and the Centre for Festival and Event Management at Napier University.

Alan Fyall

Alan is Reader in Tourism Management in the International Centre for Tourism & Hospitality Research, and Head of Research for the School of Services Management at Bournemouth University, UK. Alan has published widely with his areas of expertise spanning the management of attractions, heritage tourism and destination management. Alan has co-edited *Managing Visitor Attractions: New Directions* (2003) published by Butterworth-Heinemann, while he has co-authored *Tourism Marketing: A Collaborative Approach* (2005) and the third edition of *Tourism Principles and Practice* (2005) published by Channel View and Prentice Hall respectively. Alan has recently completed a number of projects for external clients in the South-West of England exploring suitable structures for emerging Destination Management Organizations and has conducted work in the Caribbean and Southern Africa for the Commonwealth Secretariat.

Contributors

Jesús Arias-Valencia BSc, MBA from ESAN, is former National Dean of Machupicchu Program (1997–2002). A project funded by a negotiation of a debt exchange with the governments of Peru and Finland with the main objective of helping to develop preservation processes of the natural heritage and the protection of the extraordinary archaeological environment in Machupicchu.

Professor Gregory Ashworth is Professor of Heritage Management in the Department of Planning at the Faculty of Spatial Sciences, University of Groningen, Netherlands.

Professor Stephen Boyd is Professor and Chair of Tourism in the School of Hotel, Leisure and Tourism, University of Ulster, Northern Ireland, UK. His research interests in tourism include heritage, communities, national parks, partnership, planning and management, disadvantaged regions, peripheral areas and trails. His most recent co-authored book is *Heritage Tourism*, and he is currently Associate Editor of the *Journal of Heritage Tourism*. His current research investigates community feeling on event hosting and second home development across the North Coast region in Northern Ireland, the impact of the Internet on travel agencies and the constraints of travelling with young children.

Dr Dimitrios Buhalis is Course Leader MSc in Tourism Marketing and Leader of eTourism Research at the School of Management University of Surrey and Adjunct Professor at IMHI/ESSEC in Paris. Dimitrios has been an active researcher in the areas of ICTs and Tourism and he was the UniS based Principal Investigator for a number of projects. He is a registered European Commission IST evaluator and reviewer and he was the cluster rapporteur for the IST tourism projects for the period 2000–2004. He served as Vice Chairman on the International Federation of Information Technology and Tourism (IFITT) Board and was Chair of Events and Meetings and a member of the Executive Council of the Tourism Society. He has editorial roles in a number of academic journals and he has written, edited or co-edited 12 books on eTourism, Tourism Strategic Issues and Distribution Channels of Tourism and the Future of Tourism.

Elizabeth Carnegie lectures in arts and heritage management at the University of Sheffield having previously worked at Napier University where she was a member of the Centre for Festival and Event Management. She has considerable experience of the museums and galleries sector, both as a curator with Glasgow Museums where she participated in a number of high profile, award winning projects including setting up the St Mungo Museum of Religious Life and Art (1993) and redisplaying the People's Palace in 1998; and latterly, as a museums manager. Research areas include museum audiences and public memory, community festivals and cultural identity.

Dr Janet Cochrane enjoyed a successful career in the tourism industry and in overseas consultancy, specializing in activity tourism, tourism in protected areas, and South-East Asia. Now Senior Research Fellow at Leeds Metropolitan University, recent projects have covered practical ways of strengthening the links between biodiversity conservation and tourism. Current research interests centre on understanding the interaction between tourism, biodiversity conservation and socio-economic development, on the significance of pilgrimage tourism to sacred sites in South-East Asian national parks, on the recreational needs of domestic tourists in developing countries, and on finding ways of accommodating these needs within protected areas.

Dr Hilary du Cros has interests in tourism and cultural heritage management research, scholarship and teaching. She has worked in the cultural tourism field for the past seven years and has over 20 years' experience in cultural heritage management. Dr du Cros is the Associate Asia-Pacific representative on the International Council on Monuments and Sites (ICOMOS) International Scientific Committee on Cultural Tourism. Prior to entering academia, she owned and operated one of Australia's largest cultural heritage consulting firms, where she supervised or conducted over 250 projects, including a number of projects funded by the National Estate Grants Programme. She has published over 60 scholarly books, journal articles, conference papers, monographs and book chapters. Dr du Cros is the co-author with Bob McKercher of *Cultural Tourism: The Partnership between Tourism and Cultural Heritage Management* published in 2002 by The Haworth Press, Binghamton, New York.

Dr Ros Derrett OAM is an academic at Southern Cross University, Australia. She delivers programmes in event planning and management, tourism planning and the environment, marketing and special interest tourism. She has worked extensively in education, community development, arts administration and tourism. Her research activity reflects her interest in regional consultation, cultural tourism, community cultural and economic development and tourism with a special focus on heritage, festivals and event management. She is the Project Manager of the Centre for Regional Tourism Research based at Southern Cross University and part of the CRC for Sustainable Tourism.

Reuben Grima is the curator of prehistoric sites that are inscribed on the UNESCO World Heritage List and managed by Heritage Malta. He joined the Archaeology section of the Museums Department as an assistant curator in 1992. He formed part of the management team that delivered the Hypogeum Conservation Project in 2000. Reuben has degrees in archaeology and history from the University of Malta, and a Master's degree in Roman archaeology from the University of Reading. He is presently reading for a PhD at the Institute of Archaeology, University College London, funded by a Commonwealth Scholarship. His present research interests include the landscape context of Maltese late Neolithic monuments, and the creation of archaeological narratives that are accessible to wider audiences.

Professor C. M. Hall At the time of writing Michael Hall was Professor in the Department of Tourism, University of Otago, New Zealand, and Docent, Department of Geography, University of Oulu, Finland. Co-editor of *Current Issues in Tourism* he has written widely in the areas of tourism, mobility, regional development and environmental history. He has researched World Heritage issues since the 1980s when his graduate studies focused on Tasmania and Australian approaches to wilderness conservation. Among other interests he is currently studying wilderness and nature-based tourism issues in peripheral areas of Australia, Canada, Finland, Iceland, and alpine areas of Sweden.

Dr I-Ling Kuo currently serves as Assistant Professor at the Emirates Academy of Hospitality Management in Dubai, UAE, teaching various courses in tourism programmes and statistics. She gained her MSc in Tourism Planning and Development from the University of Surrey in 1996, and PhD from Bournemouth University in 2003. Her research focuses on visitor management, interpretation and tourism management in resource-sensitive areas.

Li, Fung Mei Sarah (BSc, Dip Ed, MSc Tourism) is a graduate of the Chinese University of Hong Kong and University of Surrey, and is currently completing her doctoral degree at Murdoch University, Western Australia. She has undertaken numerous research and consultancy activities in China for more than 10 years and her lecturing career has taken her from Hong Kong to Australia. Her research activities are grounded in geography, ecotourism and cultural tourism and include countries as diverse as China, the UK and Australia.

Joanne Mackellar MBus is a PhD student at Southern Cross University, Australia. Having recently gained her Master of Business, Jo specializes her current research into areas of tourism and event planning, and the study of networks and innovation. Her previous experience in the tourism industry extends over 20 years and includes consultancy projects for local governments as well as positions in government tourism offices and in international corporations.

Dr Peter Mason is Professor of Tourism Management at the University of Luton. His early research concentrated on tourism development and impacts. More recently he has focused on tourism planning and management. He has published a number of journal articles concerned with visitor management and is known for his work on education and regulation in tourism and particularly for the first academic study that discussed and critiqued tourism codes of conduct. Recently he has researched tour guiding and interpretation in tourism. He is the author of *Tourism Impacts, Planning and Management* published by Elsevier in 2003, which discusses a number of visitor management issues.

Sue Millar is Chair of ICOMOS-UK Cultural Tourism Committee. She established a suite of MAs in Heritage, Museum, Arts and Cultural Tourism Management as Director of the University of Greenwich Business School in the late 1990s. She has lived and worked in two World Heritage Sites – Ironbridge Gorge and Maritime Greenwich – first at the Ironbridge Institute and then at the National Maritime Museum and later at the Old Royal Naval College. She currently works as an independent consultant in fields of cultural heritage and cultural tourism and is co-director of Culture Works (London) Ltd.

Ruth Owen studied for an MSc in eTourism at the University of Surrey before taking the position as a Research Officer at the University of Surrey contributing to the business plan for the Harmonise www.harmonise.org project, which created a tool to support interoperability within tourism. Her current research is involved in defining the ICT uses and needs of visitors to cultural heritage sites, as part of the FP6 EC funded EPOCH Network of Excellence www.epoch-net.org.

Bryn Parry is a Senior Lecturer in the Southampton Business School, at the Southampton Solent University, specializing in Strategy; holding qualifications in Hotel & Catering Administration and in Facilities Management, his management experience encompasses hospitality management and international consultancy. He is co-author of *Successful Event Management* and has contributed book chapters on Facilities Planning and Risk Management.

Daniël Pletinckx was trained as a civil engineer, with specialization in digital imaging and computer science. He gained extensive experience in system design, digital image processing, digital image synthesis, 3D and virtual reality through a career of 15 years in private industry. He is the author of several articles on computer graphics and cultural heritage presentation and has lectured extensively at major computer graphics and cultural heritage conferences. He was Conference Chair of the international conferences VAST2004 (Brussels) and VSMM2005 (Ghent). As Director of New Technologies, Daniel Pletinckx is responsible for designing new cultural heritage presentation systems and oversees planning, development, quality control, and management of the Ename Centre's heritage presentation projects. He also serves as chief consultant to the Ename 974 Project and is Project Coordinator for the Integrating Activities within the European 6FP IST EPOCH Network of Excellence, that deals with optimizing the use of IT technology in Cultural Heritage.

Dr László Puczkó is head of tourism at Xellum Ltd. He graduated in Business Administration at Budapest University of Economic Sciences (1993). He holds an MA in Art & Design Management (Hungarian Academy of Arts and Crafts), a PhD (Budapest University of Economics and Public Administration) and is a Certified Management Consultant. He is a Board Member of ATLAS, the Hungarian Society of Tourism, and professor at Heller Farkas College. His main areas of expertise are visitor management, health and heritage tourism, theme parks and routes. He is a co-author of books on the impacts of tourism, visitor management and tourism management in historic cities.

Tijana Rakic is a PhD student at Napier University, UK. Her current research focuses on World Heritage, tourism and national identity, while her previous research includes a global study on the future of the World Heritage List. Her research interests are heritage, tourism and national identity, heritage authenticity, post-modernity and the consumption of culture and space in tourism.

Tamara Rátz, PhD is Professor of Tourism at the Tourism Department of the Kodolányi János University College, Hungary, and Visiting Lecturer at Häme Polytechnic University of Applied Sciences, Finland. She has a particular interest in cultural and heritage tourism development and in interpretation and visitor management at heritage sites. Her recent books include *The Impacts of Tourism* (4th edition, co-authored with László Puczkó, in Hungarian, 2005), *European Tourism* (2004) and *Tourism in Historic Cities: Planning and Management* (co-authored with László Puczkó, in Hungarian, 2003).

Otto Regalado-Pezúa is Professor at ESAN of the Marketing Area and consultant for Marketing projects of sustainable tourism and development. He has a PhD in Management Sciences from the Institut d'Administration des Entreprises (IAE) of Université de

Nice-Sophia Antipolis, Nice, France; DEA in Management Sciences of Université de Nice-Sophia Antipolis; DESS in Marketing of École Supérieure des Affaires (ESA) from Université Pierre Mendès France, Grenoble, France; MBA from ESAN, Peru; Bachelor on Management Sciences from the Universidad de Lima, Peru. He has been visiting professor at CERAM, Sophia-Antipolis European Business School and ESC Troyes, France.

Martin Robertson is lecturer in the School of Marketing and Tourism, Napier University, Edinburgh. He has presented conference papers and authored published texts in the areas of urban tourism and events management; festival and event management and destination marketing; and the management of narrative as a leisure management function. He has co-edited two publications, *Managing Tourism in Cities: Policy, Process and Practice* (1998) and *Festival and Events Management: An International and Culture Perspective* (2004). His areas of research focus are urban tourism planning and development; the economic and social evaluation of the impacts of festival and events in the urban environment; strategic destination marketing, and the social science of leisure and urban tourism.

Professor Myra Shackley has a background in archaeology, geography and business management and is Professor of Culture Resource Management at Nottingham Business School, part of Nottingham Trent University. She has a particular interest in the management of visitors to historic sites and protected areas and has published thirteen books (the latest being *Managing Sacred Sites: Service Provision and Visitor Experience* published by Continuum 2001) plus many journal articles, book chapters and reports. Her most recent work deals with issues affecting World Heritage Sites, the management of sacred sites and developments in cultural tourism.

Melanie Smith is a Senior Lecturer in Cultural Tourism Management at the University of Greenwich. Her teaching and research interests include cultural tourism, heritage management, cultural regeneration, and wellness tourism. She is also Chair of ATLAS (Association for Tourism and Leisure Education). She is currently a Visiting Lecturer in Budapest, Hungary.

Dr Trevor Sofield is Professor of Tourism, School of Tourism and Leisure Management, University of Queensland, and Technical Director, Sustainable Tourism, for GRM International, one of Australia's largest consultancy companies. Dr Sofield combines degrees in social anthropology and environmental science with more than 35 years' experience in development in more than 20 countries, first as a diplomat in the Australian Foreign Service with oversight of aid programmes, and more recently as a tourism researcher and consultant, including working with UNESCO as an expert on World

Heritage Sites in the Asia Pacific. He has been undertaking research and consultancies in China for the past 12 years.

Dr Richard Tapper is an expert in sustainable tourism development, and directs the Environment Business & Development Group consultancy. He is also a Visiting Fellow at Leeds Metropolitan University, and advises the Tour Operators' Initiative for Sustainable Tourism Development. Recent projects include a programme involving tour operators in an analysis of good practices for sustainability in tourism for the United Nations Environment Programme, work for UNESCO on biodiversity conservation and tourism at World Heritage Sites, and preparation of International Guidelines on Biodiversity and Tourism Development, which were adopted by the UN in 2004. His special interests include sustainable tourism management at mass tourism destinations and in protected areas.

Dr Nadia Theuma is an anthropologist and has a doctorate degree in cultural tourism management from the Scottish Hotel School in Glasgow. She currently lectures in tourism studies at the Faculty of Economics, Management and Accountancy at the University of Malta. Nadia has conducted research on the impacts of tourism on culture and has contributed to the Tourism Carrying Capacity Assessment of the Maltese Islands. Her current research interests include the use of culture in tourism, the management of cultural events, and community development through culture and tourism activities. She has authored and co-authored articles on tourism in Malta and the Mediterranean.

Dr Dallen J. Timothy is Associate Professor of Community Resources and Development at Arizona State University, USA, and Visiting Professor of Heritage Tourism at the University of Sunderland, UK. He is the Editor of the *Journal of Heritage Tourism* and serves on editorial boards of ten international journals. Dr Timothy is also editor of Ashgate's Heritage Tourism Reference Series and co-editor of the Aspects of Tourism book series published by Channel View. His research interests in tourism include heritage, political boundaries and issues of sovereignty, shopping, planning, community empowerment, and developing world dynamics.

Dr Bart van der Aa researched World Heritage Site selection from 2000, completing a PhD in 2005 at the Faculty of Spatial Sciences, University of Groningen, Netherlands where he currently works as a lecturer.

Foreword

The UNESCO *Convention concerning the protection of the world cultural and natural heritage* came into being in 1972, at a time when some of the important economic and political powers in the world were belatedly becoming aware of the growing threats to the cultural and natural heritage of the planet. There had been inconclusive discussions for fifty years aimed at creating some mechanism whereby the more affluent countries might assist their poorer neighbours to protect and conserve the rich heritage on their territories that they were unable to finance themselves. The first faltering steps were taken in the 1920s by the League of Nations, and these continued after World War II when UNESCO took over the relevant portions of the League's remit, but nothing concrete emerged despite many years of debate and drafting.

The situation changed in the 1960s when the US Government began to take an active interest in environmental protection, spurred on by non-governmental bodies such as the Sierra Club and the World Wildlife Fund. A White House Conference in 1965 recommended that 'there be established a Trust for the World Heritage for the identification, establishment, and management of the world's superb natural and scenic areas and historic sites'. This initiative was taken up by the International Union for the Conservation of Nature (IUCN), and later by the International Council on Monuments and Sites (ICOMOS), set up with UNESCO encouragement in 1965, and the resulting Convention was adopted by the General Conference of UNESCO at its 17th Session in Paris on 16 November 1972 – an unusually rapid gestation period for an international convention.

The early years of the Convention (which came into force in 1977, when it had been ratified by twenty countries) were marked by a great deal of enthusiasm but a lack of coherent policy-making. Cultural and natural properties were nominated to be evaluated in a somewhat *ad hoc* fashion by the two Advisory Bodies to the World Heritage Committee, and the World Heritage List gradually grew. In the Convention the sole criterion for inscription on the List is 'outstanding universal value', a noble phrase but one that proved almost impossible to define, as a result of which ten more detailed criteria were painfully evolved.

By 1994 the World Heritage List had grown in an uncontrolled manner to more than 400, and the Committee recognized that a more systematic approach was needed. This resulted in a Global Strategy, which has been striving to ensure a more equitable and logical representation of the heritage of outstanding universal value, both geographically and thematically – so far, it has to be admitted, with only limited success.

The most significant development in the Convention over the past two decades has, however, been related not to its representative nature but rather to the establishment of standards and criteria for the management, presentation and promotion of World Heritage Sites. No property is now inscribed on the List unless it can show evidence that it has 'an appropriate management plan or other documented management system which should specify how the outstanding universal value of a property should be preserved, preferably through participatory means' (*Operational Guidelines for the Implementation of the World Heritage Convention*, 225, para. 108). The scrutiny of these systems by the two Advisory Bodies is now rigorous, and the inscription of a number of important sites has been deferred to await the preparation and implementation of a suitable plan. Perhaps the most significant example of this rigour was the deferral, in 2000, of the famous archaeological site of Bagan (Myanmar) because there was (and still is) no effective management plan in force.

It is axiomatic that management implies presentation to the public, at all levels from the local to the global. The mere act of listing may increase the visitor numbers at World Heritage Sites many times over: for example, visitor numbers at Sammaladenmäki, a Bronze Age cairn cemetery in Finland, rose tenfold in the first year after listing. The need for close collaboration with tourist bodies cannot therefore be too highly stressed: the approaches to Machupicchu in Peru serve to highlight the dangers of failure to develop a policy of sustainable tourism at 'honeypot' sites of this nature.

Serious consideration is now being given to what the visitor to World Heritage Sites will need (in addition to the *sine qua non* of car parking and toilets). The presentation and display techniques pioneered by the US National Park Service and more recently by English Heritage are now finding favour elsewhere around the world, providing worthwhile visitor experiences in intellectual as well as in material terms.

Only comparatively recently have specialized courses in the management of cultural sites begun to appear in universities around the world, accompanied by a slowly growing literature, both for students and for heritage managers. The present volume is an outstanding addition to the invaluable corpus.

Henry Cleere
Honorary Professor, Institute of Archaeology, UCL;
World Heritage Coordinator, ICOMOS, 1992–2002

Preface

Whenever you mention World Heritage Sites, the person you are talking to asks if there are any in that particular country. In attempting to answer them, one finds oneself trying to recall those that are inscribed and justifying both them and the properties that are not listed. On deeper questioning, few people actually know what the UNESCO designation really means and can rarely think where their own countries and properties celebrate the inscription. That said, they are never at a loss to list a lengthy catalogue of sites that they think should be listed and those that should not!

When the editors originally discussed embarking on this project we carefully considered the worth of trying to inform and contribute to the growing body of knowledge on World Heritage Sites – how could we make a valuable contribution to a complex environment where tourism is often seen as a necessary evil and is not often universally welcomed? It is our hope that we have provided both explanation of what the designation means and encouraged analysis of its impact on the successful future of the care of precious resources and sites across the globe. The content of the book will include fantastic sites such as the rainforests in Australia, historic cities in China, Europe and South America, and the role of tourism within their management. The case studies will review cultural and natural sites, those on the List of World Heritage in Danger and those considered to be 'safe'. There is significant interest in the future of these sites on both a local and global level with growing public interest and awareness in the successful sustainability of these resources. Governments recognize the value of them in the global scene, yet with a view to economic prosperity in some situations, but also their role in conservation, developing local culture and stimulating tourism activity. The text attempts to address these issues in a practical and applied manner, with use of case studies in each chapter and in-depth cases towards the end of the book to demonstrate the very individual needs of the properties on the World Heritage List (WHL). One clear aim of the text is critically to review the role of tourism activity within the issues under discussion and to encourage discussion of the positive ways to balance tourism, economic benefit, and cultural aspects and to minimize physical damage to resources.

The whole area of tourism and World Heritage Site (WHS) management has been the subject of various international academic gatherings and conference themes in recent years, with special editions in *Tourism Recreation Research* (2001) and the *International Journal of Heritage Studies* (2002), and the most recent *Current Issues in Tourism* (2005) special edition and textbook edited by Harrison and Hitchcock (2005). This collection of papers discusses World Trade Law and focuses on the contested nature of WHS and the politics that surround the whole process. Alongside the development of the academic debate has been the publication of more practical approaches, such as *The Illustrated Burra Charter Good Practice for Heritage Places Australia,* 3rd edition (ICOMOS, 2004) that 'encourages the co-existence of cultural values, particularly where they conflict and recognize the importance of interpretation', where 'conservation is an integral part of good management'. In addition, the World Heritage Centre has published *Managing Tourism at WHS: A Practical Manual for WHS Managers* (Pedersen, 2002) as part of their World Heritage Series, offering practical solutions to the variety of issues that they may encounter. The aim of this text is to combine the issues raised via the academic debate and research, with the more practical and applied results from individual properties and those involved in their management. The chapters contain broad coverage of the issues and are then followed by specific and applied case studies, thus providing a useful text for students, academics and practitioners alike.

The editors would like to recognize the considerable effort on behalf of the contributors for their initial interest and willingness to participate in the project and their continued support in submitting work to us. Their views and comments regarding the content of the chapters and text overall have led to a great wealth of content and depth throughout each section. This has contributed to the diverse range of resource and site choices, and the broad geographical spread.

The title of the book was chosen specifically to reflect the broad scope of the overall management of World Heritage Sites and the manner in which tourism activity participates in this context, rather than simply approaching tourism practice at these sites in isolation. It was not the aim of the editors only to consider tourism activity at the WHS, more to view the impacts and issues raised in combining the tourism activities within the broader context of the WHS, to establish how it results in wider socio-cultural and economic impacts and how it can contribute to the benefits gained overall. It is anticipated that this academic debate and contribution will stimulate further publications in the area. The debate over the future sustainability of the World Heritage List will continue and perhaps there is no definitive answer, more a recognition of the need to continually work towards balancing the huge variety of activities that occur at World Heritage Sites.

Anna Leask and Alan Fyall
November 2005

Abbreviations

EH	English Heritage
ICCROM	International Centre for the Study of the Preservation and Restoration of Cultural Property
ICOMOS	International Council on Monuments and Sites
IUCN	International Union for the Conservation of Nature and Natural Resources
WH	World Heritage
WHC	World Heritage Committee
WHConvention	World Heritage Convention
WHL	World Heritage List
WHS	World Heritage Site
UNESCO	United Nations Educational, Scientific and Cultural Organization

PART 1

Introduction to World Heritage Sites

Part One of this book explores the broad context within which UNESCO designated World Heritage Sites (WHS) operate. While the book considers the management issues involved in heritage sites in general, it specifically focuses on the UNESCO designated WHS as being indicative of the need successfully to manage these properties. The variety of the sites on the World Heritage List is indicative of the complex issues involved in the effective management of these natural and cultural resources. The aim of this initial section is to consider the role of tourism within the whole World Heritage process, in that it has a significant role to play but that a careful balance of activities is required to maintain the very nature of the resource that visitors seek.

The key themes and issues addressed in this Part include a précis of how a heritage property or resource becomes designated as a World Heritage Site – from the initial suggestion to the final inscription by the World Heritage Committee. In Chapter 1 Anna Leask outlines the process of inscription, before investigating the motivations for pursuing this accolade and the implications for a States Party and site. She then moves on to consider the current representation on the World Heritage List (WHL) and where the main advisory bodies of ICOMOS and IUCN have identified gaps. These bodies have identified some inequalities in the WHL across the categories of designation – natural, cultural and mixed – and geographically, with a heavy lean towards European cultural properties. There follows some discussion concerning the future of the WHL, though this is dealt with in much more detail in Chapter 11. Throughout the chapter, the author recognizes that there are varying viewpoints with regards to tourism activity at WHS. To some it is the key motivation for pursuing the status, while for others it is a marginal activity. For some it is already an established factor in the dynamics of the site, while for others the lack of infrastructure or the political situation precludes effective and appropriate tourism activity. This aspect of politicization is a recurrent theme, of relevance to the motivations for inscription, the decisions around which sites are nominated and how the World Heritage Convention operates and will be revisited throughout the book. Not least there needs to be recognition of the variety of breadth of stakeholders involved in the nomination, inscription and ongoing management of World Heritage Sites, resulting in a challenging operating environment.

In Chapter 2 C. Michael Hall explores the differences in implementation of the World Heritage Convention between States Parties, investigating what the designation means for a country as well as a site. One key theme here is that of the implications of designation – what they are, how they are measured (if at all) and how they can be optimized appropriately to the WHS. Does a site attract more visitors following WHS inscription and what other implications might there be, for example legislation? He concludes with the thought that there needs to be a change in the whole focus of WHS management, with less emphasis on the process of gaining inscription, rather to the implementation of the WHConvention following inscription. His view being that the story does not end once a site gains the status, rather that it should be the start for the improved management of the site via systematic evaluation, monitoring and reporting on the impacts of WHS listing.

CHAPTER 1

World Heritage Site designation

Anna Leask

Aims

The aims of this chapter are to:

- Introduce the concept and process of UNESCO World Heritage Site (WHS) inscription
- Outline the process and role of stakeholders involved in their designation
- Describe the current profile of the World Heritage List (WHL)
- Identify and discuss the issues surrounding WHS designation and management.

Introduction

This chapter acts as an introduction to the process of identification, nomination and inscription for WHS across the globe. This enables the future chapters to concentrate on the specific issues in relation to their implications and applications within various settings, rather than each re-examining the process. The content will cover the aims above in seeking to explain the at times complex process whereby a site deemed to be of significant worth is inscribed onto the WHL. It will consider the vast range of bodies, organizations and stakeholders who become involved in the process and the role that they play. The key management role is that of UNESCO to identify and aid the conservation of those sites deemed to be of outstanding universal value. While the sheer variety of resources protected by the designation creates its own difficulties in the application of UNESCO practices and sustainable management of the sites, a fact noted by Bandarin (2005), UNESCO recognizes this and uses its 'coveted WHS programme as a means of spreading best practice in sustainable management'. The chapter will then raise many of the controversial and political issues surrounding the whole concept of World Heritage in attempting to highlight the disparate views on the success and potential longevity of the designation process. It will then conclude with a summary of the process to act by way of introduction to later chapters that will tackle many of these points more directly.

What is a World Heritage Site?

Approved in 1972, the 'Convention concerning the Protection of the World's Cultural and Natural Heritage' was adopted by the United Nations Educational, Scientific and Cultural Organization (UNESCO) and came into force in 1976, when it had been ratified by twenty countries. It has since been ratified by 180 States Parties across the globe. The purpose of the Convention is to 'ensure the identification, protection, conservation, presentation and transmission to future generations of cultural and natural heritage of outstanding universal value' (UNESCO, 2005a). The Convention states that the World Heritage Committee (WHC) should coordinate the process of designating these sites through a system known as inscription, which includes an evaluation of the resources by experts against a set of known criteria. The aim is to encourage conservation of the resources within the designated sites and surrounding buffer zones on a local level and also to foster a sense of collective global responsibility via international cooperation, exchange and support. While designation only incurs additional legislative power in a few States Parties, South Africa and Australia for example, 'the prestige of being on the WHL is deemed such that a high level of protection will exist on the site' (Historic Scotland, 2005). Once designated, the States Party accepts responsibility for the effective management of the site and commits to adopting the 'Operational Guidelines for the Implementation of the World Heritage Convention' and the systems of reactive and periodic reporting set in place by UNESCO. If it fails to do this effectively then the threat of removal from the WHL is present, though it has not, to date, been exercised.

Sites may be nominated as cultural, natural or mixed criteria, with designation reliant upon the type of criteria that they are deemed to present in an exceptional form. The diversity of WHS is vast, including the Great Barrier Reef, Australia as the largest, former colonial cities such as the Historic Town Centre of Macau, engineering feats such as the Mountain Railways of India, artistic works such as those of Gaudi, natural phenomena such as the West Norwegian Fjords and cultural and natural resources combined in situations such as the Island of St Kilda off the coast of Scotland. Prior to 2005 nominations were evaluated against a set of six cultural and four natural criteria, though these have now been combined into one set of ten including:

> to represent a masterpiece of human genius or to contain superlative natural phenomena; or areas of exceptional natural beauty and aesthetic importance; or to bear a unique or at least exceptional testimony to a cultural tradition or to a civilisation which is living or which has disappeared (UNESCO, 2005b).

The criteria are listed in full in Table 1.1. Sites may be nominated as representing examples of one or more criteria, indeed, many of the early nominations cover all six of the cultural criteria, for example Venice. While every attempt has obviously been made to clarify what is meant by terms such as 'outstanding universal value', the

Table 1.1 Selection criteria for World Heritage Site status

(i) to represent a masterpiece of human creative genius

(ii) to exhibit an important interchange of human values, over a span of time or within a cultural area of the world, on developments in architecture or technology, monumental arts, town-planning or landscape design

(iii) to bear a unique or at least exceptional testimony to a cultural tradition or to a civilization which is living or which has disappeared

(iv) to be an outstanding example of a type of building, architectural or technological ensemble or landscape which illustrates (a) significant stage(s) in human history

(v) to be an outstanding example of a traditional human settlement, land-use, or sea-use which is representative of a culture (or cultures), or human interaction with the environment especially when it has become vulnerable under the impact of irreversible change

(vi) to be directly or tangibly associated with events or living traditions, with ideas, or with beliefs, with artistic and literary works of outstanding universal significance. (The Committee considers that this criterion should preferably be used in conjunction with other criteria.)

(vii) to contain superlative natural phenomena or areas of exceptional natural beauty and aesthetic importance

(viii) to be outstanding examples representing major stages of earth's history, including the record of life, significant on-going geological processes in the development of landforms, or significant geomorphic or physiographic features

(ix) to be outstanding examples representing significant on-going ecological and biological processes in the evolution and development of terrestrial, fresh water, coastal and marine ecosystems and communities of plants and animals

(x) to contain the most important and significant natural habitats for in-situ conservation of biological diversity, including those containing threatened species of outstanding universal value from the point of view of science or conservation

Source: UNESCO, 2005b

boundaries of 'uniqueness' and the criteria themselves, with these being the topic of debate and revision in recent years, evaluation is still essentially a subjective process. ICOMOS (2004) has commented that 'Unlike natural heritage, cultural heritage is fragmented and diverse and not predisposed to clear classification systems'.

How are WHS designated?

The initial step in the inscription process is for a site to be identified within a States Party as suitable for nomination. It is this stage that is often crucial and subject to a significant level of political negotiation, where some commentators might comment on the questionable priority given to some sites over others. Each States Party should then develop a Tentative List (TL) – an 'inventory of the cultural and natural

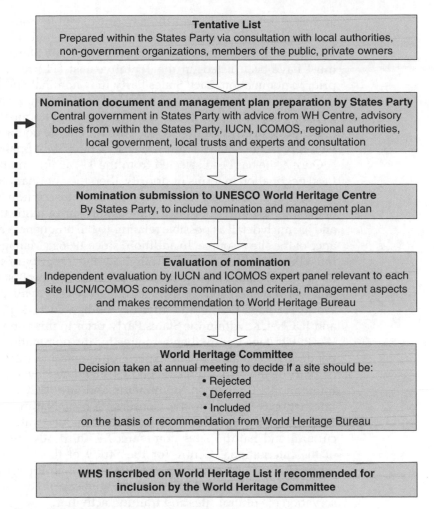

Figure 1.1 The World Heritage Site inscription process

properties of outstanding universal value within its territory, which it considers suitable for inclusion and it intends to nominate for inscription on the WHL in the following years' (UNESCO, 2005c) – though some are yet to be encouraged to develop these. Tentative Lists can be helpful in the planning process in identifying potential sites and allowing adequate preparation time for their nomination. Canada and the UK have been congratulated on their TL in their inclusion of trans-boundary (where nominations include a number of sites based on a theme but not necessarily in the same geographical area, e.g. Cave Paintings in Northern Spain) and trans-national sites (nominations where sites cross borders, such as the recently announced Frontier of the Roman Empire including Hadrian's Wall and sites in Germany) and the amount of public consultation that has been included in arriving at the list. Sites are nominated for inscription by the central government within the States Parties and must have been listed on the Tentative List (TL) for that country prior to nomination. Each States Party may nominate up to two sites each year, provided that one is a natural nomination. This represents a change from the decision taken in 2000 to limit nominations to one per annum, in an attempt to reduce the number of nominations from well-represented States Parties, such as China, Italy, Spain and India.

Once a site has been selected from the TL, again a matter of much local negotiation in terms of priority, then the nomination document can be prepared. This outlines the criteria for inscription, boundaries of the site and buffer zone (area immediately surrounding the resource) and as much detail as possible relating to the uniqueness and import-ance of the site resource. In addition, since 1996, a Management Plan must be presented to demonstrate how the integrity of the site and its universal value are to be presented, covering aspects such as trans-port, conservation and tourism activity. Advice is available from the World Heritage Centre and advisory bodies, such as ICOMOS-UK and IUCN-UK, within the States Party prior to this submission. The World Heritage Centre then arranges for the nomination to be inde-pendently evaluated by an expert representative from either one or both of the two Advisory Bodies mandated by the WHC: the International Council on Monuments and Sites (ICOMOS) and the International Union for the Conservation of Nature and Natural Resources (IUCN), which respectively provide evaluations of the cultural and natural sites nominated. A third advisory body, that of the International Centre for the Study of the Preservation and Restoration of Cultural Property (ICCROM), an intergovernmental organization, provides the Committee with expert advice on the con-servation of cultural sites and training activities.

Mission reports relating to conservation and management, reports on the cultural/scientific values, and consultations with specialists are used to produce detailed recommendations on a site. These are then studied by special panels of the respective Advisory Bodies and at these meetings recommendations are formulated which are later presented to the World Heritage Committee. The options are to rec-ommend inscription, deferral (to seek further detail) or to reject the nomination. The WHC agreed that it would consider a maximum of 45 nominations per annum at their meeting in 2004, this to include any proposed extensions to already inscribed sites. The final step is for the formal inscription of the site as a WHS and committing it to being managed in accordance with the Operational Guidelines for the Implementation of the World Heritage Convention. In some cases, sites are also immediately placed on the List of World Heritage in Danger, currently containing 34 WHS, when the resource is considered to be at substantial risk of damage from situations such as war, flood or industrial activity or in need of major conservation measures and assistance to protect and maintain the values for which it was originally inscribed. The further implications of listing will be covered in future chapters of this text.

What is the current profile of the World Heritage List?

The first 12 World Heritage Sites (WHS) were inscribed on the World Heritage List (WHL) in 1978 and the total has risen now to contain 812. The profile is varied, with 628 cultural, 160 natural and 24 mixed (those meeting both cultural and natural criteria) WHS, representing 137 States Parties (UNESCO, 2005d). Initially nominations tended to initiate from built heritage in European settings, leading to a geographic bias towards this area (Cleere, 1998), though the Global Strategy of 1994 has made some headway in attempting to redress this imbalance and encourage nominations that meet other criteria and originate from less well represented States Parties and themes. Most recent properties to be inscribed include sites from Bahrain and the Republic of Moldova appearing on the WHL for the first time. A situation has arisen whereby a few States Parties represent the majority of the properties on the WHL, while others may have none. Indeed, the number of WHS listed by States Party ranges from zero to 34, with 43 currently having no sites inscribed. This issue will be discussed in further detail later in the chapter. In recent years, attempts have been made to identify such gaps in the WHL with reports from ICOMOS and IUCN specifically addressing this issue and suggesting amelioration techniques. One such suggestion has been to increase the number of trans-boundary nominations (IUCN, 2004) and to encourage the exchange of expertise in the preparation of nomination documents and conservation techniques.

Current issues surrounding WHS designation and management

The previous paragraphs have covered the technical process involved in attaining World Heritage Site status from UNESCO. In attempting to clarify a complex political and administrative process, a huge number of issues have come to the fore and require further discussion. The author is not attempting to answer these issues, merely to raise them to inform the debate in later chapters in the text.

Motivations

Why do States Parties nominate sites for inscription? Is it for the opportunity to access international conservation expertise and exchange, the
true basis of the WHConvention, or is it for the perceived benefits of
economic growth encouraged by increased tourism activity and opportunity to access the World Heritage Fund? Perhaps it is simply to gain
the recognition and prestige associated with achieving this international accolade or maybe simply a matter of political esteem and pride.
The motivations usually relate to the specific governmental aspirations
within a States Party, be they prestige within Europe or financial in
developing countries. Whatever the reasons, they are varied, debatable
in their benefits and often politically intensified.

Implications of World Heritage listing

One of the more tangible ways of assessing the above might be to
review the actual implications of listing – the benefits and costs, the
opportunities and threats. This issue has naturally been the subject
of debate (Hall and Piggin, 2001; English Heritage, 2005) as States
Parties want to see clear benefit in exchange for the expense of mounting a nomination bid. This is a suggested list of the key implications
as summarized from these authors:

- international recognition and accountability – international prestige, increased opportunities for promotion, improved quality standards on sites and accountability if on the List of World Heritage in
  Danger
- improved protection and management of site via the system of
  site specific management plans providing a framework for decision-
  making and participation in monitoring activities and participation in periodic reporting from UNESCO
- planning implications – rarely legislative but often key material
  planning consideration or some level of recognition
- new partnerships and projects – the opportunity to form ones, for
  example at Stonehenge where 70 bodies now work together on
  the site proposals, and potential access to funding via WH Fund
  or locally, international exchange of expertise and personnel
- economic and social improvement
- political and ethnic recognition, for example in former colonial
  territories
- increased tourism activity – potential increases in visitation dependent upon the existing levels, location, theme and promotion.

What is abundantly clear is that the greatest benefits to the resources
themselves appear to follow where a clear planning structure is in

place and adherence to the site specific management plan and the UNESCO Operational Guidelines is set, rather than in countries with less developed planning and management frameworks. IUCN (2004) have commented that there is a need for national legislation relevant to World Heritage that is complementary to and supportive of other laws on protected areas and natural resource management, with management plans for each property and the inclusion of an assessment of management effectiveness as part of the management cycle.

Tourism activities at WHS

The key focus of this book concerns the role of tourism within the much wider resource management practices. The perceived benefits of tourism activity to an area are one of the key motivations for States Parties in nominating sites. Various authors (Shackley, 1998; Hall and Piggin, 2001) have debated the actual economic impacts of listing, to gauge the role of designation in any achieved increases in visitation and income generation, though none has arrived conclusively in support of such benefits – usually due to a lack of data available for even the most developed sites. The key dilemma here is that it is difficult to balance tourism activity with the conservation role, often creating a tension or conflict between the usually large number of stakeholders involved. Each of the stakeholders is likely to hold conflicting agendas and priorities, resulting in difficulties arriving at consensus of opinion on site and resource management. McKercher et al. (2005) have researched this conflict between tourism and other stakeholders, stating that 'tourism and cultural heritage management often have an awkward relationship', then go on to suggest that formal partnerships may not be the best route to success, indeed that 'successful cultural tourism is most likely to occur when both sets of stakeholders have a realistic appreciation of the tourism value of the asset, the need to conserve core cultural values and clearly defined roles'.

'The very reasons why a property is chosen for inscription on the WHL are also the reasons why millions of tourists flock to those sites year after year. So how do we merge our convictions with our concerns over the impact of tourism on World Heritage Sites?' (Pedersen, 2002). Their response has been for UNESCO and the advisory bodies of IUCN and ICOMOS to publish a range of texts and manuals to assist in directing site managers (Feilden and Jokilehto, 1998; Pederson, 2002), though often it might not be the practical management issues that require guidance, more intervention or encouragement to change attitudes from purely conservation to the wider context. Additionally, the sheer variety in resources, locations and staff expertise dictates that these publications are more generalist than specific and may not offer particularly practical solutions to each individual, 'unique' WHS. The clearest route to balancing these activities would appear to be in the effective inclusion of them within management plans and recognition of management practices that can be used to control and maximize the benefits. It is vital that the management of WHS should be integrated into tourism and land management plans at all levels – local, regional and national.

Representation and balance on the WHL

One critical flaw in the WHS listing process is that UNESCO does not nominate nor invite nominations for sites that they deem appropriate – instead it is the central governments within each States Party that do this. This inevitably leads to a situation whereby some countries are not members, do not recognize membership and designation follow- ing political changes, or indeed nominate sites at all. Additionally, the highly politicized process of Tentative List and nomination means that it is not always the most obvious resource that is nomi- nated. van der Aa (2005) suggests that this may be due to a variety of reasons including, social unrest, availability of exploitable resources on a site, overlooking suitable sites in error or attempts to exclude a minority's heritage. The political will must be there for the nomina- tion of sites to become a priority and be awarded the required funds to enable it to happen. Additionally, the political nature of UNESCO incurs a situation noted by Harrison (2005) where 'on the World Heritage List ... the outcomes will depend on the balance of status and power at any one time and on who among the numerous stake- holders has the loudest voice ... it is an inter-subjective and highly political process'.

As mentioned previously, the WHL is more biased to sites in Europe and North America and towards cultural sites. The Global Strategy, set up in 1994 to encourage a balanced, representative and credible WHL, has an action programme designed to identify and fill gaps in the WHL, and has been effective in encouraging nominations from new States Parties and a broader range of categories, for example industrial heritage, heritage routes and cultural landscapes, but there are still opportunities for improvement. Future plans include further broaden- ing of categories possibly to include community involvement and the engagement of young people in the process. Also, to encourage re- presentation from less well represented States Parties via trans-national and trans-boundary nominations, though with a precursor that they need additional assistance with the preparation and implementation of management plans, 'increasing use of serial site and trans-boundary nominations by a number of States Parties is positive but needs clearer direction and guidelines to ensure strong nomination and effective management post-inscription' (IUCN, 2005).

One further future issue for UNESCO is that of adequate funding fully to support the activities of the WH Centre. The funds raised through the WHF are inadequate, particularly as more sites are designated in less developed countries and with the increasing cost of policing the now large number of sites. Calls for further research to inform the practices of the Centre (Harrison and Hitchcock, 2005) would also require increased levels of funding, most effectively via ICOMOS and IUCN, which can call on superior professional and scientific advice in an efficient and effective manner.

The process of WHS inscription

The whole process of inscription has been criticized for its complexity, political bias and expense. These may represent the key reasons why some countries fail to have representation on the WHL. ICOMOS (2004) suggest that the structural gaps are the result of a 'lack of technical capacity to promote and prepare nominations, lack of adequate assessments of heritage properties, or lack of an appropriate legal or management framework, which either individually or collectively hinders the preparation of successful nominations' (ICOMOS, 2004) and that qualitative gaps are 'associated with certain types or themes of properties'. So, further work is required in order to overcome these issues internationally, in identifying suitable sites and assessing their cultural assets for suitability. It also may take several nomination bids and many years for some sites to be inscribed, often due to factors outside their control, such as redefinition of criteria or political wrangling. It may take years for a site even to make it onto a Tentative List, often it is particularly difficult for regions to gain recognition on national lists. Personnel changes and budgetary controls may mean that the sheer will to push for nomination may expire. Many States Parties do not have Tentative Lists in place, therefore automatically precluding them from nominating sites, while most WHS designated pre-1996 still do not have management plans in place. The lack of legislative power associated with designation is the key factor in much of this, both at international and national level. It allows questionable activities, such as planning approval for roads and housing or mining activity, to take place at or near designated WHS and frustrates experts seeking recognition and care for worthy resources. Hitchcock (2005) views this 'legal ambiguity' to be one of the key issues of the whole system. Additionally, there is also the confusion raised where a WHS is also awarded other designations. Since the WHConvention was set up there has been a great increase in the volume and applicability of other schemes for recognition and conservation of resources, such as national designations and the use of different terminology to discuss the same item, e.g. World Heritage Areas/World Heritage Sites in Australia. These designations rarely follow identical boundaries, purposes and management practices – all contributing to the multiplicity of stakeholders.

Total number of WHS and future completion of the WHL

Both IUCN and ICOMOS completed investigations into the future of the WHL and voiced, interestingly conflicting, statements regarding their positions. While ICOMOS (2004) state that there should be:

> no limit on the number of properties inscribed on WHL – the definition of potential properties to be nominated will necessarily remain an open question, subject to evolving concepts, policies, strategies and available resources … and the perception of whether or not there are gaps, cannot simply be based on numerical analysis.

IUCN (2004) counter that:

> there must be a finite number of existing and potential properties for inclusion on the WHL … IUCN considers that a number in the range of 250–300 natural and mixed WH properties should be sufficient.

The IUCN statement (IUCN, 2004) goes on to say: 'it was never intended that the WHL should ensure complete representivity of all the earth's ecosystems and habitats – other international instruments available'. One area that they do agree on, however, is that Tentative Lists need more work to assist in the further identification of potential natural and mixed properties in particular, with further harmonization at regional and thematic level between States Parties being one avenue for development. So the debate is likely to continue in terms of arriving at a fully geographically and thematically representative WHL, with continued discussion of the contentious idea of re-evaluating existing sites, removal of those no longer deemed to be of 'universal value' and of compulsory nomination of sites from non-member nations. Existing and new political situations may also become volatile and impact on the progress of WHS management, for example between Korea and China or Israel and Palestine.

A lack of public awareness surrounds the whole aspect of designation too, the author has lost count of the number of times she has been asked if Scotland even has any WHS! People often ask why sites do or do not have the status, usually in complete ignorance of what it even means – though it sounds good, doesn't it? This is particularly true in local contexts, as noted by Williams (2005).

Conclusion

An action plan to address some of these issues has been drafted by ICOMOS (2004) and includes: developing Tentative Lists for all States Parties; optimizing success of nominations; developing new Operational Guidelines; encouraging sustainable development on WHS; the introduction of periodic reporting to monitor WH; and raising awareness of the WHConvention.

The key aim of the WHConvention is to conserve cultural and natural heritage resources, but does the present structure of the WHC and associated processes actually do this? According to IUCN (2004) and ICOMOS (2004) the WHConvention is an effective framework for implementation of conservation strategies but needs better integration of Convention and international, national and regional conservation instruments, to achieve universal membership of Convention and to involve communities. This would indicate that it is effective, but then again both organizations are closely affiliated with and bound by UNESCO. Independent commentators might have reservations, but a realistic view must be taken regarding how improvements could be made to such an international, politically sensitive system. The chapters following this one investigate the issues surrounding the effective management and conservation of WHS, with the case studies then highlighting particular features of the issues applied in key WHS. In reading the following chapters and cases, it is critical to emphasize that the role of designation is not specific to tourism, rather for conservation, although there is also a need to recognize the significant role of tourism in the effective sustainable management of World Heritage Sites. As stated by Barbosa (2003), 'We have a collective responsibility to safeguard our human heritage. It is a responsibility, furthermore, that links past, present and future generations in a chain of reciprocity and care', and tourism has a vital role to play in that future.

References

Bandarin, F. (2005) Foreword. In Harrison, D. and Hitchcock, M. (eds) *The Politics of World Heritage: Negotiating Tourism and Conservation*. Clevedon: Channel View Publications.

Barbosa, M. (2003) World Heritage 2002: Shared Legacy, Common Responsibility. http://whc.unesco.org/documents/publi_report 2002_en.pdf UNESCO (accessed 21 August 2005).

Cleere, H. (1998) Europe's Cultural Heritage from a World Perspective. In ICOMOS UK Conference proceedings: *Sustaining the Cultural Heritage of Europe*. London.

English Heritage (2005) http://www.english-heritage.org.uk/server/ show/nav.8673 What are World Heritage Sites? (accessed 10 August 2005).

Feilden, B.M. and Jokilehto, J. (1998) *Management Guidelines for Cultural World Heritage Sites*. Rome: Ograro.

Hall, C.M. and Piggin, R. (2001) Tourism and World Heritage in OECD countries. *Tourism Recreation Research*, 26, 103–105.

Harrison, D. (2005) Contested narratives in the domain of World Heritage. In Harrison, D. and Hitchcock, M. (eds) *The Politics of World Heritage: Negotiating Tourism and Conservation*. Clevedon: Channel View Publications.

Harrison, D. and Hitchcock, M. (2005) (eds) *The Politics of World Heritage*. Clevedon: Channel View Publications.

Historic Scotland (2005) World Heritage Sites. www.historic-scotland.gov.uk/txtonly/index/ancientmonuments/world_ heritage (accessed 10 August 2005).

Hitchcock, M. (2005). In Harrison, D. and Hitchcock, M. (eds) *The Politics of World Heritage: Negotiating Tourism and Conservation*. Clevedon: Channel View Publications.

ICOMOS (2004) http://www.international.icomos.org/world_heritage/whlgaps.htm Executive Summary of The World Heritage List: Filling the Gaps – An Action Plan for the Future. February 2004. Paris: ICOMOS (accessed 10 August 2005).

IUCN (2004) Executive Summary of Draft Strategy Paper – The World Heritage List-future. http://www.iucn.org/themes/wcpa/wheritage/WHList_FuturePriorities.pdf (accessed 10 August 2005).

IUCN (2005) Special Expert Meeting of the World Heritage Convention. Background Paper, April. Paris: IUCN.

McKercher, B., Ho, P. and du Cros, H. (2005) Relationship between tourism and cultural heritage management: Evidence from Hong Kong. *Tourism Management*, 26 (4), 539–548.

Pedersen, A. (2002) Managing Tourism at WHS: A Practical Manual for WHS Managers World Heritage Paper 1 2002. http://whc. unesco.org/documents/publi_wh_papers_01_en.pdf   Paris: UNESCO (accessed 15 August 2005).

Shackley, M. (1998) *Visitor Management: Case Studies from World Heritage Sites*. Oxford: Butterworth-Heinemann.

UNESCO (2005a) World Heritage. http://whc.unesco.org/en/about/ (accessed 18 August 2005).

UNESCO (2005b) World Heritage Criteria. http://whc.unesco.org/ en/criteria/ (accessed 18 August 2005).

UNESCO (2005c) World Heritage Tentative List. http://whc.unesco. org/en/tentativelists/ (accessed 18 August 2005).

UNESCO (2005d) The World Heritage List. http://whc.unesco.org/ en/list/ (accessed 18 August 2005).

van der Aa, B. (2005) Preserving the heritage of humanity? Obtaining world heritage status and the impacts of listing. Netherlands Organisation for Scientific Research.

Williams, K. (2005) The meanings and effectiveness of World Heritage Designation in the USA. In Harrison, D. and Hitchcock, M. (eds) *The Politics of World Heritage: Negotiating Tourism and Conservation*. Clevedon: Channel View Publications.

CHAPTER 2

Implementing the World Heritage Convention: what happens after listing?

C. Michael Hall

Aims

The aims of this chapter are to:

- Emphasize the importance of understanding the different means by which the World Heritage Convention (WHC) is implemented in different States Parties
- Identify the importance of legislation and regulation in meeting country's obligations under the Convention
- Highlight the extent to which it is possible to say that listing actually influences visitation
- Emphasize the need for systematic evaluation strategies to be developed for WHS and the Convention as a whole.

Introduction

World Heritage Site (WHS) listing usually carries with it enormous expectation. At first glance these expectations often focus on the extent to which listing is meant to bring in extra tourists to the site or attract more government and agency support for the maintenance of the site's values. However, on closer inspection it is apparent that there are many other implications of WHS listing, including potentially changed access and use of the site, new regulatory structures, and changed economic flows. In addition, the listing of one site may also have an affect on other site nominations or even other existing sites in terms of management, the politics of heritage and even who visits. These issues can be collectively examined as issues that arise as a result of the implementation of the WHConvention. This chapter addresses some of these significant, but understudied issues with respect to two main issues: the regulatory dimension of listing and evaluation of the impacts of listing. The chapter concludes by emphasizing the need for more systematic evaluation and monitoring strategies of WHS and how States Parties meet their obligations under the Convention.

Implementation

In thinking about the implications of listing sites as WHS it is useful to draw upon the idea of implementation. Implementation refers to the process by which policies and decisions are put into effect. Implementation is often conceived of in terms of a planning/implementation dichotomy, i.e. planning occurs first then, once a document is produced, it is put into effect. However, just a conceptualization is very misleading as planning and implementation are actually two sides of the same coin. In other words, the various stakeholders and interests who sought to influence the development of policies, plans and the decision-making process do not suddenly disappear once a decision has been made – they still continue to seek to influence what happens! Therefore, planning and implementation need to be considered as part of an ongoing process (Hall, 2000). Nevertheless, the notion of implementation is still significant as it also raises issues of how it is known which policies and decisions have actually been achieved. Have they managed to achieve what was intended of them? To answer this question therefore means that one needs to evaluate plans and decisions so that their effects can be monitored.

In the case of WHS there are a wide number of factors that can be evaluated at different scales, e.g. international, national, local or regional and at specific WHS, as well as with respect to different factors or indicators as to how the obligations under the Convention have been met (Figure 2.1). For example, it is possible to evaluate the extent to which a country has implemented its responsibilities under the WHConvention, as well as the effects that WHS listing has had on individual properties and/or their surrounds. This chapter examines the implementation of the WHConvention with respect to regulatory instruments as well as make some brief comments about the effects of listing can have on particular sites.

Implementing the Convention: regulatory dimensions

The WHConvention is widely regarded as one of the most significant and successful international heritage agreements. Unlike many international treaties that deal with environmental issues it is widely ratified. Ratification of the Convention imposes obligations on those that sign it. The WHConvention is an example of 'hard' international law. Hard international law refers to firm and binding rules of law, such as the content of treaties and the provisions of customary international law, to which relevant nations are bound as a matter of obligation. However, 'soft' international law is also significant for WHS. Soft law refers to regulatory conduct which, because it is not provided for in a treaty, is not as binding as hard law (Hall, 2000). Examples of soft law include recommendations or declarations which are made by international conferences, agencies and associations, such as that of WHS cities, that are part of the institutional fabric that surrounds the Convention. Soft law is particularly important in the area of international environmental law because treaties and conventions often require parties to attend regular meetings which make recommendations for implementation, as in the case of the WHConvention.

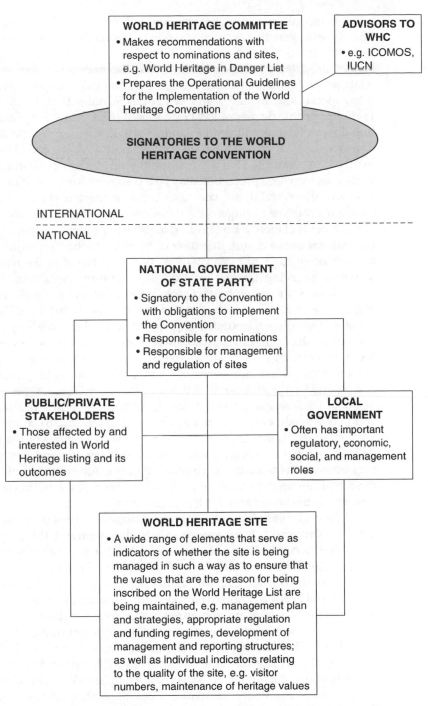

WORLD HERITAGE COMMITTEE
- Makes recommendations with respect to nominations and sites, e.g. World Heritage in Danger List
- Prepares the Operational Guidelines for the Implementation of the World Heritage Convention

ADVISORS TO WHC
- e.g. ICOMOS, IUCN

SIGNATORIES TO THE WORLD HERITAGE CONVENTION

INTERNATIONAL
- -
NATIONAL

NATIONAL GOVERNMENT OF STATE PARTY
- Signatory to the Convention with obligations to implement the Convention
- Responsible for nominations
- Responsible for management and regulation of sites

PUBLIC/PRIVATE STAKEHOLDERS
- Those affected by and interested in World Heritage listing and its outcomes

LOCAL GOVERNMENT
- Often has important regulatory, economic, social, and management roles

WORLD HERITAGE SITE
- A wide range of elements that serve as indicators of whether the site is being managed in such a way as to ensure that the values that are the reason for being inscribed on the World Heritage List are being maintained, e.g. management plan and strategies, appropriate regulation and funding regimes, development of management and reporting structures; as well as individual indicators relating to the quality of the site, e.g. visitor numbers, maintenance of heritage values

Figure 2.1 Elements in the implementation of the World Heritage Convention

International law cannot be enforced in the same manner as domestic law, because nations can only rarely be compelled to perform their legal obligations. However, the moral obligations that accrue to members of the international community and the norms of international relations are usually sufficient to gain compliance in most areas of international law. Indeed, van der Aa (2005) notes that, while most WHS have some degree of local or national legal protection, designation does not necessarily lead to an increase in legal protection under domestic law. Of the 64 sites he studied only 39 per cent (25 sites) received further protection under law although, as he noted, in certain situations, increased protection may be a precursor to nomination so as to assure the WHC that a site has suitable protected status so as to enable appropriate management strategies. Moreover, in the case of the WHConvention there is no standard legislative or regulatory approach that nations use to ensure that their obligations to the Convention are met, although the vast majority of WHS are protected at the national level under existing national and local legislation and regulation. There is no common approach to developing participatory structures in the nomination and management process for example. In fact WHS listing is not universally supported, with some stakeholders opposing nominations or the boundaries of nominated sites (e.g. van der Aa et al., 2004), particularly if they believe that it may restrict land use or development options. Instead, there is a vastly different array of regulatory and institutional instruments that States Parties utilize, ranging from National Park acts and heritage law through to planning ordinances and policy statements to manage WHS and processes. To complicate the picture even further, in some States Parties a number of the legal instruments that are used to help preserve WHS values and particular sites are derived from local or regional legislative authority even though the actual nomination must be undertaken through the national government as the State Parties to the Convention.

In England, planning policies were changed in 1994 so as to protect WH properties from inappropriate development (Rutherford, 1994; Wainwright, 2000). No additional statutory controls follow from the inclusion of a UK site in the WHS list. However, inclusion 'highlights the outstanding international importance of the site as a key material consideration to be taken into account by local planning authorities in determining planning and listed building consent applications, and by the Secretary of State in determining cases on appeal or following call-in' (Office of the Deputy Prime Minister, 2005: para.2.22). This has already occurred with respect to an application to engage in mining activities near Hadrian's Wall (Rutherford, 1994). Under the Policy Guidance from the Office of the Deputy Prime Minister each local authority, as well as other interested parties, such as other public authorities, property owners, developers, amenity bodies and all members of the public, has to recognize the implications of WHS designation as well as other statutory designation, in the formulation of

> ... specific planning policies for protecting these sites and include these policies in their development plans. Policies should reflect the fact that all these sites have been designated for their outstanding universal value, and they should place great weight on the need to protect them for the benefit of future generations as well as our own. Development proposals affecting these sites or their setting may be compatible with this objective, but should always be carefully scrutinised for their likely effect on the site or its setting in the longer term. Significant development proposals affecting [WHS] will generally require formal environmental assessment, to ensure that their immediate impact and their implications for the longer term are fully evaluated (Office of the Deputy Prime Minister, 2005: para.2.23).

Such an approach means that, in the UK, development projects that affect WHS, 'should always be carefully scrutinized for their likely effect on the site or its setting in the longer term' (Cookson, 2000: 698) before planning approval can be given. Significantly, the UK planning guidance with respect to WH specifically refers to the WHC's *Operational Guidelines for the Implementation of the World Heritage Convention* (first produced in 1978 and regularly revised) as a document that local authorities should refer to with respect to the planning and management of WHS. In addition, local planning authorities are encouraged to work with owners and managers of WHS in their areas, and with other agencies, to ensure that comprehensive management plans are developed. According to the planning guidance (Office of the Deputy Prime Minister, 2005) these plans should:

- appraise the significance and condition of the site
- ensure the physical conservation of the site to the highest standards
- protect the site and its setting from damaging development and
- provide clear policies for tourism as it may affect the site.

A similar philosophy with respect to the management and planning of WHS and values has also developed in Australia. However, unlike the UK example and unusually in global terms, WHS has been subject to the introduction of specific legislation. Indeed, WHS listing has arguably been more controversial in Australia than any other country because it has become part of debates on economic development and the relative conservation and economic values of an area, as well as debates over state and national government rights. As Suter (1991: 4) observed: 'Insofar as calculation is possible, Australia has probably had more litigation and political challenges to the Convention than all other states party to the Convention combined'. Nevertheless, despite, or perhaps because of the arguments that have raged over WHS, Australia is recognized as having one of the world's most rigorous sets of institutional arrangements for the implementation of the Convention (Hall, 2000). The development of these arrangements is detailed in the following case study.

Case study: The Development of Australia's National Regulatory Framework on World Heritage

On 16 October 1979, the Tasmanian Hydro Electric Commission (HEC) released a report that recommended state parliamentary approval for the Gordon-below-Franklin Dam as the first stage of an integrated power development. The proposal involved the flooding of a major temperate rainforest wilderness area that was part of the Wild Rivers National Park, a park of international conservation significance, as well as other impacts associated with dam construction. The proposal led to one of the most controversial and bitter environmental issues in Australia's history (Hall, 1992).

On 7 and 15 September 1982, the newly elected state Liberal government revoked sections of the Wild Rivers National Park vesting the area in the HEC and, as a result, the proposed dam construction become a national issue. The Tasmanian government launched an Australia-wide advertising campaign explaining its decision and warned federal politicians not to interfere in the state's development schemes. In line with previous statements, the Liberal Commonwealth (national/federal) government announced its decision on 8 December to nominate the wilderness area affected by the dam to the WHS List, but refused to exercise its authority to prevent the dam being built, instead offering financial compensation, which the state government refused.

From 12 December to March 1983, the Franklin Dam issue became one of open confrontation between conservationists and the Tasmanian government, as the Tasmanian Wilderness Society launched a dam-site blockade designed to hinder construction and maintain national and international media interest. As a Commonwealth election loomed, the Labour opposition followed the lead of the Australian Democrats and gave a firm undertaking that they would prevent dam construction if elected to office. Conservation groups all around Australia then decided to campaign openly against the federal Liberal government.

On 5 May 1983, the Labour Party won the Federal election and immediately passed regulations under the *National Parks and Wildlife Conservation Act 1975* and passed the *World Heritage Properties Conservation Act 1983* in order to prohibit the construction of the dam in an area of WHS quality with the Act also being applicable to other WHS. The WHC (1983: 11) commended 'the Australian government for enacting the necessary protective legislation so rapidly'. In a landmark decision, the Australian High Court decided in favour of the Commonwealth's power to intervene. The decision effectively prevented construction work on the dam scheme and helped to preserve one of the world's last remaining temperate wildernesses. Nevertheless, the fact that the Commonwealth overrode state policy and law in order to stop certain activities that were regarded as being at odds with WHS values meant that the debate over WHS became more than just a conservation issue and instead focused on issues of state and political rights. For example, despite the apparent willingness of the Commonwealth to work with the states and territories to nominate areas to the WHS List, severe resistance emerged from the Queensland and Tasmanian state governments. The Queensland Minister for Tourism, National Parks and Sport, Bob McKechnie, stated in 1985 that 'not one more square inch' of Queensland would be added to the list (*Weekend Australian*, 13–14 April 1985: 16). Similarly, the Tasmanian Minister for the Environment said that the 31 per cent of Tasmania already included on the National Estate Register or the WHS List was 'quite enough' (*Weekend Australian*, 13–14 April 1985: 16).

In 1986 and 1987, the Labour Federal government made three major unilateral decisions regarding the preservation of natural heritage, all of which can be regarded as wilderness. First was the Commonwealth's announcement of intent in June 1987, to nominate the North Queensland rainforest to the WHS List, despite the likelihood of a Queensland government challenge in the High Court. Second was the declaration of Federal legislation to prevent timber-felling in the Southern and Lemonthyme Forests in Tasmania until an examination of the area's WHS properties has been completed. Third, the Commonwealth nominated the second stage of Kakadu to the WHS List. All three actions were opposed in court and all three cases were won by the Federal (Commonwealth) government, thereby reinforcing their powers to regulate WHS. As Boer (1989) commented with respect to the Queensland government's action in the High Court to determine whether the areas that were subject to nomination came within the meaning of 'natural heritage' as found in the WHConvention (*State of Queensland v. The Commonwealth* 1988), the case represented:

> a transparently clear statement of the Commonwealth power to fulfil its obligations under the World Heritage Convention, and it appears that further challenges brought by the states against the Commonwealth in this area will have little chance of success. ... It has become clear that the Federal government has the power to nominate to the World Heritage List any area which it identifies as being of World Heritage status. The protestations and challenges of state

governments and private companies, though impeding the nomination process, have not been able to stop it (Boer, 1989: 144, 143).

WHS listing and the maintenance of WHS values that could be potentially listed continued to be a significant issue in federal-state relations during the 1990s and into the new century. However, the election of a Liberal federal government in 1996 led to the development of new institutional approaches to WHS. In November 1997, a Heads of Agreement on Commonwealth and State Roles and Responsibilities for the Environment (Council of Australian Governments, 1997) was signed by all heads of federal and state government and by the Australian Local Government Association. Part I of the Agreement states that 'The Commonwealth has a responsibility and an interest in relation to meeting the obligations of the *Convention for the Protection of the World Cultural and Natural Heritage'*. A new Act governing the Commonwealth's responsibilities with respect to WHS, as well as other significant environmental matters of national interest, was also introduced. The *Environment Protection and Biodiversity Conservation Act 1999* came in force from 16 July 2000, arguably enhancing the management and protection of Australia's WHS properties. Some of the key dimensions introduced by the Act included:

- greater up-front protection for WH properties
- a modified assessment and approvals process
- application of consistent WH management principles for all WH properties regardless of location and
- a new set of Commonwealth/State government arrangements.

Following the legal precedents set in the 1980s, the 1999 Act protects all Australian properties that are inscribed on the WHS List; where a site has been nominated for, but not yet inscribed on, the WHS List; and where, even though a site has not been nominated for WHS, the Minister believes that the property contains WHS values that are under threat. The Act regulates actions that will, or are likely to, have a significant negative impact on the WHS values of a declared WHS property, including those actions that occur outside the boundaries of a WHS. Actions that are taken in contravention of the Act can attract a civil penalty of up to Aus.$5.5 million, or a criminal penalty of up to seven years imprisonment.

Regulations pursuant to the Act (*Environment Protection and Biodiversity Conservation Regulations 2000*) outline the Australian WHS management principles for the management of natural heritage and cultural heritage (Table 2.1). The regulations also state that at least one management plan must be prepared for each declared WHS property which includes a number of specific elements that must be included (Table 2.2), as well as the environmental impact assessment and approval process. Under the regulations, the assessment of an action

Table 2.1 General principles for the management of natural and cultural heritage in Australia's World Heritage Sites

- The primary purpose of management of natural heritage and cultural heritage of a declared World Heritage property must be, in accordance with Australia's obligations under the World Heritage Convention, to identify, protect, conserve, present, transmit to future generations and, if appropriate, rehabilitate the World Heritage values of the property
- The management should provide for public consultation on decisions and actions that may have a significant impact on the property
- The management should make special provision, if appropriate, for the involvement in managing the property of people who have a particular interest in the property and may be affected by the management of the property
- The management should provide for continuing community and technical input in managing the property

Source: Environment Protection and Biodiversity Conservation Regulations 2000: regulation 10.1

Table 2.2 What management plans for a declared Australian World Heritage Site should include

(a) State the World Heritage values of the property for which it is prepared
(b) Include adequate processes for public consultation on proposed elements of the plan
(c) State what must be done to ensure that the World Heritage values of the property are identified, conserved, protected, presented, transmitted to future generations and, if appropriate, rehabilitated
(d) State mechanisms to deal with the impacts of actions that individually or cumulatively degrade, or threaten to degrade, the World Heritage values of the property
(e) Provide that management actions for values, that are not World Heritage values, are consistent with the management of the World Heritage values of the property
(f) Promote the integration of Commonwealth, State or Territory and local government responsibilities for the property
(g) Provide for continuing monitoring and reporting on the state of the World Heritage values of the property
(h) Be reviewed at intervals of not more than 7 years

Source: Environment Protection and Biodiversity Conservation Regulations 2000: regulation 10.2.02

that is likely to have a significant impact on the WHS values of a property occurs whether the action is inside the property or not (reg. 10.3.03). The assessment process should identify the WHS values of the property that are likely to be affected by the action; examine how the WHS values of the property might be affected; and provide adequate opportunities for public consultation. Finally, the regulations state that,

'An action should not be approved if it would be inconsistent with the protection, conservation, presentation or transmission to future generations of the WHS values of the property' (reg. 10.3.04) with monitoring of compliance with respect to actions also identified under the regulations.

The Department of the Environment and Heritage (2004) provides an example of how the Act and the regulations pursuant to the Act serve to protect WHS values in Australia. During 2003–04, an industrial minerals company proposed to develop the Mourilyan silica sand deposit situated between Mourilyan Harbour and Kurrimine Beach, approximately 20 km south of Innisfail in North Queensland. The proposed boundary was situated 3 km west of the Great Barrier Reef World Heritage Site at Kurrimine Beach and 1 km west of the boundary of Kurrimine Beach National Park, which is part of the Wet Tropics World Heritage Area. The proponent referred the development to the Department of the Environment and Heritage in July 2003 claiming that it was not a controlled action under the Act. However, under Section 12 and Section 15A of the Act, the Department considered that significant impacts were likely on the WHS values provisions. On the basis of consultations with the Great Barrier Reef Marine Park Authority and the Wet Tropics Management Authority, the mining operation was therefore determined to be a controlled action and was prohibited.

The case study indicates how implementation of the WHConvention has been undertaken in Australia with respect to its obligations. New regulatory procedures have been developed rather than using existing legislation. Just as significantly, the Australian example indicates the importance of taking a long-term perspective on the nature and relative success of implementation.

Evaluating the effects of designation

Another significant aspect of understanding the implementation of the WHC is identifying the effects of listing on various sites. Despite the various positive claims that are made with respect to WHS listing, particularly with respect to their tourism impact, there is a lack of effective consistent evaluation and monitoring strategies not only between sites but in specific sites over time (Buckley, 2004). Tourism is just one area in which there is inadequate monitoring and evaluation at WHS. For example, Buckley (2004: 82) noted that, 'even for Australia's largest and best-known WHS, past data on visitor numbers and origins are generally too incomplete to track historical trends except at the broadest scale'.

Despite the enthusiasm of authors such as Shackley (1998: preface) who claimed that WHS designation was 'virtually a guarantee that visitor numbers will increase', there is substantial evidence to suggest that this is not necessarily the case. For example, Rodwell (2002) noted that with respect to cultural heritage sites in the UK there was no proven relationship between status and visitor numbers. Similarly, Hall and Piggin (2001), in a survey of tourism and WHS in OECD States Parties reported that, while two-thirds of the 44 sites they examined did report an increase in visitor numbers since listing usually of the order of 1–5 per cent per annum, this figure was not significantly different from that of the average rate of tourism growth in those States Parties anyway. Indeed, with respect to the Australian data Buckley (2004: 82) reported

> In so far as can be determined from available data, any significant increases in the growth of visitor numbers at WHSs seems to have coincided more closely with periods of major environmental contro-versy rather than the date of WHS listing, as such, though there are too many factors and inadequate data to establish this pattern definitively. If so, it seems that the tourism industry of today should be indebted to the conservation activists of the past not only for pro-tecting one of their primary resources, but also for advertising it.

Substantial questions can be asked as to whether people sometimes even know that they are visiting a WHS. For example, Hall and Piggin (2001) also noted that less than half of the sites in their survey had spe-cific areas for the explanation of the WHConvention and why the sites were granted WHS status, even though this is one of the elements of the WHC's guidelines for the implementation of the Convention. This may lead to a situation in which local stakeholders have little under-standing of the Convention and of the values that site designation rec-ognizes and seeks to preserve (Hall and Piggin, 2002). In many cases significant conservation and heritage sites were recognized well before WHS status was provided, and people visit the site with those pre-existing values in mind rather than the values identified by WHS sta-tus. Another interesting study on the effects of WHS listing on visitor numbers is that of Wall (2004) who surveyed visitors to the Laponian WHS in north-western Sweden which was declared a WHS in 1996. According to Wall only 3.7 per cent of respondents stated that the visit would never have occurred or would have had different travel plans if it had not been a WHS. Nevertheless, 64 per cent agreed in part or com-pletely that WHS designation had value for the surroundings, with 51 per cent agreeing in part or completely that designation was of value for visitors. Interestingly, in this Swedish example, only 26 per cent agreed in part or completely that designation restricted human use.

Conclusions

The WHConvention has been in existence for over 30 years. Yet, despite the large number of sites that have been declared, the evolution of criteria and systems for listing, and the development of guidelines for implementation of the Convention, the wider understanding of the effectiveness of listing, particularly in terms of how countries implement the Convention on a national and site basis and the impacts of designation, are actually very poor. As van der Aa (2005: 140) observed, 'most actors involved in the [WHConvention] – UNESCO, countries and stakeholders of world heritage sites alike – have been able to use the convention for their own purposes'. Although such an approach may further the goals of some stakeholders, there are substantial questions about how the qualities that are being sought to protect are being managed as well as the wider impact of designation.

To undertake a systematic programme for the evaluation and monitoring of WHS would seem to be a logical progression in the development of the Convention and in ensuring that State Parties' obligations are being met. However, to do this effectively requires not just the development of appropriate indicators, which is arguably a relatively easy part of the process given the precedents set by impact assessment processes around the world, but also the development of regulatory and institutional processes that provide for such regulation to occur on an on-going basis as well as the funding for such actions. Such measures are being gradually developed by the WHC as part of a regular cycle of reporting, although the value of such reporting measures in implementation terms is dependent on selection of indicators, monitoring procedures and capacity to respond to issues identified in reporting procedures. As Hall and Piggin (2001) reported, lack of funding was one of the most significant management issues at WHS in the wealthier States Parties of the OECD, let alone those in less developed countries.

It is becoming increasingly apparent that some of the assumptions regarding the benefits of listing, for example with respect to visitor numbers, are increasingly being questioned. Much attention has focused on the nominations and policies of WHS listing rather than how effectively the Convention is implemented. However, if WHS listing is to remain more than a symbolic act, it is vital that not only is the nomination process subject to greater rigour (van der Aa, 2005), but also the means by which countries' obligations are met through a systemic evaluation, monitoring and reporting process of the impacts of listing.

References

Boer, B. (1989) Natural resources and the National Estate. *Environmental and Planning Law Journal*, 6 (2), 134–144.

Buckley, R.C. (2004) The effects of World Heritage listing on tourism to Australian national parks. *Journal of Sustainable Tourism*, 12, 70–84.

Cookson, N. (2000) *Archeological Heritage Law*. Chichester: Barry Rose Law Publishers.

Council of Australian Governments (1997) *Heads of Agreement on Commonwealth and State Roles and Responsibilities for the Environment*. Canberra: Council of Australian Governments.

Department of the Environment and Heritage (2004) *Department of the Environment and Heritage, Annual Report 2004*. Canberra: Department of the Environment and Heritage.

Hall, C.M. (2000) *Tourism Planning*. Harlow: Prentice-Hall.

Hall, C.M. and Piggin, R. (2001) Tourism and World Heritage in OECD countries. *Tourism Recreation Research*, 26 (1), 103–105.

Hall, C.M. and Piggin, R. (2002) Tourism business knowledge of World Heritage Sites: a New Zealand case study. *International Journal of Tourism Research*, 4, 401–411.

Office of the Deputy Prime Minister (2005) *Planning Policy Guidance 15: Planning and the Historic Environment*. London: Office of the Deputy Prime Minister.

Rodwell, D. (2002) The World Heritage Convention and the exemplary management of complex heritage sites. *Journal of Architectural Conservation*, 3, 40–60.

Rutherford, L. (1994) Protecting World Heritage sites: Coal Contractors Limited v Secretary of State for the Environment and Northumberland County Council. *Journal of Environmental Law*, 6 (2), 369–384.

Shackley, M. (1998) *Visitor Management: Case Studies from World Heritage Sites*. Oxford: Butterworth-Heinemann.

Suter, K.D. (1991) The UNESCO World Heritage Convention. *Environmental and Planning Law Journal*, 8 (1), 4–15.

van der Aa, B.J.M. (2005) Preserving the Heritage of Humanity? Obtaining World Heritage Status and the Impacts of Listing, Doctoral Thesis, Faculty of Spatial Sciences, University of Groningen, Groningen.

van der Aa, B.J.M., Groote, P.D. and Huigen, P.P.P. (2004) World heritage as NIMBY: the case of the Dutch part of the Wadden Sea. *Current Issues in Tourism*, 7 (4–5), 291–302.

Wainwright, G.J. (2000) The Stonehenge we deserve. *Antiquity*, 74, 334–342.

Wall, S. (2004) Protected areas as tourist attractions. Paper presented at *Tourism Crossroads – Global Influences, Local Responses*, 13th Nordic Symposium in Tourism and Hospitality Research, Aalborg, 4–7 November.

World Heritage Committee (UNESCO, Intergovernmental Committee for the Protection of the World Cultural and Natural Heritage) (1978) Operational Guidelines for the Implementation of the World Heritage Convention. Paris: UNESCO.

World Heritage Committee (UNESCO, Intergovernmental Committee for the Protection of the World Cultural and Natural Heritage) (1983) Report of the Rapporteur, Sixth Session of the World Heritage Committee, Paris, 27–30 June 1983, CLT-83/CONF.021/8. Paris: UNESCO.

PART 2

Management of World Heritage Sites

Part Two concentrates on the operational management of the WHS, with a particular emphasis on the fundamental interdependencies involved in managing the various components and stakeholders associated with important heritage resources. Managing heritage resources requires the integration of a wide range of complex and interrelated management considerations, which arise both from within and outwith the resource itself. While tourism activity at some sites is well developed and recognized, at others it is marginal and not a significant management consideration. However, external factors, such as improvements in infrastructure, increased propensity to travel and political instability, mean that growth in visitor access may well be an inevitable result. The very significance of the heritage resources means that the sites all require individual approaches to their effective management. This section of the text aims to highlight the issues and suggest appropriate mechanisms for this.

In Chapter 3, Sue Millar tackles the issue of managing stakeholders at WHS – an issue that remains an obstacle to the successful future of many sites currently listed on the WHL. The importance of forging an effective stakeholder system is critical from the initial stages of World Heritage nomination, since sites cannot even be nominated until they have appeared on a States Parties Tentative List – this requiring at the very least a consensus of opinion on the significance of the resource from local, regional and central government bodies, in conjunction with resource owners, members of the public and visitors. Naturally this relationship will vary in effectiveness and participation, but is essential in then following through with the development of a nomination document and management plan specifically written for the World Heritage Site. This chapter considers the issues in a variety of UK settings including the Lake District, Stonehenge and Hadrian's Wall, examining the role of the local community within the planning process in balancing the contrasting views of stakeholders to encourage effective resource management.

In Chapter 4, Stephen Boyd and Dallen Timothy examine the marketing issues that surround the designation of a WHS. They challenge commonly held tourism marketing principles and critically appraise the application of the marketing mix within a WHS setting. Their case study on the Giant's Causeway in Northern Ireland demonstrates the value of marketing the wider context of a resource, rather than simply focusing on the WHS itself. In Chapter 5, Bryn Parry then examines the destination management at Liverpool Maritime Mercantile City to demonstrate how a holistic framework can enable the multiple aspects of a WHS to combine successfully, again taking the view that the resource should not be seen in isolation from the surrounding context and dimensions. The final chapter in Part Two is written by Myra Shackley and focuses on Visitor Management at WHS. Key issues such as maintaining 'spirit of place', managing security and cultural sensitivity are identified, with examples of both positive and negative techniques at a host of WHS being used as exemplars.

CHAPTER 3

Stakeholders and community participation

Sue Millar

Aims

The aims of this chapter are to investigate:

- Stakeholders' views, value systems and interpretations of heritage significance
- Collaboration, consensus and conflict among stakeholders
- Layers and levels of community participation
- Re-branding World Heritage Sites.

Introduction

Stakeholders and community participation

> Memory is vital to creativity: that holds true for individuals and for peoples, who find in their heritage − natural and cultural, tangible and intangible − the key to their identity and the source of their inspiration. (UNESCO, 2005a)

How can a multitude of stakeholders be actively involved in managing World Heritage Sites (WHS) to ensure they are inspirational places for individuals and peoples both now and in the future? In particular, how can different communities be involved in the process? What kind of interface should there be between the aspirations and values of local community groups, communities of interest, communities of practice and the aspirations and values of local councils, national governments, national and international cultural heritage organizations and tourism organizations? On what terms should the local people meet visitors to World Heritage Sites? What does the real involvement of local people mean in terms of management structures, management styles and brand image? Can the question be answered 'Whose heritage is it anyway?' in relation to the management and interpretation of World Heritage Sites?

A quiet sea change is taking place in the approach to the inscription and management of World Heritage Sites in the first decade of the 21st century. Theoretically 'all the peoples of the world' are stakeholders in World Heritage. In practice, until recently, a limited number of stakeholders − governments, conservation experts and local authorities − were involved in the process. Local people, local amenity and community groups, local businesses, tour companies and visitors were largely left out of the consultation and management processes. In numerous countries and at many World Heritage Sites around the world they still are. In the UK in the 20th century, many people often did not know they lived or worked in or near a World Heritage Site and cared less. In states with weak economies World Heritage Site status was eagerly sought as a kite mark for the promotion of mass tourism, under the guise of international cultural tourism, without any consideration as to whether the local people and local infrastructure had the capacity to respond effectively to the demands.

The focus of responsibilities concerning the protection and conservation of World Heritage is shifting from a forum of conservation experts and national and local government representatives to a partnership approach involving an expanded list of local and regional stakeholders covering a wide spectrum of interests located both inside and outside the boundaries and buffer zones of a World Heritage Site. These new stakeholders include private sector businesses, developers, owners, non-governmental organizations (NGOs) and community groups (see paragraphs 39 & 40 *Operational Guidelines for the Implementation of the World Heritage Convention*, UNESCO, 2003).

The World Heritage Committee acknowledges that there must be a link between universal and local values for a WHS to have a sustainable future. The ambition for world ownership of the world's special and diverse natural and cultural heritage remains strong. 'What makes the concept of World Heritage exceptional is its universal application. World Heritage Sites belong to all the peoples of the world, irrespective of the territory on which they are located' (UNESCO, 2005b). Yet such idealistic rhetoric, such global aspirations can create problems when they are transposed into the reality of the local context on the ground. If, in fact, WHS status encourages indiscriminate mass tourism, compromises authenticity, distorts traditional values, gives rise to the need for congestion management at 'honeypot' tourist destinations and thereby creates a need for additional conservation management, then inscription – however well intended – is problematic. The World Heritage Committee now accepts that such grandiose statements of aspiration are incontrovertible, but it also recognizes that they can no longer remain in the stratosphere of European international diplomacy in an era of global economic interdependency, global cultural tourism, global migration, global terrorism and the increasing homogeneity of culture and cultures.

The urgency of the need for communities of all types – international, national, regional, local, business, learning, leisure, tourism, conservation – and individuals worldwide to participate in celebrating cultural diversity and in developing a sense of cultural identity as a springboard for the future has placed World Heritage Sites centre stage. Paradoxically, the shift in the emphasis of cultural significance from the tangible to the intangible heritage that is taking place is putting 'people' into the heart of the WHS debate. People are important not only in terms of their commitment to the inscription and management of a WHS, but also in terms of their contribution to the intangible aspects of a site in the first place. The International Committee of Monuments and Sites (ICOMOS) Report *The World*

Heritage List. Filling the Gaps – an Action Plan for the Future states, 'While the List based on the 1972 Convention generally expects some physical evidence on a site, the need to acknowledge intangible aspects is one of the current challenges of the listing process ...' (ICOMOS, 2004). In every country around the world there is one over-riding guiding principle: the support of local people as well as world visitors is the key to a dynamic sustainable future for World Heritage Sites.

Case study: Stakeholders' views, value systems and interpretations of heritage significance – The Lake District, UK

World Heritage Sites are not like 'motherhood and apple pie'. They are not entirely wholesome. World Heritage Sites are deeply political entities that arrive in local communities with clearly defined boundaries and 'buffer zones' following inscription on the World Heritage List. They come with baggage and have not always been welcomed. Therefore, current nominations must have the full support of the principal stakeholders and this is not always easy to obtain. For example, the UK nomination of the Lake District as a cultural landscape is seen variously as a new opportunity and yet another burden. The area is already a National Park. Some conservation bodies remain sceptical. In 2002, the five main partners were brought together as the World Heritage Liaison Group under the leadership of ICOMOS-UK: the Countryside Agency, English Heritage, English Nature, the Lake District National Park Authority, and the National Trust. They explored what additional benefits World Heritage status would bring and whether the boundaries of the proposed World Heritage Site should be the same as the National Park.

There is a considerable amount of political pressure at national level. The UK Government is keen to pursue the Lake District's nomination as a Cultural Landscape: it is on the Government's Tentative List. However, as part of the nomination process, the main parties must not only agree the boundaries and buffer zones, taking into consideration the perceptions of user groups, they must also subscribe to a management plan. The management plan has to be based on a clear understanding of what is significant about the site, why and how it is vulnerable and come to a consensus on what needs to be managed.

The Lake District is a complex cultural landscape. It is viewed as both quintessentially English and of international importance. Since the 18th century it has been a place for spiritual refreshment and quiet countryside recreation. The strong associations with Wordsworth and other Lake Poets, and influential figures, such as Ruskin and Beatrix Potter, are reflected in the preservation of the places where they lived.

Considerable areas are protected by national and international nature conservation designations. Herdwick sheep have heritage significance for farmers and the tourism industry in terms of preserving the landscape as a romantic idyll. Their role became fully apparent during the foot and mouth crisis. Keith Twentyman comments, 'A lot of people, particularly visitors, think the Lake District is natural. It isn't. It is a managed environment and the management is done by these sheep' (Smart, 2001). They are sometimes called the Lake District's gardeners.

The 'universal significance' of the physical location of the Lake District as a whole as we know it today is difficult to define. The special significance of the Lake District is not just the sum of individual aspects of its landscape, but rather a remarkable alliance between the aesthetic appeal of its farming and mining traditions, and the output of painters and poets who, inspired by the landscape, showed how it could appeal to the higher senses and be accessible to all. It relates to the inter-relationships between the physical, social, economic and cultural impacts placed in the context of a set of core values – aesthetic, ethical, spiritual and intellectual. These close interdependencies have created the overarching 'universal significance' of the Lake District.

The difficulty of defining the area of the Lake District as a cultural landscape combining tangible and intangible values and attributes, as well as a number of practical management factors, means that enthusiasm on the ground among local people has been somewhat muted. The National Park and the National Trust already manage the area in a sustainable manner. However, since 2004 the National Park Service has made a firm commitment to World Heritage Site inscription providing £50 000 towards the cost of the Project. It now believes 'inscription can help renew local pride in the area and focus attention and resources on actions that will benefit the local community in a variety of ways' (Lake District, 2005). A cross-partnership group will produce a budget, create a project team, identify a boundary and prepare a management plan. From the National Park's point of view, the main benefit of inscription is its social and economic value to the community. Although the National Park Service is in one sense the mouthpiece of current government policy, the wholesale commitment of such a major partner at local level is essential if the nomination is to have any chance of success with the World Heritage Committee.

The expansion of World Heritage

The major stakeholder in World Heritage Sites in the UK is the Government. Like other States Parties worldwide who have signed up to the World Heritage Convention, the UK Government nominates one site for inscription each year. Practical pressures of 'realpolitik' can be seen to sit uncomfortably with the notion that World

Heritage Sites must be of 'outstanding value to humanity' and of 'universal significance'. One glance at the map of World Heritage properties shows that the overwhelming number and the highest density of World Heritage Sites currently inscribed on the World Heritage List are in Europe. Therefore Europe and European States Parties are the largest stakeholders.

States Parties from the developing world are under-represented as stakeholders. At the World Heritage Committee meeting in Australia in 2000, it was decided to develop a global strategy for a credible, representative and balanced List. ICOMOS was commissioned to analyse the World Heritage List and the Tentative List on a regional, chronological, geographical and thematic basis. Their report *Filling the Gaps – an Action Plan for the Future* (ICOMOS, 2004) lists some 48 states which do not yet have any properties on the List and cites two main reasons. First, these states lack the technical capacity to prepare a nomination and second, among World Heritage experts there is a qualitatively different understanding of value systems that do not fit the European norm. This situation is changing.

Philippe Segadika explains that the intangible heritage of the Tsodilo, Botswana – inscribed on the World Heritage List in 2001 – continues to be of great cultural significance today.

> The Ju/hoansi and Hambukushu communities living at Tsodilo know that Tsodilo is the ancestral home to the spirits of all living creatures. As proof to this, the local shamans, guides and herbalists point to specific areas, which are testimony to the marks of the first animals, the first people, first sex spot as well as the first and eternal water spring in the Tsodilo landscape. (ICOMOS, 2003)

Yet the focus of the description from the World Heritage Centre remains Eurocentric and primarily refers to the tangible heritage assets.

> With one of the highest concentrations of rock art in the world, Tsodilo has been called the 'Louvre of the Desert' … Local communities in this hostile environment respect Tsodilo as a place of worship frequented by ancestral spirits. (UNESCO, 2005c)

The ICOMOS Report provides an irrefutable rationale and justification for the continuing expansion of the concept of a monument or site, building on the Venice Charter, in order to include a large spectrum of stakeholders worldwide. 'Monuments and sites can encompass the authentic spirit of a holy place, possibly only tangible in weak traces, as well as witnesses of the past erected of seemingly indestructible stone material'. The definition reflects UNESCO's adoption of the International Convention for the Safeguarding of the Intangible Cultural Heritage (17 October 2003). Some major cultures, such as the Bantu States in Central Africa, have not yet been recognized. Approximately half (49 per cent) of the Sites on the Tentative

List in 2002 were from Europe while Sub-Saharan Africa had less than 5 per cent and the Near and Middle East, North Africa, Asia and the Americas each had just over 10 per cent.

Equity and excellence are admirable, ethically sound principles. But it is open to debate whether they are applicable to a division of universal world heritage largely within modern state boundaries. Andorra, the Democratic People's Republic of Korea, Iceland, Saint Lucia and Togo made their first appearance on the List in 2004. Trans-boundary properties are increasing. Togo is one of these. The inscription indicates a deeper level of understanding, respect for and sensitivity to the combined tangible and intangible values within an historic cultural landscape that is vibrant and sustainable today.

> The Koutammakou landscape in northeastern Togo, which extends into neighbouring Benin, is home to the Batammariba whose remarkable mud Takienta tower-houses have come to be seen as a symbol of Togo. In this landscape, nature is strongly associated with the rituals and beliefs of society. The 50 000-ha cultural landscape is remarkable due to the architecture of its Takienta tower-houses, which are a reflection of social structure, its farmland and forest, and the associations between people and landscape. Many of the buildings are two storeys high and those with granaries feature an almost spherical form above a cylindrical base. They are grouped in villages, which also include ceremonial spaces, springs, rocks and sites reserved for initiation ceremonies. (UNESCO, 2005c)

The viability of the World Heritage Committee's approach as the international stakeholder of World Heritage remains fundamentally flawed. First, there is the possibility of devaluing the meaning of the term 'universal significance' by placing it so firmly within the context of an equitable division across State Parties. Second, by correcting the imbalance of inscriptions in favour of State Parties in the developing world, there is a real possibility of seriously increasing the number of World Heritage properties in danger with limited resources for political intervention and remedial action. Failure to take action to delete sites from the List further devalues the notion of a WHS as a uniquely special place owned by the peoples of the world rather than just another meaningless label. The majority of the WHS inscribed on the List of World Heritage in Danger in 2004 came from the developing world. Already poor in terms of economic and technical resources to protect their World Heritage Sites, many of these countries were further affected by natural or man-made disasters – earthquakes and war. They include the Iranian City of Bam; Bamiyan Valley, Afghanistan; Katmandu Valley, Nepal and the historic towns of Baku in Azerbaijan and Zabid in Yemen. Money is available from the World Heritage Fund.

If the number of World Heritage Sites in the developing world increases – as it rightly should – the cost of their upkeep in terms of conservation and management has to be addressed. The local community who live in or near a World Heritage Site and visitors arriving as tourists become the most significant stakeholders in this new arena. They need to be trained and nurtured. As the UK Government juggles with the competing priorities of economic development and competing interpretations of sustainable communities their commitment to World Heritage is measured. Their position becomes vividly apparent in the Stonehenge 'Sound Bite' case study.

Case study: Collaboration, consensus and conflict among stakeholders – the case of Stonehenge

World Heritage Site inscription can be the impetus for cooperation and collaboration among key stakeholders, but also the complexities and animosities can lead to atrophy and inaction. In the UK World Heritage designation currently carries no formal status in terms of designation and organizational management. No additional finance is attached to being a World Heritage Site. Cooperation depends on the goodwill of the stakeholders coming together in a loose knit fashion under the auspices of the World Heritage Site coordinator. The locus of power and control at WHS is difficult to determine, it often shifts and is different at each site both in the UK and in other countries round the world.

Stonehenge is an icon of international importance and a symbol of national pride. It has been a popular visitor attraction for generations of English people and international tourists travelling to Cornwall and the West Country. It is on the coach route for day trips from London. Recently, part of the stone circle featured on the Royal Mail stamps. Yet plans to improve the visitor facilities, the visitor experience and the road – the infamous A303 – have stalled.

Much of the conflict among stakeholders stems from the fact that interpretations of cultural heritage conservation and visitor management are dynamic processes. Ideas change. But decisions affecting Stonehenge are so important to the British sense of cultural identity and national pride that progress is slow and currently non-existent. Simultaneously, the costs of building dual carriageways, tunnels and roundabouts are escalating exponentially. The Master Plan 2000 involved an extensive and wide-reaching but unmanageable consultation process as indicated by the long list of invitees. Stonehenge and Avebury were inscribed on the World Heritage List as prehistoric monuments and not as cultural landscapes. At the Public Enquiry into the Highways Agency's plans, February 2004, ICOMOS-UK took an entirely different stance from English Heritage. ICOMOS-UK viewed Stonehenge as a group of monuments in their setting – a ceremonial cultural landscape – and stated that any intrusion of a dual carriageway into two-thirds of the World Heritage Site was entirely unacceptable.

English Heritage along with the Department of Culture, Media and Sport (DCMS) took a strict view of World Heritage status and the inscription referring to the pre-historic monuments. They were primarily concerned that the iconic stone circle should be free of traffic and seen in an appropriately restored landscape by taking a 2.1 km short-bored tunnel underground.

The proposed Visitor Centre – a state-of-the art modern structure designed by Australian architect Denton Corker Marshall of Melbourne – to be located outside the boundaries of the World Heritage Site on the far side of Countess Roundabout, was the subject of a second enquiry. The main issues for residents and visitors alike were that this new facility, to be placed approximately 1.6 km (one mile) from the stone circle would mean taking a bus ride (from the Visitor Centre), walking or cycling to see it. Car parking will only be available officially at the Visitor Centre. Passions run high.

This case study explores the reasons for the opposition to the proposed road, landscape and visitor centre developments from the point of view of different stakeholders. It consists of sound-bites juxtaposed to enable the reader to listen to their voices and examine their comments. The approach reveals what little thought government agencies gave to the needs of local people who were not involved in the planning process; how alliances of convenience are made; how throwing money at a problem via consultants and working groups solves nothing unless it is accompanied by an overall vision; that the real long-term solution to the roads issue – a long-bored tunnel mooted in 1995 – is getting further and further away on grounds of cost. But the Summer Solstice Festival is still happening with car parking adjacent to the Stone Circle while the English Heritage Stonehenge Project remains on the drawing board.

'Sound-bites' on Stonehenge

English Heritage: the facts

> Stonehenge and Avebury were inscribed on the World Heritage List in 1986 for their outstanding prehistoric monuments. At Stonehenge, the unparalleled stone circle (3000 BC–1600 BC) is surrounded by a ceremonial landscape comprising more than 300 burial mounds and many other prehistoric remains. The Stonehenge World Heritage Site is owned by English Heritage, the National Trust, the Ministry of Defence, farmers and householders. (English Heritage, 2005a)

English Heritage: The Stonehenge Project

> Stonehenge is one of the country's most important prehistoric monuments, but has been famously described by a United Kingdom government committee as a 'national disgrace' (English Heritage,

2005b). It is currently surrounded by roads and its visitor facilities are inadequate for today's needs.

The Stonehenge Project will rescue this iconic World Heritage Site from the noise and clutter of the 21st century and give it the dignified setting it deserves. Roads will be removed or tunnelled and ploughed fields returned to open grassland. A new world-class visitor centre will be built outside the World Heritage Site and there will be improved access through the Stonehenge World Heritage Site landscape. Summer 2005

Countess Road Residents Group

Here is some more good news! Previously we reported that visitors would have to spend a minimum of about half a day to visit the Stones, with a 1 mile/1.8 km walk each way. The good news is that new routes are under consideration that have a 15 minute journey in a land train and only a 0.75 mile/1.2 km walk each way. So you won't get quite so wet or muddy, the children won't get quite so fractious, and the buggy won't feel quite such a drag (CRRG, 2003).

Please tell us, on the 'contact us' page, your views about having to walk this distance, in all weathers, with a minimum visit of about 2 hours if one includes getting from your transport, going through the visitor centre, the shop, toilets and café (not necessarily in that order!). March 2003

Stonehenge Public Enquiry: Pre-historic Society

A public inquiry was held in Salisbury between 17 February and 5 May 2004 into the Highways Agency's £200 million proposal for a short-bored tunnel and 3.4 km of four-lane dual carriageway on the A303 road line through the World Heritage Site (UCL, 2004). The Prehistoric Society is just one of many archaeological and conservation organizations – including the National Trust, the Royal Archaeological Institute, the World Archaeological Congress, Rescue, ICOMOS-UK and the CBA (Council of British Archaeology) – to be unhappy with the scheme because of its negative impact on archaeological remains and landscape within the World Heritage Site. The Prehistoric Society formed part of a loose coalition with the CBA and the Wiltshire Archaeological and Natural History Society. June 2004

Save Stonehenge

World Heritage Site threatened by road building scheme! One of the world's most famous heritage sites, Stonehenge, is threatened by a massive and highly destructive road-building scheme. ... barbaric ... No other country in the world would contemplate treating a site which is a world icon in such a way. (Lord Kennet, February 2004)

Statement from the Member of Parliament for Salisbury

Following the Public Enquiry, the Inspector delivered his report on 31 January 2005. Meanwhile estimates of the cost have been spiralling.

In a clever wheeze that kicked the whole thing into the long grass, in December last the Secretary of State for Transport announced that a decision on the financing of the Stonehenge project would now be put to a 'regional consultative body' and it will have to compete with funds for other road improvements in the whole of The South West.

Then came the big one. The current 'approved' budget for Countess Flyover, the 2.1 km tunnel and the Winterbourne Stoke bypass stands at £223 m. You won't be surprised to hear that unattributable sources close to the truth have whispered to me that the estimated (as opposed to the approved) budget is fast approaching £400 m. (Robert Key MP, February 2005)

'Managed Open Access' to Stonehenge for the Summer Solstice ... a free festival 2005

English Heritage is likely to again provide 'Managed Open Access' to Stonehenge for the Summer Solstice. Please help to create a peaceful occasion by taking personal responsibility and following the conditions. The car park (on the Western side, enter off the A303 from the roundabout – it's signposted) will open at around 8pm on 20th June, and close at around 1pm on 21st June. Access to the stones themselves is from around 10pm until 9am (efestivals, 2005).

There's likely to be entertainment from samba bands and drummers but no amplified music is allowed. Van loads of police have been present in the area in the past in case of any trouble, but generally a jovial mood prevails. Sunrise is at around 4:45am. April 2005

Salisbury District Council Press Release

Stonehenge Visitor Centre is Refused

Salisbury District Council has thrown out English Heritage's plans to develop a new visitor centre for Stonehenge. The council's Planning and Regulatory Committee refused the scheme when it met on Tuesday night (July 26th). Their reason for refusing the plans was related to the proposed land train and access to the site. (SDC, 2005)

Layers and levels of community participation

In the UK once a site is on the Tentative List the hard work begins – defining the boundaries and buffer zones, ensuring that community support is in place and writing the nomination and management plan documents. Increasingly, there is an emphasis on the economic, social, environmental and cultural impacts of inscription – the benefits and disbenefits to the community. Wearmouth–Jarrow's candidature for WHS status is supported by both Local Authorities and the Government Office for the North East. A coordinator is in place to liaise with different stakeholders and prepare the necessary documentation.

The cost to the Local Authority is substantial, not only at the outset, but also in terms of their on-going responsibilities. In England, Local Authorities usually employ a WHS coordinator who is a cultural heritage manager. The Local Authority World Heritage Forum, LAWHF, is available for peer support. In Scotland, Historic Scotland has assumed many of these responsibilities and currently employs the World Heritage coordinator at New Lanark.

At Ironbridge Gorge in the late 1990s, The Ironbridge Gorge Initiative Framework for Managing the WHS was circulated widely in the valley. It was a large glossy brochure and represented a real attempt to seek comments from local people in order to 'work together to care for the WHS for our and future generations'. At Greenwich, at the same time, a secondee from English Heritage wrote the management plan. Community involvement was minimal. A leaflet was circulated to residents, but the boundaries were set by the cultural heritage expert without wide consultation and were based on traditional art-historical architectural and landscape criteria. The WHS Coordinator now employed by the Local Authority has set up Executive, Education and Marketing Groups. The WHS Steering Committee, chaired by a Greenwich councillor, ensures WHS issues are discussed on a regular basis. Initiatives for the joint marketing of Corporate Hospitality and the very existence of the Cutty Sark Docklands Light Railway station would probably not have happened without pressure from this Committee. However, at Greenwich, as elsewhere, individual heritage organizations are conscious of maintaining their own identities, visitor numbers and separate applications for funds.

Similarly, volunteers are committed to individual organizations. Therefore sites such as Kew or Canterbury benefit from the services of volunteers who are not directly involved in WHS matters. Perhaps there is an opportunity for an international organization of Friends of World Heritage Sites with local branches, but it does not exist at present. Amenity societies find World Heritage status useful in challenging unsuitable developments from the height and density of buildings to the quality of design. During 2005 The Greenwich Society has been watching the Stockwell Street Development intended to provide 'A New Square' and the redevelopment of the last large site in Greenwich Town Centre within the WHS. It is working alongside the World Heritage Committee. The Society responded to the planning application for tower blocks on the Lovells Wharf site saying: 'The height of the two towers is unacceptable. They will loom over East Greenwich and over the Park and the World Heritage Site'. Pressure group politics succeeded. A revised plan eliminating the two high-rise towers has been submitted by the developers. At Ironbridge Gorge in the late 1980s, not long after inscription, Residents' Groups from the Jackfield, Broseley, Coalport and Ironbridge communities – using

World Heritage status – were effective in overturning Shropshire County Council's plans for an undistinguished design for a bridge to replace the worn out ferro-concrete 'Free Bridge'. Instead, a modern bridge of distinctive design was erected scarcely visible from the famous Iron Bridge ancient monument in the heart of the World Heritage Site.

Visitor expectations of World Heritage Sites are high. Tourists in general and cultural tourists in particular are generally amorphous intractable stakeholders. Yet tourists are the 'peoples of the world' to whom world heritage belongs. At World Heritage Sites tourists anticipate having an interesting time that is guaranteed to be authentic. The precise quality of the visitors' experience, however, is influenced by their own expectations about the place prior to their visit. McKercher and du Cros (2001) have identified five major categories of cultural tourists:

1 The 'purposeful cultural tourist' for whom cultural tourism is the primary motive for visiting a destination, and the individual has a deep cultural experience
2 The 'sightseeing cultural tourist' for whom cultural tourism is a primary or major reason for visiting a destination, but the experience is more shallow
3 The 'serendipitous cultural tourist', who does not travel for cultural tourism reasons, but who, after participating, ends up having a deep cultural tourism experience
4 The 'casual cultural tourist', for whom cultural tourism is a weak motive for visiting a destination, and the resultant experience is shallow
5 The 'incidental cultural tourist', who does not travel for cultural tourism reasons but, nonetheless, participates in some activities and has shallow experiences.

Heritage sites, they suggest, are likely to have all five categories of tourists at any one time, with the mix dependent on the nature of the place and the origin of the majority of the visitors.

This research is a helpful starting point in terms of how it might be possible to engage all visitors and all tourists in different ways and at different levels more fully, more effectively and more actively as stakeholders in World Heritage. Cultural tourists need improved visitor management at WHSs. Individual cultural heritage organizations within World Heritage Sites need visitors and the money they bring with them. But, the World Heritage conservation movement also needs a myriad of committed stakeholders world-wide who understand and care about the future viability and sustainability of World Heritage. Cultural tourists to World Heritage Sites, as much as local people, have a significant role to play. The development of strategies to encourage the participation of visitors – and especially 'cultural tourists' – as stakeholders in World Heritage conservation remains an opportunity to be grasped by the World Heritage movement. Because States Parties agree to safeguard the World Heritage Sites in their care, there is an added expectation by visitors that these States Parties, as the principal stakeholders within a nation state, will take their responsibilities seriously. There is a belief among visitors to World Heritage Sites that they are – or should be – carefully managed and controlled, often at a national level, to protect the values for which they were first recognized. In reality the reverse is often the case. Many World Heritage Sites experience extreme tourism pressures, particularly in regard to their more sensitive characteristics or heritage values. Recently, *The Times* newspaper highlighted the dilemma of Hadrian's Wall: 'The World Heritage Site survived invasions and battles but is being wrecked by a surge in tourism'. Professor Peter Fowler's report *Hadrian's Wall and the National Trail* addresses the issues. Peter commented in *The Times* interview: 'To put it mildly, I was somewhat disconcerted at what I found ... serious inadequacies in the management of the Trail are apparent ... the commitment by the Countryside Agency and the Highways authorities "to manage the Trail effectively" was not apparent on the ground' (Alberge, 2005). States Parties and national agencies can no longer operate effectively independently, either individually or together, at a strategic or an operational level as has been illustrated at Hadrian's Wall. A broader operational stakeholder partnership arrangement is necessary for effective action with clear accountable shared leadership.

Only by developing a positive, dynamic interface between local people and tourists as key stakeholders will it be possible to continue to provide a distinctive cultural tourism experience celebrating cultural diversity at each World Heritage Site as well as improved visitor management. The *ICOMOS International Charter for Cultural Tourism* addresses the primary relationships between the cultural identity and cultural heritage of the host community and the interests, expectations and behaviour of visitors, both domestic and international (ICOMOS, 1999). It promotes the engagement of the host community in all aspects of planning and managing for tourism. At sites where the managed engagement between the host community and the visitor is strongest, visitor management is also the most successful.

Many natural and cultural World Heritage Sites are highly valued by the local community who identify with the character and qualities of these places. As committed stakeholders local people combine an understanding and appreciation of the heritage assets and willingness to communicate this sensibility and knowledge to others. Canterbury Cathedral – located within a World Heritage Site – appoints an ordained minister to manage Visitor Services. The principle adopted by the first incumbent, Canon Peter Brett, was in sympathy with the spirit of a place of worship: it was one of winning over visitors not pushing them around. 'Spaces were formed for pause and reflection ... It was a bold, but extremely effective, decision to make the whole of the massive Crypt a place where silence was expected. Signage which indicates that the Crypt has its own silence which is there already, and to be felt by being quiet oneself, proved a subtle and generally successful appeal. The quietness itself, paradoxically, facilitates movement' (Brett, 2001). The significance of maintaining spiritual values in a cathedral of world significance in architectural heritage terms and the importance of involving and training members of the congregation as volunteer guides to communicate with visitors from around the world are essential aspects of developing a working, workable stakeholder partnership at local level.

Communities are often keen to present their World Heritage Sites to visitors or to exploit them as tourism resources in the anticipation of economic gain. They are also likely to be protective of their own privacy and lifestyles, which can be overwhelmed during peak tourism seasons. At both natural and cultural World Heritage Sites local people are often the tour guides and interpreters. At others they are the guardians and purveyors of the intangible heritage in the form of priests, musicians, dancers, story-tellers, craftspeople, demonstrators, cooks and farmers or gardeners. The quality of the tourism experience is greatly enhanced if members of the local community are engaged as key stakeholders and encouraged to welcome visitors. The confidence of communities to invite strangers to join in with their local festivals held within the boundaries of a World Heritage Site often means that they can benefit directly from the financial rewards tourism brings. In addition, genuine community support can ensure that the promotional images of the destination presented to the outside world are those actually experienced by the visitors as they interact with local people during their visit.

Re-branding World Heritage Sites

The development of an approach to branding World Heritage Sites in the UK and elsewhere, based on the fundamental sets of experiences offered to visitors by the local community in the setting of a World Heritage Site, is a new opportunity. Where a World Heritage Site achieves the full integration of the community into the appreciation, interpretation and operation of the cultural heritage assets it is able to enhance its local distinctiveness, manage better and appeal successfully directly to a wide audience. When the local community is perceived by cultural heritage professionals as just 'the workforce' or 'the vocal minority' getting in the way of the development of grandiose schemes, such as at Stonehenge, then cultural heritage values themselves are in danger of being ridiculed, even under the umbrella of World Heritage Sites.

Early attempts at branding World Heritage Sites were a useful exercise but missed the essence of the special significance of World Heritage Sites – the reason for nomination in the first place. Hadrian's Wall Tourism Partnership explored some options with a model dividing the audiences into two, external and internal. The External Audience was the consumer, media, community and the Internal Audience the Partnership, funders, community, partners, suppliers, and media (Partnership based stories).

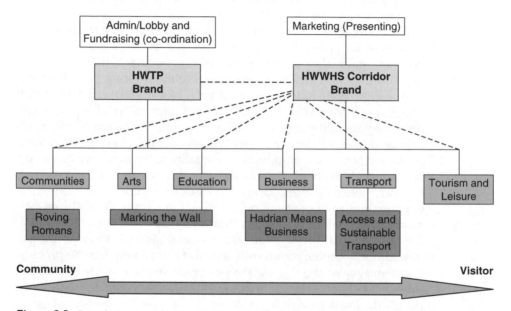

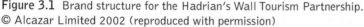

Figure 3.1 Brand structure for the Hadrian's Wall Tourism Partnership.
© Alcazar Limited 2002 (reproduced with permission)

In moving towards establishing a new approach to branding World Heritage Sites, where the values and attributes of the people and the place are combined, in turn an agenda is set whereby the confidence and creativity of the community and visitors alike can flourish. Brand identity is based on cultural identity and becomes a source of inspiration for all. A new brand can give a new sense of pride for local people and visitors something they never dreamed of needing or wanting – something beyond their expectations. This is good business sense. It maintains market differentiation and allows an organization or partnership to become a market leader. But it is also good heritage sense as it can provide a platform for a dynamic, sustainable heritage for the future. It is no accident that the Regional Development Agencies see the benefits of World Heritage status as an opportunity to bring people living in adjacent communities together, to develop a sense of self-worth and civic pride. As a caveat, development initiatives based on a new-found brand identity must take place in tandem with and in the context of a robust community-based conservation programme, if the opportunities are to be maximized and disasters averted.

Conclusions

Communities have moved centre stage in the World Heritage debate. Their roles have yet to be defined in detail. But in the process of the democratization of heritage, a greater emphasis on intangible values and the pressing need to conserve and celebrate cultural diversity across the world, World Heritage Sites have the chance – both in the UK and elsewhere – to engage their stakeholders, community sup- porters and visitors alike in a new agenda. This new agenda is one that is more exciting, more fulfilling, more refreshing and more par- ticipatory than in the past. In establishing an environment for mutual exploration, investigation and learning at World Heritage Sites, the conservation of cultural heritage assets will be secure, for the time being at least.

References

Alberge, D. (2005) Walkers put Hadrian's Wall on road to ruin. *The Times*, 9 August.

Alcazar (2002) Hadrian's Wall Tourism Partnership Combined Brand Strategy Report Stages 1 and 2, Helen Powell, Director, Alcazar Limited, November.

Brett, P. (2001) Case Study on Canterbury Cathedral. (Unpublished) Prepared on behalf of ICOMOS – UK Cultural Tourism Committee.

CRRG (2003) Article, Countess Road Residents' Group Newsletter, 21 March.

efestivals (2005) 'Managed Open Access' to Stonehenge for the Summer Solstice ... a free festival 2005 (www.efestivals.co.uk, accessed 20 April 2005).

English Heritage (2005a) The Facts, Background Information on Stonehenge, English Heritage website (www.english-heritage. org.uk/stonehenge accessed 12 April 2005).

English Heritage (2005b) The Stonehenge Project, English Heritage website (www.english-heritage.org.uk/stonehenge 12 April 2005).

ICOMOS (1999) ICOMOS International Charter for Cultural Tourism, Adopted by ICOMOS, 12th General Assembly, Mexico, October.

ICOMOS (2003) Mapping and Managing the Intangible Heritage at World Heritage Sites. Proceedings of the ICOMOS Scientific Symposium Place, memory, meaning: preserving intangible values in monuments and sites, Victoria Falls, Zimbabwe 27–31 October. ICOMOS CD-ROM.

ICOMOS (2004) The World Heritage List: Filling the Gaps – an Action Plan for the Future, An Analysis by ICOMOS (International Committee of Monuments and Sites), February 2004 (www. International.icomos.org accessed 22 March 2005).

Key, R. (2005) The Stonehenge Saga: A View from the Commons, Robert Key MP for Salisbury, 12th February 2005 (www.druidnetwork.org accessed 12 April 2005).

Lake District (2005) Statement by the Lake District National Parks Service, A Special Place, World Heritage Status, April 2005 (www.lake-district.gov.uk accessed 3 May 2005).

Lord Kennet (2004) Save Stonehenge, Lord Kennet, Save Stonehenge Society, February 2004 (www.savestonehenge.org.uk accessed 23 March 2004).

McKercher, B. and du Cros, H. (2001) *Cultural Tourism: The Partnership between Tourism and Cultural Heritage Management*. Binghamton, New York: Haworth Press.

SDC (2005) Stonehenge Visitor Centre is Refused, Salisbury District Council Press Release, 26 July.

Smart, K. (2001) 'The irreplaceable 'wild' sheep who are the Lake District's gardeners' quotes Keith Twentyman, Cumbria NFU Group Secretary, K. Smart, *News and Star*, 24 March.

UCL (2004) Stonehenge Public Enquiry: Prehistoric Society Statement, June (www.ucl.ac.uk/prehistoric accessed 23 March 2005).

UNESCO (2003) Operational Guidelines for the Implementation of the World Heritage Convention, paras. 39 & 40, Intergovernmental Committee for the Protection of the World's Cultural and Natural Heritage, World Heritage Centre, (Revised) 2 February, 2005 (www.whc.unesco.org/archive/opguide05.en.pdf accessed 11 April 2005).

UNESCO (2005a) *Tangible Cultural Heritage*, UNESCO (www.unesco. org accessed 11 April 2005).

UNESCO (2005b) *The World Heritage Centre*, UNESCO (www.whc.org accessed 12 April 2005).

UNESCO (2005c) *The List* UNESCO (http://whc.unesco.org/en/list/1140 accessed 5 October 2005).

CHAPTER 4

Marketing issues and World Heritage Sites

Stephen W. Boyd and
Dallen J. Timothy

Aims

The aims of this chapter are to:

- Examine a range of marketing issues relevant to World Heritage Sites (WHS)
- Challenge commonly held tourism marketing principles, particularly the marketing mix as to its value where WHS are concerned
- Examine critically the role that factors such as scale and accessibility play in how sites are marketed
- Through application of a case study to present the merits of marketing not just the site, but the wider setting in which it is situated.

Introduction

Marketing is a highly complex topic that holds an important place within tourism (Holloway, 2004). Conventional thinking has often focused on the development of a market as central to successful tourism development as opposed to the development of an attraction base that has long-term potential. World Heritage Sites are often the icons used to market destinations. For example Australia deliberately makes use of its WHS in its tourism image making, whereas at the same time, the sites themselves stand as exemplars of long-term visitor attractions that have come to represent powerful evocative symbols of a country's identity, helping to acknowledge the presence of properties ascribed for their outstanding natural and cultural properties. As leading attractions in many parts of the world, their success in terms of tourism is not often the result of their designation as having World Heritage status, but rather other factors, such as how the sites are marketed and how accessible they are to the marketplace (Shackley, 1998). Furthermore, there is the irony that the success of many sites as places heavily visited is at the expense of why they were initially inscribed, namely to protect and conserve 'valued' heritage resources.

This chapter explores a plethora of issues associated with marketing of WHS, including the role marketing plays as only one dimension against issues such as conservation, interpretation, sales, customer provision; the extent to which the marketing mix concept can be applied to WHS; the prominence of scale and peripherality in determining site level visitation; the role of branding and the merits of de-marketing of sites; the need to market sites as part of wider attraction spaces and the value of strategic thinking in terms of marketing of World Heritage Sites. An in-depth case study of the Giant's Causeway in Northern Ireland is presented at the end of the chapter in which many of the above issues are addressed, albeit within a site that has peculiarities and factors that make its marketing distinctive.

Marketing issues

Type, scale and market reach

The type of site matters when it comes to how world heritage sites are marketed. The reality that sites can be nominated for their natural or cultural attributes, or in some cases both, has marketing implications. Natural sites are often marketed as part of wider systems of protected areas and national parks, where issues of peripherality, sensitivity, and threshold use levels take on importance along with the multi-purpose behind visiting either passively to enjoy outstanding natural scenery or to use that backdrop as the venue for thrill-seeking activity. In contrast, in many cases cultural sites situated in urban areas are on the agenda of many urban tourists, have better access, are often parts of diverse and modern world cultural spaces, where issues of interpretation and education assume importance. As such, in both contexts, appeal is to both the passive heritage visitor (akin to the mass tourist) and the serious heritage visitor (akin to the special interest traveller) market, and the challenge is to market to different ends of the visitor spectrum.

Heritage is not homogeneous; it exists at different levels or scales, namely world, national, local and personal (Timothy, 1997; Timothy and Boyd, 2003). Many WHS draw large masses of tourists from many countries, for which a visit to these sites themselves is likely to be only a small part of a more extensive itinerary, and as such the amount of time spent at a WHS is often as short as a few hours. For many international visitors, while WHS are viewed as attractions that may invoke feelings of awe, they probably do not invoke feelings of personal attachment. Visits to ancient monuments are largely motivated by the belief that such objects really are linked to the remote past. Indeed, for many tourists, visiting international heritage attractions that have been accorded WHS status is a way of appreciating universal civilization and achieving some degree of human unity (Moulin, 1991). In contrast, while local residents and domestic visitors are an important part of the market to WHS, these people also serve the function of supporting heritage spaces that are of a local, regional and national scale, and their attachment to sites of international significance is often indirect as a result of visiting as part of the visiting friends and relatives (VFR) market where they feel obligated to show WHS to their international guests (Robinson et al., 1994).

Psychographic characteristics also apply when it comes to marketing WHS. Plog (1973, 1991) proposed that tourism places develop differently as a result of the types of visitors they attract. He argued that tourists could fall between two extreme poles on a psychographic spectrum, where psychocentrics display tendencies towards nearness, comforts of home, and familiarity in their surroundings. At the other end of the spectrum, allocentrics seek out the distant, unusual and challenging experiences. In a similar way, psychographic thinking can be applied to visitors interested in WHS. By visiting sites within cities on the original Grand Tour circuit and for example, UK sites within or close to modern urban places, modern-day visitors to Europe are displaying psychographic tendencies to visit WHS within well established tourism places. In contrast, visitors keen to explore the cultural sites (e.g. temples of Asia, the ruins of the Mayan and Aztec civilizations), experience the culture of first peoples and their traditions (e.g. sites in the interior of Australia, and peripheral regions of Canada and the Pacific Ocean) and are, in essence, creating new Grand Tours including international heritage sites they prefer to explore, thus displaying more allocentric tendencies. Marketers of WHS should take note of these trends (Timothy and Boyd, 2003).

Branding

Branding has become common in marketing speak today, developing its own lexicon of terms: equity, identity, positioning, personality, essence, character, soul, culture and image. In the context of this chapter attention is given over to positioning and image. Positioning refers to what a brand stands for in the minds of its customers and prospects, relative to its competition, in terms of benefits and promises. The brand is obvious here, namely that of examples of outstanding value worthy of universal recognition for their cultural and/or natural heritage, as compared to other attractions within the vicinity. Provided issues such as accessibility to site are not problematic, many Destination Marketing Organizations have capitalized on using the brand as the means to sell the experience of that particular area. Travel to the Red Centre of Australia is not complete without visiting Uluru, or a visit to the Agra region of India requires a stopover to view the Taj Mahal. The dangers of using the WHS logo are the possible exclusion of recognition of many other opportunities and hence experiences WHS regions have to offer visitors, namely the experiences derived from visiting non-WHS attractions. As such, the brand becomes too myopic and centred around a visit and experience of only the world heritage site. Brand 'image' is referred to as generally synonymous with the reputation of the brand as a whole. Reputation may be taken and read as visitor experience. What 'experience' do visitors expect when they visit sites that have been accorded international heritage status? Surely, they expect to see evidence of why the site has received this highest accolade, and then the visitor experience that is created around it. The challenge therefore for many site managers is to provide a quality product for a market that they intentionally never expected to entertain, namely the tourist. The mandate of WHS is one of protection and conservation, and furthermore, member states who ratified the convention do not nominate sites because of their tourism draw, but rather because they satisfy a number of the natural and cultural criteria needed in order to be considered for WHS status. Unfortunately, many sites have turned to tourism and its market as a means of financing themselves, and ensuring the necessary conservation measures are carried out. Being proudly allowed to display the UNESCO logo at sites does not come with monies or personnel to assist in its operation. As such, tourism has become a necessary evil in many cases, albeit with the consequences this market brings, such as visitor pressure, congestion at peak times, and possible site damage. These consequences have led to thinking that de-marketing of some sites is the preferred alternative.

De-marketing

With the rise in interest of things cultural and heritage, it is hard to conceive how WHS can take a de-marketing option given that such destinations are on visitors' 'must see' list. Horner and Swarbrooke (1996) refer to the term as meaning action that is designed to discourage consumers from buying particular goods and services. In the case of WHS, this would involve not producing any promotional material, developing messages within advertisements and brochures with the intent of discouraging certain people from visiting in general or not to visit at certain times, or promotion of alternative places. De-marketing is not an option to be applied to all WHS as many do not receive visitors given they are not highly accessible, Easter Island being a good case in point. The above strategies, while evidentially positive in terms of what they aim to accomplish, would be very hard to apply to WHS that are heavily visited by tourists. To many Destination Management Organizations (DMOs) the idea of not using the site in advertisements would not get widespread support, and to suggest an alternative site to visit would in many cases be unworkable in terms of finding sites and other attractions that would be suitable substitutes. The concept of substitution of attraction and place is untenable in most cases by visitors as why should they be forced to view secondary sites in order to maintain the 'real' one? The risk in achieving this substitution of experience is that the market may choose then not to return to the WHS itself. While this action is applicable for many tourism destinations, it is unlikely to apply in the case of visitation patterns to WHS. In an ideal world, sites that face extreme pressure from high levels of visitation at peak times would benefit from de-marketing, if only to alleviate concerns over the loss of ecological and cultural integrity within the site itself, and in this case, one approach to de-marketing would be selectively to market sites for niche markets, appealing to those that would be classed as special interest travellers over those akin to mass tourists with a passing interest in heritage and culture. In order to achieve this, DMOs have to engage in a deliberate marketing campaign that identifies those segments of the international and domestic market they most want to reach. While de-marketing is a concept that receives limited attention within the tourism marketing literature, it is an issue that has merit in this chapter.

Peripherality and accessibility

Another issue that has received mention above is that of peripherality. Peripheral regions are attractive for tourism, and many WHS, particularly those classified as 'natural sites', are found in peripheral regions. Hall and Boyd (2005) noted the paradox that exists for tourism in peripheral regions, namely that is the peripheral characteristics of destinations such as naturalness, remoteness, isolation, outstanding flora and fauna, to name a few, can be affected by the influx of too much tourism to the extent that what originally attracted visitors to the region is lost as a result of rising visitor numbers. The irony, however, is that many of these peripheral regions rely on tourism as the only viable form of economic development open to them and have to accept getting the balance right between numbers and maintaining the quality and integrity of sites. In the case of many natural WHS, these are often found to be part of wider systems of protected areas and national parks, and as such fall under the jurisdiction of the public sector management agency and their respective managerial approaches and strategies to control visitor numbers so that sites are not too severely impacted upon. Accessibility, or the relative absence of it, can be as strong a factor as marketing in terms of determining how important individual sites will be as tourism attractions. The inability to get to sites will be a strong enough incentive to limit the type of visitor, and the volume of visitation. In the case of 'natural' WHS, those areas selected from within wider systems of protected spaces are often the most well known parks within the system and irrespective of location attract large numbers of visitors. Yellowstone National Park and Grand Canyon National Park in the USA, Rocky Mountain Parks in Canada and Tongariro National Park in New Zealand are apt examples of sites that are relatively isolated and distant from large centres of population, but which yet receive large numbers of visitors. While accessibility is central to tourism, what is also important is the product at the destination itself and its composite parts.

Marketing as one dimension of sites

Marketing is only one dimension of WHS, and others such as education, information, on-site sales, and service provision need to be considered. While many of these will be addressed in other chapters of this book, the purpose of alluding to them in this chapter is to make the point that, while the purpose behind marketing is to sell the site to a potential customer base, these other factors, when combined, have an important role in creating an overall visitor experience. A 'designate sites and they will come' mentality requires that sites are furnished with quality interpretation and educational facilities, things to do and see as well as service provision that caters to the basic needs of visitors to eat, sleep and shop. In many cases, where sites are found in peripheral areas, some of these basic requirements are not met, making it difficult to sell the site to visitors, and often in this case, numbers of visitors are small. Uluru is popular as a destination as there is accommodation relatively nearby, good interpretation and educational facilities are on hand, along with a cultural centre where authentic and locally produced products are available to purchase. It is these tangible elements, as well as the intangible of the experience of being at the place, and the meaning behind the visit that combine to make up what is ultimately being marketed in the first place.

Marketing mix

This is a well known concept within marketing, known to involve the traditional four Ps of product, place, promotion and price, and is often referred to as the 'core' of marketing (Holloway, 2004). Product is referring to what is actually delivered to the consumer and the benefits that a consumer can gain to suit their needs and wants. Goeldner et al. (2000) state that product also includes product planning, product development, breadth of the line, branding and packaging. In the case of WHS, the product is self-explanatory. The market is brought to either a natural and/or cultural product which has been deemed of international status; a product borne out of the need to safeguard sites of outstanding human value and a product line that is constantly being added to on a regular basis each year by those nations that have ratified the convention. In the case of WHS, there is no such thing as 'coming up with the right product' as the product exists not as a result of tourism, but rather as a by-product of the need to protect and conserve them for current and future generations. Place is concerned with distribution, and the channels by which consumers are given access to the product. In the case of WHS, consumers are brought to the product through advertisement, and selling sites as iconic and must visit places. The status that many WHS hold in the minds of visitors often means that name recognition alone is often sufficient when it comes to satisfying the place element of the mix. Promotion communicates the benefits of the product to customers, and includes the techniques used to accomplish this. In some cases, tourism businesses within the vicinity of sites have used the WHS brand to promote their ventures and sell their experience as part of the wider opportunity the WHS region offers. Research by Hall and Piggin (2003) noted that in the case of Tongariro National Park and Te Wahi Pounamu (Southwest New Zealand) WHS, the majority of tourism businesses surveyed recognized the benefits of World Heritage listing for the wider region, and that almost half of the businesses surveyed stated they believed such status attracted visitors to the region and therefore used the term 'World Heritage' in their promotional materials. The last of the 4 Ps 'price' is the critical variable in the marketing mix. Goeldner et al. (2000) state that the price set must both satisfy customers and meet profit objectives. In many cases, admission is free, whereas in many national parks, admission is based on a differential fee system between international and domestic visitors. Other Ps have been added, but often have limited bearing on marketing. For example, Boyd and Timothy (2001) noted that partnership can be an effective tool in terms of both interpretation and management of sites irrespective of whether they are found within a mixed-use landscape or a protected landscape. Mill and Morrison (1998) noted that other Ps included programming and people, with other new ones being added to the original mix, namely passion, purpose, performance, potential, pass-along, position, practice and, lastly, profit. Regardless of whether it is acknowledged that there are 4 or 13 Ps, what emerges is that the thinking behind the marketing mix is not well suited when applied to sites of World Heritage status.

Strategic approach to marketing

Marketing of heritage places should not necessarily entail attempts to increase visitor numbers through advertising (Timothy and Boyd, 2003). Instead it means that managers of WHS, for instance, have opportunities to target certain consumers and control their visits while, at the same time, improve conservation standards (Pearson and Sullivan, 1995). One useful way of looking at marketing is to consider the value of adopting a strategic approach. Hall and McArthur (1998) argue that there are essentially three elements and questions involved in strategic marketing planning:

1 Where are we now?
2 Where do we want to be in the future?
3 How do we get there?

To get answers to these questions, a five-stage marketing planning process emerged: situational analysis; establishing objectives and strategies; marketing activities; marketing management; and marketing evaluation. Space does not permit a detailed discussion of each here, except for the following brief comments as each applies to World Heritage Sites. Understanding the present situation involves realizing that WHS cannot be all things to all people, so tough decisions are required as to what the target audience is and what type of experience is being created for them. Also important here is how much of a competitive advantage do WHS have over other heritage attractions in the region in terms of accessibility, market segments, facilities and services, marketing strategies, cost and maintenance. As for marketing objectives and strategies, what is critical here is the extent to which goals and objectives can deviate from selling the key attributes of the site itself and on what its WHS status is based. Developing marketing strategies is to translate current conditions into desired situations (Heath and Wall, 1992), for instance, promoting awareness of newly established sites through an advertising campaign, or targeting specific market segments as a way of bringing more money into the local region. Marketing activities refer back to determining the most correct marketing mix for achieving the stated goals and objectives of managers. Marketing management involves the implementation of use of effective marketing strategies, often requiring hiring more staff and spending more money, two items that are often lacking where WHS are involved. Lastly, marketing evaluation is useful in determining if strategies were successful against initial marketing objectives. The most effective methods to carry this out where WHS are concerned is measuring usage and establishing visitor profiles – activities that have a long history for natural heritage sites as opposed to cultural heritage sites. Timothy and Boyd (2003) note that the primary purpose of evaluation is to assist managers in understanding issues such as marketing effectiveness, image creation/enhancement, and the number of people who visited the heritage sites based on advertising efforts and media usage, not necessarily to develop broad-based theories.

The following case study addresses many of the marketing issues raised in this chapter.

Case study: Marketing of the Giant's Causeway World Heritage Site

The Giant's Causeway, the UK's first WHS was inscribed in 1986 under the following natural properties:

- be outstanding examples representing major stages of Earth's history, including the record of life, significant on-going geological processes in the development of landforms, or significant geomorphic or physiographic features
- contain superlative natural phenomena or areas of exceptional natural beauty and aesthetic importance.

The Giant's Causeway lies at the foot of the basalt cliffs along the sea coast on the edge of the Antrim plateau on the North Coast of Northern Ireland. It comprises some 40 000 black basalt columns protruding out of the sea. Geological studies of these formations over the last 300 years have greatly contributed to the development of the earth sciences and show that this striking landscape was caused by volcanic activity during the Tertiary period some 50–60 million years ago.

While the Giant's Causeway was noted for its unique natural properties, it has had a long history of being a leading tourist attraction. Ever since a Dublin woman's realistic sketches publicized the Giant's Causeway in 1740, it has been a magnet for visitors to Northern Ireland. Europe's first hydro-electric tram operated between the key resort community of Portrush on the North Coast to the Causeway between 1883 and 1949, enabling early visitors to travel to see the famous stone columns, as well as take leisurely journeys around the coast. In more modern times, a visitor centre was built in 1986 that symbolizes a rural cottage design and housed an interpretative centre that explains the geological enigma of the Causeway and tells the stories of the legendary Irish giant, Finn MaCool who, it is claimed, had a hand in the creation of the causeway. As early as accurate visitor records were kept for attractions in Northern Ireland, the Giant's Causeway has been the Province's leading visitor attraction. In 1986, the year the visitor centre was constructed and WHS status was achieved, visitor numbers were approximately 100 000, rising to 400 000 a decade later. By 2004, visitor numbers recorded at the Giant's Causeway visitor centre reached 450 000 visitors. High visitation levels have been maintained as the hexagonal columns have not been extensively altered. Apart from a paved road leading to the causeway and a series of steps up from the base of the causeway to the cliff top, the attraction has been pretty well left in its natural state. The souvenir shacks that were a common feature of the route down to the causeway during the 19th century have since been removed and are now present in a modern form within the visitor centre.

In May 2000, part of the original visitor centre was damaged by fire and an international competition at present is underway to replace the visitor facilities at the Causeway site, with the new visitor centre to be open for the 2007 summer peak tourism season. There is some concern by the owners of the World Heritage Site (jointly owned and managed by the National Trust which is responsible for the stones, headlands and cliff top paths, and Moyle District Council which is responsible for the car park and site of the visitor centre) about over-crowding during peak holiday periods, particularly bank holiday weekends, the dangers of being swept into the sea off the rocks and rising levels of graffiti on many of the columns, all aspects which were addressed in a management plan that was prepared and sub-mitted to UNESCO in February 2005.

The Giant's Causeway is indirectly marketed by the Northern Ireland Tourist Board (NITB) as the hexagon is a prominent part of the logo for the Board. The hexagon 'brand' has become synonymous with tourism in Northern Ireland. Recently, the NITB, along with the Department of Enterprise, Trade and Investment (DETI), have com-missioned a Causeway Coast Tourism Masterplan which aims to place the Giant's Causeway within the larger Causeway Coast and Glens Area of Outstanding Natural Beauty (AONB), but with the Giant's Causeway being deemed as a priority area for the NITB (McBride, 2005). The Giant's Causeway is an essential part of the long-term visioning of the NITB and this is presented within their Strategic Framework for Action 2004–07 document (NITB, 2003). The strategy comprises three broad themes: growing visitor numbers; business enhancement; and effective communication. Under the business enhancement section, the following signature projects are to be pur-sued with the goal of delivering international 'stand out' for Northern Ireland:

- Giant's Causeway/Antrim and Causeway Coast Area
- Titanic Quarter
- Walled City of Derry
- Christian Heritage/St Patrick
- Mournes National Park Area.

The Giant's Causeway WHS has been linked to its wider setting of the Antrim and Causeway Coast Area and is being marketed as part of a wider tourism space. The actual site of the Giant's Causeway is relatively small, comprising 6 km of sheer cliffs, rising to over 90 m, forming a series of bays and a coastal path 8 km long. It is, therefore, appropriate to market the site as part of a larger and more diverse coastal tourism space. Marketing is noted as an important element of the Causeway Coast and Glens Tourism Masterplan 2004–2013, with a strategic recommendation committing over £5 million to a market-ing budget over the first 3 years of the Masterplan, to target priority markets of Great Britain, Republic of Ireland, Mainland Europe, North America and Domestic/Northern Ireland. The marketing strategy has the following marketing objectives:

- to increase the number of out-of-state visitors to the region (407 000 staying visitors were recorded in 2002)
- to increase the level of awareness of the Causeway Coast and Glens in priority markets
- to promote a coastal tourist trail as a major new product for the island of Ireland (see below)
- to increase the economic contribution from tourism by extending visitor dwell time and, as a consequence, visitor expenditure (out-of-state visitors spent an estimated £56.4 million in 2002)
- to achieve spatial distribution of visitors throughout the region through the promotion of a range of activity and rural holidays and attractions (DETI, 2004).

The marketing strategy for the Causeway Coast and Glens will be to focus on the following segment of the market:

- independent travellers/car touring
- short breaks/cultural holidays
- activity holidays (golf, walking, cycling, diving, surfing, sea fishing)
- rural breaks
- coach tours.

This marketing strategy is in keeping with many of the Winning Themes (another element of the 'Business Enhancement' section of the Strategic Framework for Action), which were identified as delivering a competitive advantage for Northern Ireland, namely through short breaks, excellent events, business tourism, activity tourism and cultural and heritage tourism. The strategy will be overseen by the Causeway Coast and Glens Regional Tourism Organization (RTO), which will work in close cooperation with the NITB in the design and production of literature, advertising, packaging, trade marketing, cooperative marketing with neighbouring regions (e.g. the Republic of Ireland and Scotland) and operate familiarization trips and engage in event marketing and other programmes.

The Giant's Causeway, as part of the wider Causeway Coast and Glens (CCAG) region, will also be marketed through the creation of a Coastal Tourism Route that will take in the whole of the CCAG AONB, and thereby link the three signature projects of the Titanic Quarter in the Docks of Belfast, the Giant's Causeway on the North Coast and the Walled City of Derry at the western tip of the region (Wilmont, 2005). This is another example of how the actual WHS is being promoted as part of a wider tourism space. In so doing, tourism businesses and activities can associate themselves with being part of the Causeway region and use the World Heritage status as part of their wider marketing literature to encourage visitors to their specific attraction.

Conclusions

This chapter has raised a number of wider considerations when it comes to marketing of World Heritage Sites. While many of the issues have general application to most WHS, the uniqueness of each site will mean that the degree of application will vary considerably. Issues of branding and the WHS label, market reach, access, and the relevance of the marketing mix, need to be assessed on a site-specific basis, taking in the context of place and the characteristics of each designated site. The selection of the case example of the Giant's Causeway WHS demonstrates the value of broadening marketing beyond the parameters of the site itself to incorporate the wider tourism space in which it is part. Tourism marketing is an essential element to tourism in general, and while the extent to which various issues vary when considered in the case of WHS, marketing is a necessity given many of these destinations have evolved as key tourist spaces out of an initial interest to protect and conserve them.

References

Boyd, S.W. and Timothy, D.J. (2001) Developing partnerships: tools for interpretation and management. *Tourism Recreation Research*, 26 (1), 47–53.

Department of Enterprise, Trade and Investment (DETI) (2004) *Causeway Coast and Glens Tourism Masterplan 2004–2013*. Belfast: Netherleigh House.

Goeldner, C.R., Ritchie, J.R.B. and McIntosh, R.W. (2000) *Tourism: Principles, Practices, Philosophies*, 8th edn. New York: John Wiley & Sons.

Hall, C.M. and Boyd, S.W. (2005) *Nature-based Tourism in Peripheral Areas: Development or Disaster?* Clevedon: Channel View Publications.

Hall, C.M. and McArthur, S. (1998) *Integrated Heritage Management*. London: Stationery Office.

Hall, C.M. and Piggin, R. (2003) World heritage sites: managing the brand. In Fyall, A., Garrod, B. and Leask, A. (eds) *Managing Visitor Attractions: New Directions*. Oxford: Butterworth-Heinemann, pp. 203–219.

Heath, E. and Wall, G. (1992) *Marketing Tourism Destinations: A Strategic Planning Approach*. Chichester: John Wiley & Sons.

Holloway, J.C. (2004) *Marketing for Tourism*, 4th edn. Harlow: Prentice Hall.

Horner, S. and Swarbrooke, J. (1996) *Marketing Tourism, Hospitality and Leisure in Europe*. London: Thomson Business Press.

McBride, K. (2005) Causeway Coast and Glens Signature Project Manager, Northern Ireland Tourist Board, personal correspondence.

Mill, R.C. and Morrison, A.M. (1998) *The Tourism System: An Introductory Text*. Dubuque: Kendall/Hunt Publishing Company.

Moulin, C. (1991) Cultural heritage and tourism development in Canada. *Tourism Recreation Research*, 16 (1), 50–55.

Northern Ireland Tourist Board (NITB) (2003) *Strategic Framework for Action 2004–2007*. Belfast: NITB.

Pearson, M. and Sullivan, S. (1995) *Looking After Heritage Places*. Melbourne: Melbourne University Publishing.

Plog, S.C. (1973) Why destinations areas rise and fall in popularity. *Cornell Hotel and Restaurant Administration Quarterly*, 14 (3), 13–16.

Plog, S.C. (1991) *Leisure Travel: Making it a Growth Market ... Again!* New York: John Wiley & Sons.

Robinson, R., Wertheim, M. and Senior, G. (1994) Selling the heritage product. In Harrison, R. (ed.) *Manual of Heritage Management*. Oxford: Butterworth-Heinemann, pp. 381–399.

Shackley, M. (1998) Introduction: world heritage sites. In Shackley, M. (ed.) *Visitor Management: Case Studies from World Heritage Sites*. Oxford: Butterworth-Heinemann, pp. 1–9.

Timothy, D.J. (1997) Tourism and the personal heritage experience. *Annals of Tourism Research*, 34 (3), 751–754.

Timothy, D.J. and Boyd, S.W. (2003) *Heritage Tourism*. Harlow: Prentice Hall.

Wilmont, D. (2005) Causeway Coasts and Glens. Personal correspondence.

CHAPTER 5

Destination management: a holistic approach. Liverpool – Maritime Mercantile City

Bryn Parry

Aims

The aims of this chapter are to:

- Illustrate how new ways of looking at the central themes of World Heritage Sites (WHS) can enhance their management
- Demonstrate how a holistic framework can encompass multiple interpretations of a WHS
- Demonstrate how a holistic model of destination management can enable one to learn from the strategic, operational and tactical issues of differing WHS.

Introduction

The key ingredient for many World Heritage Sites (WHS) is their profound sense of being in an iconic space. However, WHS do not derive their power purely from the amount of ground, or just from the surface of the surrounding buildings/environment, nor purely from the people within that space. This chapter demonstrates that successful management of a WHS is dependent upon managing the interplay of all of these factors (in addition to others) each and every day and over extended periods of time.

The framework used in this chapter to focus debate integrates and enhances the existing 'threads' of activity and weaves them into the 'bigger picture'; hence, the focus is not on the detail of any specific aspect, but on how these can be woven together more effectively. The framework enables lessons to be transferred to any WHS, but the chapter focuses on a single example. As one of the newer WHS, Liverpool – Maritime Mercantile City (LMMC) can draw upon lessons learned by its predecessors. However, its urban site, with competing stakeholders, throws the tensions often seen in other WHS into sharp contrast. Those not familiar with Liverpool, or the specific LMMC site, can access an online map via LCC (Liverpool City Council, 2005).

Context and challenges

UNESCO's World Heritage Mission (UNESCO, 2005) is necessarily ambitious and the criteria for individual WHS can be the subject of heated debate. Hence, translating these into the management plan required for each WHS and then getting that plan actually to work requires great creativity.

The laudable aim of living with our legacy and passing it on to future generations is quickly embroiled in questions of contested interpretations and competing imperatives. The sheer range of WHS on the World Heritage List (WHL) accentuates these challenges. Urban city sites are charged with 'spiritual, emotional and symbolic values' that can divide the very groups that a successful management plan needs to unite it, while natural sites might find the most fragile of ecologies set in extremely volatile physical surroundings.

The very nature of inscripted sites can put them among the rarest and most finely balanced parts of our heritage. As with other forms of tourism, the enhanced profile that can protect a site can also set in train its erosion; the current length of the WHS 'in danger' list is already unacceptably long.

The aims of this chapter are to demonstrate how it should be possible to evaluate critically the central themes of managing WHS in a holistic way. The model used is deliberately simplistic. This allows one quickly to ensure that the overall thrust of the intended approach is sound, before using it as the basis for fleshing out critical aspects of the management plan with what is essential for a specific WHS.

Motivation and engagement

The issues of motivation and engagement (Trauer and Ryan, 2005: 481–491) with a destination have been explored elsewhere in the tourism literature. For a WHS, this can be thrown into further complexity as to how one should serve serendipitous and incidental tourists alongside the provision of the all-encompassing experience that purposeful tourists are looking for. One only has to think of the recent furore over Wal-Mart seeking to site a supermarket near the WHS at Teotihuacan, Mexico to see how not managing this aspect can cause unnecessary conflict.

Figure 5.1 illustrates the range of tourist experiences that each WHS must take into consideration. In Figure 5.1, the level of Intimacy is used as a measure, rather than knowledge or engagement, as it denotes a more accurate understanding of what is at the heart of a place. When you are closer to a person, you not only have a better understanding of how different people perceive them, but you have an insight into their 'true' character. Initially, 'blinded by love' to their faults, you grow to recognize these as well, but see them as an inherent part of that person's essential character. Hence, asking how intimate we feel with a particular WHS requires us to reflect on whether we really know it, as others might, and on whether the flaws that we might seek to remove are really 'defects' (to be removed) or part of its inherent character (to be addressed as such).

Dicks (2003: 1) recognizes that:

> Places today have become exhibitions of themselves. Through heavy investment in architecture, art, design, exhibition space, landscaping

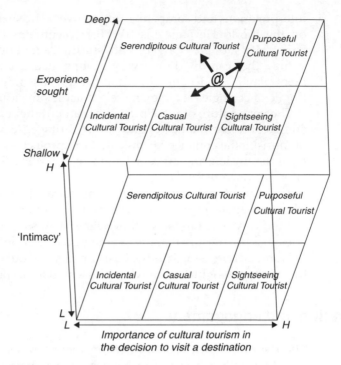

Figure 5.1 A cultural tourist typology.
Source: Amended from McKercher and du Cros, 2003: 46
(Copyright John Wiley & Sons, reproduced with permission)

> and various kinds of redevelopment towns, cities and countryside proclaim their possession of cultural values ... and this identity is expected to be easily accessed by ... visitors ... to be legible.

How far should a WHS go in managing this process? Not to engage with it would mean that the WHS loses ground in the increasingly competitive marketplace for visitors' time and money; while too commercial an approach might undermine the very uniqueness of the heritage that it was set up to protect.

As Figure 5.1 illustrates, it might be that a purposeful cultural tourist lacks the 'intimacy' with a site's heritage really to appreciate its fundamentals, while an incidental tourist is actually much more aware of detailed aspects of the site's true heritage, but merely has more pressing deadlines during their visit.

Destination management model

Having identified the broad themes and competing imperatives, an easily identifiable framework on which to structure an approach that

DESTINATION MANAGEMENT IS THE MANAGEMENT OF CHANGE
DESTINATION MANAGEMENT INTEGRATES OVERLAPPING LIFE-CYCLES

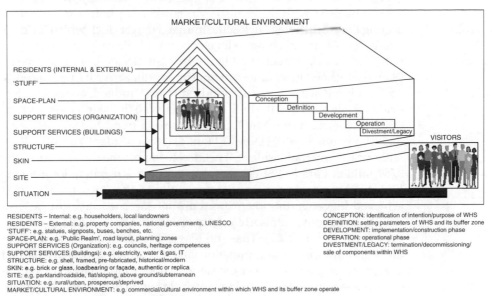

RESIDENTS – Internal: e.g. householders, local landowners
RESIDENTS – External: e.g. property companies, national governments, UNESCO
'STUFF': e.g. statues, signposts, buses, benches, etc.
SPACE-PLAN: e.g. 'Public Realm', road layout, planning zones
SUPPORT SERVICES (Organization): e.g. councils, heritage competences
SUPPORT SERVICES (Buildings): e.g. electricity, water & gas, IT
STRUCTURE: e.g. shell, framed, pre-fabricated, historical/modern
SKIN: e.g. brick or glass, loadbearing or façade, authentic or replica
SITE: e.g. parkland/roadside, flat/sloping, above ground/subterranean
SITUATION: e.g. rural/urban, prosperous/deprived
MARKET/CULTURAL ENVIRONMENT: e.g. commercial/cultural environment within which WHS and its buffer zone operate

CONCEPTION: identification of intention/purpose of WHS
DEFINITION: setting parameters of WHS and its buffer zone
DEVELOPMENT: implementation/construction phase
OPERATION: operational phase
DIVESTMENT/LEGACY: termination/decommissioning/
sale of components within WHS

Figure 5.2 Destination management is the management of change

enables the various inputs and outputs of WHS to be addressed holistically is required. Figure 5.2 provides such a framework. Its evolution and application to single settings has been dealt with elsewhere (Parry and Norman, 1996; Parry, 2004).

Since some elements seem 'obvious' and others just seem to raise questions, this framework helps to identify the critical components and internal conflicts that will need to be fully addressed when developing the management plan. As with Figure 5.1, it also serves as a catalyst to reflect on the true nature of the WHS that is being perpetuated and whether the intention is to sustain its heartland characteristics or merely preserve its ephemera.

Although the first attempt may take some thought and a little time, such an approach has several advantages. It enables those managing WHS to make the overlapping interactions, inherent within any destination, much clearer to the various stakeholders, while highlighting the emergence of critical trends. Further, it enables one to reconsider and challenge the fundamentals that actually underpin the distinctiveness of each WHS. For instance, Choi (2002) noted that a failure to recognize the unique acoustics of ancient monuments can lead to their loss, recounting the argument that the determining factor in the look of some Mayan buildings was actually the echo that they generated and not the aesthetic look of them.

Since this chapter is going to explore the LMMC in more detail, one aspect of this WHS gives us an example of the means by which Figure 5.2 can be used with the critical evaluation of options for commemorating the world's first enclosed commercial, wet-dock which, in 2005, was a cleared site awaiting redevelopment. While no visible remnants of the 'Old Dock' remain the site can be easily located, since its 'space-plan' was echoed in a number of buildings built above it (most recently by Canning Place and its surrounding roads). Indeed, archaeological evidence suggests that the bulk of the dock wall (its 'skin') has survived under the ground (the 'site'). Since there is a trend to leave archaeological remains *in situ*, UNESCO (an 'external resident') and the local authorities ('internal residents') needed to enable the developers of the £750 million Paradise Street Development Area regeneration scheme (PSDA) that envelopes the site to continue this preservation; best achieved by converting them from an unconcerned investor (a 'visitor') to somebody intimately engaged with the site's heritage (a 'resident') (Grosvenor, 2005). That still leaves the question of what might form an appropriate interpretation above ground, especially as that interpretation cannot deliver the same richness and nuances of experience as a tangible site might. However, strong links with local agencies (support services organization) and the creative use of information technology (support services buildings) ought to go a long way in solving the problem.

Having become comfortable with the different 'layers' of the model and how they interact, it is now appropriate to turn to the different stages of the life cycle. Liverpool's 'Old Dock' has clearly undergone a number of redevelopments and thus can be treated either as a single life cycle or as a number of life cycles, each passing on to the next. The original concept was 'defined' by its architects' drawings and 'developed' by its construction, before entering the 'operation' phase, and before being 'divested' as ships outgrew it and leaving its 'legacy'; space for dock-related buildings and heritage above ground, plus industrial archaeology below ground. The WHS management plan must, therefore, decide if sustaining the LMMC can encompass both the commercial imperative of the PSDA development above ground and the preservation of the physical heritage below ground.

Managing the life cycle – LMMC

Concept

In most projects, the concept that won approval is often markedly different from that which goes into operation. While that may not be critical for a tourist attraction it cuts to the very heart of WHS and their purpose; hence, a holistic approach should help to ensure that

the heartland characteristics of the concept proposed in the nomination documentation encompass the twin objectives of communicat-
ing the significance of the WHS and establishing a concept that has
the potential to sustain that significance over its full life cycle.

The interplay of layers should help in critically evaluating what
actually goes into creating and sustaining the LMMC. Is it the collective history, the remaining artefacts, the evolving culture, or its future
potential? The heated debates over whether such high profile projects as the European Capital of Culture 2008 initiative, or the PSDA,
actually reflect the 'true' nature of the city illustrates the need for a
structured approach to the multi-layered concept of WHS, many of
which can involve contested heritages.

Justification for the inscription of LMMC as a WHS (Liverpool
City Council, 2002: 25) stems from the city's:

> ... historic role as an eminent international seaport ... and the sur-
> viving urban landscape that testifies to the role ... The nominated
> site is a complete and integral urban landscape that encompasses
> much of the very heart of the City of Liverpool and provides tangible
> and coherent evidence of the city's historic character and signifi-
> cance ... [whilst recognising that] the city is at the forefront of the
> urban regeneration movement.

This is where the level of Intimacy from Figure 5.1 becomes critical
when evaluating the heartland characteristics of the concept for
WHS. For, while much of the recent and proposed urban regeneration involves the opening up of access between the city centre and
the docks, this does not reflect the reality of its heritage. As Sharples
(2004: 123–124) observed, a dock wall evolved:

> ... until it stretched the length of the docks, a physical and psycho-
> logical barrier c.18ft (5.5 metres) high, behind which the docks were
> a mysterious world to most Liverpudlians. The novelist Nathaniel
> Hawthorne, American consul in Liverpool in the 1850s, likened it to
> the Great Wall of China.

Indeed, such were the divisions that, during one of the many riots
that have punctuated Liverpool's history, sailors fired a cannon at
the town hall, while employers sheltered inside. So, how should the
concept for the LMMC balance the need to present a unified and easily accessible interpretation for the WHS with the need to commemorate the often divided and contested nature of that heritage?

Definition

If the challenges in agreeing the central concept for a WHS are so
stark, the complexities of translating that concept into a workable
definition should not come as any surprise. The definition of a WHS,

both in terms of its characteristics and its boundaries, might be influenced by political and topographical issues as much as by historical or heritage issues. Further, the level of definition put into place at this stage can heavily influence both the levels of interaction by visitors (something explored in Figure 5.1) and the potential length of the destination life cycle that the WHC might expect.

All WHS need not only to demonstrate clearly the criteria required for inscription but also to balance the management of these with the requirements of sustainability and other elements of UNESCO's World Heritage Mission. As such, the management plan required for each WHS involves a 'buffer zone' around the WHS itself, to mitigate some of the interactions with surrounding areas. Initially, the definition of the buffer zone in the map of the LMMC Management Plan (Liverpool City Council, 2005) looks fairly obvious; however, one quickly begins to ask how easy it will be to manage the heritage of LMMC when:

- only one half of the River Mersey actually falls within the buffer zone
- a significant part of that buffer zone overlaps with other significant initiatives, such as the £750 million PSDA regeneration scheme (Grosvenor, 2005).

Although Liverpool's maritime heritage is unquestioned, the definition of LMMC initiatives should not succeed at the expense of smothering other aspects of the city's rich heritages; after all, this is the city that gave the world the radio, goal-nets, prefabricated concrete buildings, purpose-built department stores, dual-carriageways, district nurses, scheduled steam-powered railways, and a host of other innovations.

To show how Figure 5.1 and Figure 5.2 can be combined to help thread through these difficult issues, one can look at the issues involved in addressing the heritage of Liverpool's 'Chinatown'. Since shipping companies like the 'Blue Funnel line' were seen as instrumental in the city becoming the site of Britain's first 'Chinatown', the link with the LMMC is clear. However, while the imposing arch and street furniture (the 'stuff') of the modern 'Chinatown' area provide an easily accessible guide for the average tourist, those with a more intimate understanding of the heritage would know that the original site is actually located a few streets away.

Just as decisions on how to define appropriately the 'Chinatown' aspect of LMMC will impact on both the concept and the operation of the LMMC, so will similar management decisions on comparable aspects of other WHS.

It is at this stage that one 'opens' and 'closes' critical doors to later success and so it is vital that one considers the full life cycle. The realities (Towner, 1996: 68) of the much-quoted 'Tourism Area Life cycle' need to be understood if the production of a flawed Definition phase is not to lock a WHS into an unsuitable future. Voase (1995: 40) helps to explain why it is that initially hated characteristics can often end up being the most loved and, so, receive an unwarranted amount of interpretation.

Production

In addition to the issues of conservation and redevelopment, this phase will also encompass the effective integration of the diverse range of stakeholders upon which the success of any WHS depends. Further, it is here that the difficult process of developing appropriate means of making the WHS more 'legible' to visitors, without imposing bias on the competing interpretations of its heritage, takes place. For most WHS, compromise and re-interpretation will be inevitable during the later operational phases of each layer and so the expertise with which the concept of each layer is defined and made tangible is likely to be critical to its success. This is why the multi-layered approach in Figure 5.2 is recommended.

Like many British cities, Liverpool was boldly redeveloped during the 1960s (Sharples, 2004: 36–37), a wide-scale production phase of the city's fabric that swept away much of its historical space-plan and altered the city's natural rhythms. Ironically, as the LMMC was being confirmed, many of the city's Victorian terraced houses were again threatened with demolition, this time under the government's 'Pathfinder' housing regeneration scheme. The public debate that followed echoed many of the themes already explored, namely whether the heartland of an area can be found in its people, its space-plan, in its texture (the 'skin'), or in a combination of these. It also brought into focus the competing beliefs of those who argue that community spirit is embedded in the fabric of structures and those that believe that rebuilding with the community in mind is the best way forward. Success for Liverpool lies in whether heritage can make its voice heard and find champions among the key stakeholders in the critical decisions. Figure 5.2 should ease the challenge of integrating the design and management principles laid out by the city for its 'public realm' (Liverpool Vision, 2004: 3) with the similar objectives of the WHS and in managing the differing life cycles of each layer.

The evolution of the two cathedrals (Sharples, 2004) that overlook the WHS are a constant reminder of how much can change between the start and end of the production phase of a project. The Roman Catholic cathedral demonstrates that it is possible to change tack radically during the production phase and to reinterpret a building's purpose, while the Anglican cathedral's fabric contains many official and unofficial commemorations of key events, such as the loss of the RMS Titanic, during construction.

Among WHS across the world, similar tensions are being felt. Using the dynamics emerging from Figure 5.1 and Figure 5.2 to identify them correctly as they emerge should help to provide the best opportunity for being in a position to manage the decision, as opposed merely to mitigate the impact of the decision. As already discussed, this chapter can only provide the framework for such an approach with many of the case studies included in the second half of this book serving as additional material with which to test the framework.

Operation

It costs more to run a building than it does to build it (Brand, 1994) and so the simplest of all interventions is to guard against the overspending and false-economies that are prevalent with most projects. If the awareness and understanding of what is required to integrate a successful WHS into a community has been effectively communicated to key stakeholders during the previous phases then this phase should be more about focusing and fine-tuning effort rather than rectifying mistakes. The target of the WHS management team should be to facilitate the interplay of the different layers seen in Figure 5.2, so as to strike an optimum balance between effective visitor interpretations and resident satisfaction.

Since each stage of each layer is undertaken by a set of stakeholders, the WHS management team can use Figure 5.2 to identify where the dynamics of the destination are already flowing freely, where they can be unblocked and where an intervention might stimulate a beneficial outcome. Jacobs (1961: 431) argues that:

> The invention required is not a device for coordination at the generalized top, but rather an invention to make coordination possible where the need is most acute – in specific and unique localities.

Jacobs (1961: 161), also, reminds us that merely putting large numbers of people together does not make them residents:

> At the other extreme, huge city settlements of people exist without their presence generating anything much except stagnation and, ultimately, a fatal discontent with the place.

Jacobs (1961: 156) recognizes that well-balanced destinations become home to the clusters of activities that provide the right environments for innovation and sustained development; thus ensuring the best possible chance for the operational phase to be a suitably lengthy one and one that is in line with UNESCO's World Heritage Mission.

Freeman (1990: 260–261) notes that:

> Evidence also suggests that external firms erected buildings of greater height than local firms ... External firms have further disrupted

the traditional townscape by their use of external cladding materials out of harmony with those already existing … These observations suggest that non-local firms are less imbued with a 'sense of place' than local firms, many of which are of small size, often family-run and with a long period of association with a particular town.

This supports the comment, made earlier, that WHS are likely to have more success if critical stakeholders are made to feel more like 'residents' than 'visitors'. The tendency for many buildings within the LMMC area to be built to an international scale was a key reason for the LMMC being designated in the first place, but the sustained development of this area is still likely to reflect the tensions explored above. Those managing the LMMC need to balance medium-scale refurbishment projects that are sympathetic with Liverpool's current fabric with the more radical and innovative developments that (although at odds with the current cityscape) reflect the city's bold heritage.

Jacobs (1961: 271) recognized some time ago that 'single-use areas' are not attractive to outsiders ('visitors') and that the borders of such areas have the weakest appeal to the 'residents' within them. So the management of the LMMC should seek to avoid it becoming a heritage ghetto and to focus on managing the tensions between the full range of resident and visitor expectations that Figure 5.1 and Figure 5.2 have highlighted.

Divestment/legacy

Although previous phases have been shown to govern the effective management of a destination, this phase is likely to be the most controversial for a WHS. If, having guided the area's heritage through the myriad competing tensions of previous phases, the legacy passed on to future generations is seen as irrelevant or 'false' in any way, then the WHS is likely to be judged a failure. Since the sustained evolution of any WHS, inevitably, results in aspects of it becoming redundant for their original purposes, the debate over what components it is critical to retain and what might be sacrificed is always likely to be a heated one.

The destruction in 1980 of the initially derided, but later muchadmired, Firestone Factory in London is viewed as a milestone in raising the profile of conserving 20th century industrial archaeology. However, since the factory's architect was on record as saying that his factories should be demolished when their usefulness is outlived (Jones and Woodward, 1992: 379), one wonders whether he would view the survival of his Hoover Factory façade as the wrapping around a Tesco supermarket with much pride. Like many WHS, the

LMMC needs to find appropriate ways to conserve the nuances of a building's heritage along with the fabric that encases it.

Liverpool's Pier Head and its famous trio of buildings, the 'Three Graces', help to illustrate some of the complexities facing the LMMC. Once at the bustling heart of passenger services crossing the Atlantic and the ferry services crossing the River Mersey, with the ground-breaking railway and road tunnels running beneath, it is now more likely to be seen as a windswept space braved mainly by those taking the 'heritage cruise' that sustains the world famous ferries. Exciting plans envision a nearby cruise terminal that could revive Liverpool's cruise liner heritage and a riverside canal, though a metro system linking it all with the city centre failed to find funding.

The challenge is deciding whether the priority should go to preserving the site's maritime heritage or ensuring its continued mercantile use and whether priority in the 'space-plan' should go to the planned uses or to retaining the poignancy of the avenue of trees that commemorate the Canadian sailors and airmen who gave their lives protecting the vital World War II convoys. Working as a team that sees the issues holistically is much more likely to deliver a solution that enables the full range of visitors to the WHS to coexist alongside the full range of residents within a vibrant maritime city.

Conclusions

This chapter set out to demonstrate that while the lessons learned in other chapters will enhance the management of WHS, the approaches recommended will work best when supported by a robust and well thought through framework that furthers understanding of the dynamics of a destination. Jacobs (1961: 155) argued that:

> It is too easy to fall into the trap of contemplating a city's uses one at a time, by categories ... To understand cities, we have to deal outright with combinations of mixtures of uses, not separate uses, as the essential phenomena ...

going on to argue (Jacobs, 1961: 422) that,

> For this kind of planning, it is not enough for administrators in most fields to understand specific services and techniques. They must understand, and understand thoroughly, specific places.

Reflecting on the level of Intimacy that both the management and the visitors might have with a site can lead to one asking searching questions as to what might reflect the 'true' heritage. Many books note the influential Oriel Chambers building in Liverpool and that severe criticism of it curtailed the career of its architect. Few though mention a statue depicting a gorilla applying make-up that was added as a humorous riposte to the criticism that 'Art is to architecture, like lipstick is to a gorilla'. The debate as to which is the more accurate reflection of Liverpool's heritage is a rich one.

The framework in Figure 5.2 should be seen as a first step in deepening the level of understanding needed to enable a better insight into what constitutes the heartland characteristics that WHS seek to protect. Recognizing the full range of visitor experiences, illustrated by Figure 5.1, will help to keep vibrant those heartland characteristics, the ones that inscription sought to protect in the first place.

References

Brand, S. (1994) *How Buildings Learn: What Happens After They're Built*. London: Viking.

Choi, C. (2002) Saving the sounds of our distant past. *New Scientist*, December 7, p. 7.

Dicks, B. (2003) *Culture on Display, the Production of Contemporary Visitability*. Maidenhead: Open University Press, McGraw-Hill.

Freeman (1990) Commencing building development: the agents of change. In Slater, T. (ed) *The Built Form of Western Cities*. Leicester: Leicester University Press.

Grosvenor (2005) *Liverpool Paradise Street Development Area*. Grosvenor Group http://www.liverpoolpsda.co.uk (accessed 4 April 2005).

Jacobs, J. (1961) *The Death and Life of Great American Cities*. London: Penguin.

Jones, E. and Woodward, C. (1992) *A Guide to the Architecture of London*. London: Weidenfeld and Nicolson.

Liverpool City Council (2002) *Liverpool – Maritime Mercantile City: Nomination of Liverpool Maritime Mercantile City for Inscription on the World Heritage List*. Liverpool: Liverpool City Council/DCMS. http://www.liverpoolworldheritage.com/nomination.asp (accessed 4 April 2005).

Liverpool City Council (2005) Liverpool Maritime Mercantile City Management Plan. Liverpool: Liverpool City Council. http://www.liverpoolworldheritage.com/management.asp (accessed 4 April 2005).

Liverpool Vision (2004) *Liverpool City Centre: Public Realm Implementation Framework*. Liverpool: Liverpool Vision. http://www.liverpoolvision.co.uk/documents/corearea.pdf (accessed 4 April 2005).

McKercher, B. and du Cros, H. (2003) Testing a cultural tourism typology. *International Journal of Tourism Research*, 5 (1), 45–58.

Parry, B. (2004) Facilities planning. In MacMahon-Beattie, U. and Yeoman, I. (eds) *Sport & Leisure Operations Management*. London: Thomson Learning.

Parry, B. and Norman, P. (1996) Facility performance in the European hospitality industry. Euro FM Conference, Barcelona.

Sharples, J. (2004) *Pevsner Architectural Guides: Liverpool*. London: Yale University Press.

Towner, J. (1996) *An Historical Geography of Recreation and Tourism in the Western World 1540–1940*. Chichester: John Wiley & Sons.

Trauer, B. and Ryan, C. (2005) Destination image, romance and place experience: An application of intimacy theory in tourism. *Tourism Management*, 26, 481–491.

UNESCO (2005) UNESCO World Heritage Mission. http:// whc.unesco. org/en/home (accessed 5 August 2005).

Voase, R. (1995) *Tourism: The Human Perspective*. London: Hodder & Stoughton.

CHAPTER 6

Visitor management at World Heritage Sites

Myra Shackley

Aims

The aims of this chapter are to consider:

- Contemporary visitor management issues at World Heritage Sites (WHS)
- The ways in which WHS have responded to growing visitor numbers
- Methods being utilized to increase visitor security
- Issues surrounding cultural sensitivity at WHS.

Introduction

Increased interest in, and awareness of, WHS has led inevitably to an overall increase in visitor numbers, although this is not evenly spread throughout the world. However, easier access, the growth of low-cost airlines (not only in Europe but also in Australia and Asia), more diverse use of discretionary time, increased consumer confidence in making travel bookings and the extensive publicity given to WHS have all contributed to this phenomenon. Even political or security crises only pose temporary interruptions to this upward trend, as discussed elsewhere in this chapter, where the effect of temporary closure of Uluru (Ayers Rock) actually produced more publicity (and more visitors) for the site. All WHS confronted by a growth in visitor numbers also face the same set of problems and issues, centred, inevitably, upon the dual need to balance conservation with generating revenue from visitors, either directly or indirectly (ICOMOS, 1993). Most WHS now attract increasingly mature and experienced consumers of heritage tourism products whose requirements for facilities and interpretation have become steadily more sophisticated. Moreover, visitors accustomed to the highly professional levels of site interpretation often offered in the developed world are increasingly expecting similar standards to be available universally. This is sometimes difficult for WHS site managers in the developing world who may have restricted access to finance and expertise. In addition to these general issues, over the last decade two other factors have become significant in visitor management, namely crime and security and cultural sensitivity. The reasons behind this are not hard to seek. Uncertainty created by ongoing acts of global terrorism has meant that many visitors have become increasingly concerned about their personal security at major visitor attractions and site managers are concerned about possible threats to the site. Arguments over the 'ownership' of world heritage and the increasing diversity of the travelling public have meant that more attention is being paid to the cultural sensitivities surrounding WHS interpretation. The same factors, combined with an increasingly high media profile for WHS, have resulted in increased visitor numbers.

This chapter aims to illustrate these points by introducing several specific WHS where these problems appear, and offering some comments and conclusions. It is widely recognized that most World Heritage Sites are major cultural tourism attractions and several are icons of national identity. Although it is assumed that the 'average' visitor to World Heritage Sites is motivated either by an interest in cultural heritage or by a love of the natural world, this is not necessarily the case. Visitors to WHS can also be motivated by adventure (see Uluru, below), or simply by the desire to use the site as a backdrop for some social function (see Mogdao, below), a phenomenon long recognized at Asian sites such as the Taj Mahal, but increasingly seen at Chinese sites including giant panda reserves (Urry, 1990). This diversity of visitor motivation makes it quite difficult to generalize about visitor management trends in a worldwide context, especially as sites vary so widely in the standard of visitor facilities that they are able to offer to the public.

Contemporary visitor management issues at WHS

Maintaining the 'Spirit of Place'

The UK's network of World Heritage Sites illustrates many of the issues mentioned above. Of the 26 UK sites, some on the WH List have very low levels of visitation (such as Gough and inaccessible islands in the South Atlantic or St Kilda, a protected island bird sanctuary in the Outer Hebrides). However, others are the lynchpins of the UK's cultural tourism industry such as Westminster Abbey, Canterbury Cathedral and the cities of Bath and Edinburgh whose visitors probably do not realize that they are in a World Heritage Site (Borg et al., 1996). Some recent additions to the WH List such as the Dorset and East Devon Coast (2001) have not seen significant increases in visitor pressure since designation and have lower levels of visitation than the urban sites, although they do not escape the need to deal with adverse visitor impacts. However, WHS status has undoubtedly led to increased interest in the environmental significance of these sites. Of all the UK locations, the most controversial cultural site is undoubtedly the oldest, namely Stonehenge, one of the country's most important prehistoric monuments but famously described by a UK government committee as a 'national disgrace'. Although located in the middle of Salisbury Plain, the monument is surrounded by roads, creating traffic problems, and its visitor facilities are inadequate for today's needs. Over the last 20 years various plans have been produced to improve the quality of the visitor experience, the latest being 'The Stonehenge Project' which supposedly would remove the traffic noise and enable the visitor to appreciate the site in its archaeological context (see Chapters 3 and 12 for further insights into the contemporary management of Stonehenge in the UK).

The solutions proposed for Stonehenge are not unique, most have been tried elsewhere – the Valley of the Kings in Egypt (Sinai) uses a non-polluting land train, for example, and St Katherine's Protectorate has established a new visitor centre to focus the visitor on the entire cultural landscape rather than just on the site. However, if one day it is successfully implemented, the Stonehenge Project will undeniably provide a spectacular new set of visitor facilities for Stonehenge and enable visitors to see the monument within its proper context, appreciating the full extent of the cultural landscape in which it is contextualized. The experience quality will be maximized, but is the massive cost justifiable? Getting the balance right between providing a quality experience for the visitor and ensuring the long-term sustainability of the site is a very delicate matter and mistakes can often be made. It is not always easy to reconcile the needs and wants of the various WHS stakeholders.

An interesting example of this can be seen at quite another type of site, the grove of giant cedar trees (*Cedrus libani*) in the Quadisha valley in North Lebanon (Shackley, 2004b). Lebanon receives about 750 000 visitors/year, attracted by a diverse tourism portfolio including WHS such as Baalbeck and Tyre (Berraine, 1997). The most significant survivors of Lebanon's once magnificent cedar forests are the 'Forest of the Cedars of God (Horsh Arz al-Ra)' in a managed grove near the mountain village of Becharre, at the head of Ouadi Quadisha (the Holy Valley). Valley and cedars were inscribed on the WH list in 1998, under criteria C (iii)(iv). The grove includes about 375 cedars of great age with four trees more than 1500 years old and 35 m high, and receives around 200 000 visitors/year, about 20 per cent of the total visitors to Lebanon. The cedars survive in a walled grove located anomalously in the middle of a bleak over-grazed landscape near a ski resort, and are managed not as a small living forest but as a tree museum. Visitors access the grove via a smart new entry/exit post, with the site being policed by members of the Committee of Friends of the Cedars who ask for a voluntary donation on entry (replacing a former admissions charge). The visitor experience is highly controlled. In order to protect the cedars visitors must walk only on the 3 km of surfaced paths, which have been laid through the 102 hectare enclosure and delineated by posts and hemp ropes, and which are highly unsuitable for the disabled or for small children. The general impression given is that both cedars and visitors are fiercely regimented. The grove is afflicted by loud Middle Eastern pop music from the nearby complex of souvenir shops and cafés.

The resulting experience does not give the visitor any taste of what it was like in the original forest. Shackley (2004b: 422) concluded that 'the grove has preserved the trees, but without the spirit of place' and contrasted the grove with the Chouf cedar reserve in southern Lebanon. This reserve, which is not a WHS, receives only 30 visitors/day who are allowed to wander through the quiet, spectacular misty forests just with a naturalist guide. But the WHS at Becharre has turned an ecological attraction into a sanitized tree museum, mostly for the protection of the trees, but also to regiment and commercialize the experience. Visitors can see the trees but not experience them, which is unusual in a cultural landscape, although distressingly common where buildings have been over-reconstructed so that architecture has survived in a lifeless, sterile environment. The unhappy post-Soviet reconstructions of Silk Road cities of Bukhara and Samarkhand are excellent examples here (Shackley, 1998). However, there is actually no evidence that the majority of visitors to Becharre are disappointed. Expectations are poorly formed and differ between incoming international tourists and local people. The initial WHS management plan recommended that attention be paid not just to the conservation needs of the indigenous flora and fauna but also to displaying the trees in as natural a manner as possible. Supporters of the present plan have clearly conserved the trees but provided little interpretation and a poor quality experience – with the Chouf reserve (not a WHS) demonstrating how it could be done better.

Visitor numbers to Lebanon are increasing steadily as confidence builds in the stability of the country, but its WH Sites are certainly in no danger of being swamped by huge numbers. However, this is not true elsewhere and real anxieties exist over visitor management issues at some sites under pressure. This can also be exacerbated by government policies promoting access to such sites, and by technologies through which visitor information is widely disseminated. The Mogao Caves in China, one of the most splendid of hundreds of Buddhist sites that studded the Silk Road linking China and the West, are an excellent example here. Over the course of 1000 years, from AD 336, more than 700 caves were carved into a mile-long sandstone cliff and most are covered with magnificent paintings. Although sporadically visited over the centuries by pilgrims, it is only now that mass tourism has reached the site, which comes under intolerable pressure, particularly in the Chinese 'golden week' holidays of May and October when as many as 5000 Chinese tourists crowd into the caves, causing an increase in humidity levels with the leaching of salts through layers of plaster, damaging the painted surfaces. When the proposed desert railway from Liuyuan to Dunhuang is completed this problem will escalate – just as the deterioration of the Potala Palace in Lhasa, Tibet will be affected when the Qinghai-Tibet railway to Lhasa is completed in 2007. It is Chinese government policy actively to promote tourism to marginal areas, including the desert sites of the Silk Road. Factories in the booming coastal belts are encouraged to send their workers there on holiday trips and, in June 2004, China announced plans to intensify desert area tourism, ostensibly to raise funds for combating desertification. This is likely to damage permanently the Silk Road sites. Although there is an attempt by a local conservation organization to control tourist numbers and monitor the impact, this seems doomed because it is partially financed by revenue from ticket sales. China wants to be the world's number one tourist destination and of the 812 sites on the WH List China has 30, just behind Italy and Spain, but Beijing is reputed to want 100 more. Tourist revenue can increase up to 25-fold after World Heritage listing, as it did in the walled city of Pingyao in Shanxi province, with income now reaching $2 billion per year, of which foreigners contribute only $42 million, the rest resulting from a huge growth in poorly-controlled domestic tourism (Righter, 2004). It is far from uncommon to see major buildings that had been destroyed being rebuilt when it was realized that they could attract more visitors. This is exactly what is happening in part of the old town of Lhasa in Tibet at present, with cosmetic facings being applied to buildings in the central historic area to create a more authentically Tibetan appearance (Tibet Information Network, 2004).

The difficult balance between needing to earn revenue from sites by increasing visitation, which may potentially damage the site, is managed differently elsewhere. Twenty years ago the Indian Supreme Court banned night-time visits to the Taj Mahal, which had been popular with tourists wishing to see the sight by moonlight. This ban has now been lifted, ostensibly as part of the celebration of the 350th anniversary of the monument, with a three-month trial which took place between December 2004 and February 2005 for five nights around each full moon. Cynics might say that the relaxation of the rules was less to celebrate a birthday but more to compensate for the fact that Agra hotel occupancy has been down since the Taj Mahal was closed at night in 1984, as a result of worries over internal political security and external issues. Without the inducement to stay overnight many tourists now visit Agra (250 km from Delhi) only for the day, reducing visitor revenue and having a serious impact on employment. The new opening policy will partially redress this balance, but the cost on the fabric of the Taj Mahal may be high.

Crime and security

The events of the past few years, including 9/11 and subsequent terrorist activities, have increased levels of security virtually everywhere. WHS, by virtue of their cultural uniqueness and high level of awareness are vulnerabe to terrorist attacks and those that are national icons particularly so. During the aftermath of 9/11 the Taj Mahal (discussed above) was felt to be a potential target for extremist attacks, and many large and spectacular sites, which would normally welcome thousands of visitors in the course of a day, experienced a drop in visitor numbers as they are places where visitors feel vulnerable, despite high levels of security. This effect has even been felt in the churches and cathedrals of London. Nor is terrorism the only kind of crime to which WHS are vulnerable, and the last decade has showed increasingly high levels of looting, especially at locations whose remoteness means that they are difficult to police. For example, in December 2004 it was reported that five German tourists had gone missing in the Sahara Desert in southern Algeria, which caused concern since this was an area where 32 European tourists were held captive for several months by Army rebels in 2003. However, in this case the tourists were found safely but it transpired that they had stolen 130 artefacts from the Tassili n'Ajjer National Park, famous for its prehistoric cave art. In December 2004 they were tried, found guilty, jailed for three months and fined £262 000. Nor is this an isolated example. For nearly 400 years, Robben Island, 12 km from Cape Town, was a place of banishment, exile, isolation and imprisonment. It was here that rulers sent those they regarded as political troublemakers, social outcasts and the unwanted of society. During the apartheid years, Robben Island became internationally known for its institutional brutality. The duty of those who ran the Island and its prison was to isolate opponents of apartheid and to crush their morale. Robben Island came to symbolize, not only for South Africa and the African continent, but also for the entire world, the triumph of the human spirit over enormous hardship and adversity, most notably personified in Nelson Mandela who was imprisoned there for 27 years. Mandela's prison was turned into a museum and national monument in 1997, and is also a WHS. However, Cape Town authorities are considering posting police there to crack down on crime that threatens to deter tourists from visiting the former prison as reports of rape, vandalism and drug-related crimes threatened to ruin its tourist trade (Shackley, 2001b). There have also been concerns that tourists themselves are vandalizing the island by illegally taking away mementos. Nor is the issue of illegal taking of souvenirs restricted to Robben Island; there are examples of this from Hawaii, where tourists remove rocks from the volcanoes of Mauna Loa and Kilauea, and from the Taj Mahal, where visitors (and guards) remove fragments of inlay for sale. However, incidents of theft and vandalism by visitors to World Heritage Sites still remain (fortunately) extremely rare, although professional theft is far more common, such as the removal of Khmer statues from the temples at Angkor in Cambodia, but is usually carried out by professional gangs. Looting at the former Khmer capital had been a problem since the 1980s. The Cambodian government sought the help of UNESCO, which placed Angkor on its List of World Heritage in Danger in 1992. The listing caught tourist attention, and the money they brought in has allowed the Angkor protection group to hire local guards to prevent looting, a policy which has been so successful that the site has been removed from the endangered list.

In some cases, the need to ensure visitor safety and protect the monument has resulted in a diminution of experience quality, and this has been claimed by visitors to the Statue of Liberty in New York, which re-opened on 3 August 2004, nearly three years after the effects of 11 September 2001. It was that noticeable that after re-opening there was a marked change both in the interpretation of the monument and in the level of security for visitors. The decision had been taken to divide tourists into smaller groups and to close off the body of the Statue to visitors so that it is no longer possible to go up the winding 21-storey staircase. Visitors are now only able to view inside the Statue through a glass ceiling, guided by a park ranger and with an enhanced lighting and new video system. However, they can once again walk out onto the Statue's observation deck to see the panoramic views of New York City and the Harbour. Previously, visitors had been able to climb from the toe of the Statue to the crown but now they can only stand just below the staircase in the pedestal, and stare up at the interior structure.

According to members of the National Parks Service, the decision to close off the body of the Statue had to do with the heat, which can apparently reach 40.5°C (105°F) in summer, but other sources suggest that the Parks Service determined that it would be impossible to protect the winding staircases and relatively narrow interior of the Statue adequately from terrorist attack. New staff training programmes have been devised including 'Behavior Pattern Recognition™' which focuses on the observation of people and suspicious behaviour, including spotting what visitors are wearing, bags they are carrying and any mannerisms that seem suspicious. Other innovations within the Statue include additional emergency lighting and exits, upgraded and expanded fire detection and suppression systems and a series of compartmentalized spaces, expanded smoke detection and speaker systems on and around the Island, additional communication systems to alert visitors with safety messages, and new and upgraded elevators, ramps and evacuation routes. But is this technology gone mad?

National Parks Service employees have been trying to put a positive spin on the changes claiming that, in the past, it had been a very long climb just to see out of three small windows and that today's experience is more educational, more exciting and queue free. Tourists are not all happy with this – some feeling that the Statue stands for freedom and it should therefore be able to be freely visited. Some claim that security procedures can take two hours involving two security checkpoints and an 'air puffer' for possible biological contaminants, which seems a little excessive. Others complained about the confiscation of unopened water bottles, although this is a common precaution elsewhere, including Vatican City. Even with timed tickets the visit now requires visitors to arrive two hours in advance to get through the security screenings, the ferry and the queues for the tour. A visitor also wanting to see nearby Ellis Island must now allocate an entire day. Other visitors see the increased presence of Park Rangers as a plus, with visitors assigned timed tours, each led by a Park Ranger in groups of 15 to 20 booked either in advance, over the Internet, or when they buy ferry tickets and are given an assigned time to show up and begin. But undeniably the visitor experience now includes the very antithesis of that freedom for which the Statue stands.

Cultural sensitivity

In the case of Robben Island (above), it might have reasonably been assumed that visitors to a site, which has now become virtually a secular pilgrimage destination because of its connections with Nelson Mandela, would treat the site with great respect. However, there are many examples of sites where visitors demonstrate unexpectedly high levels of cultural insensitivity, of which an excellent example is the great monolith of Uluru (Ayers Rock), which lies at the heart of the WHS landscape in central Australia and is sacred to the Anangu aboriginal people who have lived there for 30 000 years. It receives more than 350 000 visitors per year and is probably the most familiar visual landscape element in Australia. Visiting Uluru is a unique opportunity to encounter aboriginal art, mythology and culture and visitors consume its landscape in a variety of different ways, from guided walks to helicopter flights, some of which may be inappropriate for a sacred site. The most contentious of these is climbing the monolith itself, a procedure discouraged but not forbidden by its Anangu custodians. Temporary closure of the climb in 2001, as the result of the death of a tribal elder, resulted in increased awareness of the sacredness of the Uluru landscape, a process already started by Anangu-led tours. The Anangu would like visitors to appreciate Uluru as a node in a sacred landscape rather than just a monolith to be climbed, although many tourists visit the site solely to climb the rock. For the Anangu, Uluru is the focus of several 'dreaming tracks' and ceremonial exchange routes; climbing it is seen as impious and spiritually dangerous. Both Uluru and Kata Tjuta are full of sacred sites, some accessible only to particular social groups. For the Anangu, it is both unsafe and forbidden for men to look at women's sites and vice versa. Some sites, such as the Kantju waterhole at Uluru, require special behaviour, where visitors are asked to approach quietly and remain respectful. Photography of such sites of special spiritual significance is forbidden, with clear notices to inform visitors. Parks Australia has produced a new management plan for Uluru which confirms that crowding is considered by them to be a significant problem within the park. Visitors' safety and the provision of visitor facilities also figure highly. Twenty-seven people have died on Uluru since 1965 and there have been many accidents despite restrictions on the climb when the temperature exceeds 35°C or when the rock is windy or slippery.

Conclusions

As discussed above, this case study of Uluru encapsulates the three main elements of contemporary visitor management already identified. Uluru has issues of visitor safety and security, it has problems with managing the large numbers of visitors to the site and in maintaining and interpreting its sacredness to visitors. Uluru is a landscape icon for Australia and of huge cultural significance, not just as an archaeological site and visitor attraction. The identification of crowding as a major problem has become common. The issue of site degradation at Mogao, as a result of visitor pressure, has already been referred to. Strategies to manage large numbers of visitors are only successful where they can be adequately policed – for example the booking system for the tomb of Nefertari in the Valley of the Kings, and crowding impacts on both visitor experience and visitor safety.

As the writer has discussed before (Shackley, 1998, 2001a) crowding is often made worse by the way in which tours are organized and this can also vary with the kind of activities that visitors to the sites partake in. At Uluru, for example, crowding is made worse by coach company itineraries taking visitors to the same places at the same times of day, with around 40 per cent of Uluru's visitors coming on such organized tours which are very tightly scheduled. But it is often difficult to regulate visitor flows at WHS and, indeed, there may be pressure to increase visitor flows for political reasons, as can be seen from the Chinese example (above). WHS stakeholders want different things, as was seen at Stonehenge, and such visitor management issues may take years, and sometimes decades, to resolve. Just as at Uluru, where visitor infrastructure is to be relocated away from culturally sensitive places including the development of new visitor notes near the climb and new walks diverting visitors from culturally sensitive locations (Parks Australia, 2000), the new centre at Stonehenge would enable visitors to appreciate the site in its landscape setting, to consume it appropriately and to reflect on its meaning. This, after all, must be the ultimate aim of managing visitors at WHS which provide unique opportunities for displaying the very best of our global heritage. Inevitably, in a world where cultural tourism is becoming more popular and its participants better informed, issues of visitor pressure, security and safety are going to remain significant, but it can be seen from the above examples that it is perfectly possible to deal with these at a local level and arrive at acceptable solutions. The issue of balancing conservation and visitor pressure will always be contentious for WHS managers but there is room for optimism that new vision and new technologies will result in continued improvements over the next decade, just as greater levels of awareness have raised their profile over the last.

References

Berraine, M. (1997) *Tourisme, culture et developpement dans la Region Arabe*. Rabat: UNESCO.

Borg, J. van der, Costa, P. and Gotti, G. (1996) Tourism in European heritage cities. *Annals of Tourism Research*, 23, 306–321.

ICOMOS (1993) *Tourism and World Heritage Cultural Sites: The Site Manager's Handbook*. Madrid: World Tourism Organization.

Parks Australia (2000) *Uluru-Kata Tjuta National Park Visitor Infrastructure Master Plan*. Canberra: Parks Australia.

Righter, R. (2004) The greatest show on earth. *Time Magazine*, 4 December, pp. 45–48.

Shackley, M. (1998) *Visitor Management: Case Studies from World Heritage Sites*. Oxford: Butterworth-Heinemann.

Shackley, M. (2001a) *Managing Sacred Sites: Service Provision and Visitor Experience*. London: Continuum Press.

Shackley, M. (2001b) Potential futures for Robben Island; shrine, museum or theme park? *International Journal of Heritage Studies*, 7 (4), 355–365.

Shackley, M. (2004a) Tourist consumption of sacred landscapes: space, time and vision. *Tourism Recreation Research*, 29 (1), 67–75.

Shackley, M. (2004b) Managing the Cedars of Lebanon. *Current Issues in Tourism*, 7 (4–5), 417–426.

Tibet Information Network (2004) Central Lhasa Gets Facelift with 'Tibetan Characteristics'. http://www.tew.org/development/lhasa.facelift.html (accessed 13 March 2005).

Urry, J (1990) *The Tourist Gaze*. London: Sage.

Whittaker, E. (1999) Indigenous tourism; reclaiming knowledge, culture and intellectual property in Australia. In Robinson, M. and Boniface, P. (eds) *Tourism and Cultural Conflicts*. Wallingford: CABI Publishing.

PART 3

Generating and managing revenue

Part Three focuses on the operational and practical aspects of providing financially sustainable heritage properties. The majority of heritage sites suffer from a basic lack of funding, resources and expertise, though part of the purpose of the World Heritage Convention is to encourage international cooperation and exchange of knowledge, expertise and funds. Recognition of the conflict between conservation and tourism activities is required, in conjunction with recognition of the necessity of generating revenue to ensure resource sustainability and meet visitor expectations. The heritage sector is undergoing a significant period of change in terms of central government support, so appreciation of the option to involve the private sector in the future management of public-owned sites and the associated issues would be appropriate.

In Chapter 7, Janet Cochrane and Richard Tapper examine partnership approaches and other management initiatives which can maximize potential revenues and conservation benefits from tourism. They appraise the often conflicting views of WHS managers and the tourism sector, leading to suggestions of how stronger links between the two can be forged. Opportunities to build relationships between tour operators and tourists, plus WHS managers in enhancing the contribution of tourism to the maintenance of sites, are discussed. With reference to a range of WHS, including the Bunaken Marine National Park in Indonesia they demonstrate how this relationship can be enhanced to the mutual benefit of both parties.

A popular route for generating revenue at heritage sites is hosting events and festivals. This next chapter, written by Melanie Smith, Elizabeth Carnegie and Martin Robertson, provides an overview of the conflicts inherent in organizing temporary events in heritage spaces such as WHS. This chapter attempts to assess the degree of local community engagement with festivals and events that often have a wider national or international remit. The use of Edinburgh Old and New Towns and Maritime Greenwich WHS as case studies demonstrates these issues and argues that many of the issues could be addressed through integration of ideas within the WHS Management Plans.

The final chapter in Part Three offers a concise and accessible exploration into the use of Information Communication Technology applications (ICT) in WHS settings. The text is well supported visually, allowing the non-technical reader easily to absorb the huge variety of opportunities and developments in this field. Dimitrios Buhalis, Ruth Owen and Daniël Pletinckx examine the concept of ICT, before presenting some current uses of ICTs at WHS such as Olympia in Greece and the Uffizi in Florence, Italy. These indicate how the advances in communications technology and increased market forces present sites with a number of challenges, as well as opportunities, as WHS managers attempt to meet the needs of the resource and the stakeholders. The chapter ends with consideration of the extent to which ICTs can be applied to WHS and how the cost of this type of development does not need to be prohibitive or compromise the resource itself.

CHAPTER 7

Tourism's contribution to World Heritage Site management

Janet Cochrane and Richard Tapper

Aims

The aims of this chapter are to:

- Show how changes in approaches to the strategic and delivery mechanisms for socioeconomic development are affecting tourism management at World Heritage Sites (WHS)
- Examine partnership approaches and other management initiatives which can maximize potential revenues and conservation and development benefits from tourism
- Suggest ways that WHS managers can forge stronger links with the tourism sector
- Outline specific means of generating income from tourism
- Provide case studies which illustrate successful management approaches.

Introduction

Tourism to WHS and other protected areas is increasing, bringing with it challenges to the sites from wear-and-tear and the impacts that large numbers of visitors can have on their 'spirit of place'. In turn, this is forcing a search for methods of balancing conservation with the livelihood needs of local people and the right of tourists to enjoy such places. WHS and other protected areas can benefit from tourism in several ways, in that additional funds for conservation can be generated from tourism, and the profile of the site can be raised, both of which help to generate greater government support. Furthermore, where local people experience economic benefits from these sites, they are also more likely to become aware of the importance of conservation.

Historically, funding for many WHS has often been inadequate, and most have received their funding from the national or international public sector. Now, increasing emphasis is being placed on the role of other groups in civil society in contributing to their management. One obvious way of encouraging the participation of other groups is to maximize non-damaging forms of using the sites for revenue generation which, for many places, means tourism. This chapter will add to the many existing studies on the economic value of tourism to conservation by suggesting practical ways of ensuring that tourism provides greater support to WHS. Information from published material has been supplemented with primary research carried out among outbound tour operators based in several countries into actual experiences of links between WHS and tourism companies.

Support from tourism for conservation and management of World Heritage Sites

The sometimes uneasy relationship and mutual dependence between tourism and heritage attractions has been explored in a number of academic and practical texts, including Prentice (1993), Nuryanti (1997), Shackley (1998), Robinson et al. (2000), McKercher and du Cros (2002), Pedersen (2002) and Tapper and Cochrane (2005). The management of attractions important enough to be listed as WHS presents particular challenges because of the sites' international significance: by their designation, they become part of the global heritage, and demand resources consistent with this status. Further challenges are provided by the fact that cultural artefacts and natural areas designated as WHS require very different management techniques, although there is an overlap where sites include elements of both. In many cases, an attraction which is overtly natural is actually a creation of human endeavour, and Howard (2003) makes the useful point that nature – or at least interpretations of it and assessment of its value – is itself a cultural construct.

The ideal situation is a symbiotic relationship between tourism and WHS, in which tour operators use them to add value to their products and local service providers earn money from tourists, while the sites earn higher revenues and achieve a higher profile nationally, which can encourage government bodies to devote stronger protection measures to them. However, at the same time, tourism can add to the costs of managing protected areas, since sites have to invest in, manage and maintain tourism facilities in order to prevent damage to sensitive areas, while the presence of visitors can threaten the integrity of ecosystems, of fragile buildings or other cultural artefacts, or the 'spirit of place', which is often a hugely significant element of the site. Tourism has therefore to be managed with care: it is essential for site managers to assess and balance the costs and benefits of visitation, and it is equally important for local people and communities to benefit from tourism, as this will demonstrate the economic value of resources which have been protected under a World Heritage designation and, in some cases, alienated from other forms of exploitation which might have been of more immediate benefit to the resident population.

There is a range of goals and means for maximizing the benefits of tourism to biodiversity and to economic and social development, and the benefits of biodiversity to tourism, while minimizing negative social and environmental impacts. These include:

- generating sufficient revenues to reduce threats to biodiversity from local communities

- encouraging all stakeholders, particularly the private sector, to support the active conservation of biodiversity and the sustainable use of its components
- ensuring the effective participation of local communities in the development, operation and monitoring of tourism activities
- channelling tourism revenues towards conservation, for example through management of protected areas, education, research programmes, or local community development
- zoning and control of tourism developments and activities
- diversification of economic activities to reduce dependency on tourism
- encouraging the role of protected areas as key locations for good practices in the management of sustainable tourism and biodiversity.

Some WHS are unsuitable for use as tourist attractions because of geographical or political factors, which make them inaccessible, or because of their fragility. In the case of other places, while site-specific management will vary considerably depending on their type and location, some common features can be identified. These relate to the underlying principles which guide the approach to revenue creation and to the range of methods available to generate this revenue.

Management structures and the partnership approach

Traditionally, government departments have had sole responsibility for the administration of WHS, with funds for managing them allocated from the national budget or from international bodies. However, in countries with budgetary constraints, conservation is not generally prioritized and levels of funding are likely to be low. Furthermore, some countries have legal restrictions that prevent government departments from generating their own incomes – for example, by selling concessions to businesses – or which require revenues raised by government departments to be returned to the national treasury. Restrictions of this type may inhibit WHS from supplementing their government funding with other sources of income. In consequence, sites managed through government departments are often under-funded.

Recognition of these limitations has meant that a partnership approach is increasingly applied in managing WHS. Generally, the partnership philosophy is assuming a wider influence at a strategic level because project-based or single-sector initiatives aimed at addressing economic decline often fail to achieve lasting results; the approach is relevant to many spheres and is becoming increasingly common in tourism (WTO, 2003). Even greater opportunities arise where the tourism and conservation sectors join forces, with the advantages revolving around economies of scale in human resources and marketing, greater effectiveness in product development, improved quality of service, increased community awareness of conservation, resolution of potential conflicts of interest, and a reduction in overlapping initiatives.

Increased focus on partnerships is an example of how the current rationale of heritage site management is informed by international trends in governance, one aspect of which is the devolution of resource management. Local communities are increasingly being given the opportunity to make decisions over their own resources and livelihood infrastructure. This reflects the policy shift, both nationally and internationally, away from a paradigm of managerialism and 'government' towards entrepreneurialism and 'governance' (Scott, 2004: 50). Another aspect of this is the greater integration of private and public sectors. Practical outcomes are the increasing privatization of service delivery, and the development of cross-sectoral partnerships between the public and private sector and with community and voluntary groups. In the UK, for instance, the delivery of much government policy now depends on Local Strategic Partnerships, which often unite different government departments as well as private and community groups.

There are many different types of partnership, ranging from simple marketing alliances between neighbouring attractions to more complex management arrangements. In 2004, seven historic houses in Yorkshire, in the UK, created a joint marketing strategy around a single product theme. Some of the individual properties were in private ownership while others were owned by English Heritage or the National Trust, an important NGO. In some cases there was initial reluctance to participate in the scheme because of fears that smaller or less well-known properties would suffer competitive disadvantage. However, in the event, the results of the scheme were excellent in that marketing budgets were used more efficiently, while the target market proved keen to visit each of the seven properties over the course of the season in order to follow through each aspect of the theme.

The shifting approach to heritage site management is also evident in the increasing adoption of parastatals as a form of management structure. Parastatals are essentially public sector organizations which incorporate some elements commonly found in private sector organizations. English Heritage, which has responsibility for managing many of England's historic monuments – including the WHS of Stonehenge and Hadrian's Wall – is an example of this. Parastatals have much greater flexibility than government departments to set fees and charges, establish funding mechanisms such as concessions, implement staffing policies based on efficiency and market salaries, and respond to customer needs, while their ability to retain the money they earn gives more incentive to generate funds through greater entrepreneurship. Another example of a parastatal is the KwaZulu-Natal Nature Conservation Service, in South Africa, which manages its protected areas under cooperative agreements with landowners. Again, such arrangements are effectively a partnership between the public and private sector.

WHS can benefit from the partnership approach through more sophisticated and cost-effective marketing, acquiring additional managerial capacity, and ensuring good relations with local communities. So, while government departments may still maintain overall responsibility for protected areas and important cultural sites, a variety of more flexible management structures is being developed. At the Indonesian WHS of Komodo, for instance, a collaborative management scheme, initiated in 2002, involves the national park authority, the local government, an international conservation NGO, and a local tourism company as well as local communities, government agencies, and private sector organizations. Through the initiative, the capacity of the park authority to implement conservation management, sustainable livelihood activities and conservation awareness is strengthened, while improved channels for funding conservation through tourism are being created. A looser partnership has been formed at the Jurassic Coast WHS in southern Britain, where a steering group oversees management of the site and includes local council officers, business representatives, landowners, and the chairs of various working groups covering science and conservation, education, tourism, museums, and local towns, which use their proximity to the site to capture tourism revenues.

Building links with the tourism sector

In many cases it may not be appropriate for WHS to create a formal partnership with other agencies, but there are still many advantages in building a closer cooperation with the tourism industry. WHS offer tourism companies important possibilities to add value to their holiday products, since global recognition of the World Heritage 'brand' can be an important selling point. Specialist operators may include visits to sites as an integral part of their itineraries, while mass tourism companies increasingly offer cultural excursions as add-on options to their holiday packages. For example, one German mass tour operator provides excursions from its main destinations to around 120 different WHS (Tapper and Cochrane, 2005).

While the benefits to the tourism industry of WHS are fairly obvious, however, the advantages to WHS of tourism are less well appreciated. A study of tourism at the WHS of Luang Prabang, Laos, examined the relationship between various stakeholders and found low levels of communication between the tourism sector and heritage agencies, with the heritage sector more reluctant to engage in dialogue than the tourism industry, and poor levels of political will to increase the contribution of tourism to local heritage through a proposed bed-tax. On the other hand, the tourism industry was pro-active in encouraging donations from clients which went towards restoration work (Aas et al., 2005).

The unwillingness of the heritage sector to work with the industry is symptomatic of the traditional lack of a marketing philosophy among heritage site managers (Prentice, 1993) and to a dichotomy between 'preservers' and 'users': in other words, the suspicion of people charged with looking after heritage sites towards greater public access. This has come about partly because the wear and tear caused by tourism is often only too clear, and partly because the advantages tourism can bring are under-recognized. These benefits derive not only from the increased finances, which can be channelled directly from tourism into conservation, but also from the indirect benefits of improving acceptance of the site among local populations through ensuring economic benefits to them.

Even where these benefits are accepted, however, and a site is convinced of the need to encourage tourism, the opportunities may not be fully exploited because of poor understanding of the complex structure and operation of the tourism industry. While the basic requirements considered by tour operators when assessing a new tour or excursion include the quality of a site's cultural attraction or wildlife, its accessibility, the 'fit' with the company's existing products, its marketability, and the standard of food, accommodation and infrastructure, including reliable local ground handling agents, an additional factor is that the relationship between the tourism and conservation sectors has to be long term and on a firm basis of trust. One reason for this is that tour operators are legally responsible for the quality of every element of the tour packages they assemble and, to avoid fear of litigation, have to know that the product matches what was represented to their clients through the brochure, and that high standards are maintained by all their suppliers. Also, because of the cycle of product development and marketing, it can be two years between the initial idea for a new product and the time clients start arriving, and this means establishing long-term agreements between tour operators and sites: for example, tour operators need firm information about entry fees at least 12 months in advance, so that these can be factored into holiday costs that are published in their brochures. Even in the case of independent travellers, sites must offer a good quality, consistent experience if they are to maintain or increase market share.

Having an understanding of the industry will put WHS managers in a much better position to encourage tour operators to visit. It is also important to have a basic knowledge of the market for the attraction, so that the most appropriate visitor segments or tour operators can be targeted and catered for. Once a relationship has been formed with tourism personnel from local or overseas tour operators or from the local tourist board, it should be possible to take advantage of this. For instance, tour company personnel can be asked to help with specific aspects of enhancing the possibilities for tourism, such as devising tour circuits, identifying key target markets, and advising on pricing structures and the appropriate design of visitor facilities; many tour operators will be interested in doing this if they see the potential for including the site in future tours.

Naturally, the main purpose of creating closer links with the tourism sector is not just to promote the site to a wider audience but also to maximize the financial benefits. There are a number of mechanisms for doing this.

Maximizing revenues from tourism

The standard way of collecting revenues for WHS and other protected areas is through entrance fees. However, these rarely cover the operational costs other than in exceptional cases such as the Galapagos Islands, where visitor fees make a major contribution to Ecuador's national budget. Nevertheless, studies have shown that entry fees can often be raised without affecting visitor numbers, resulting in an overall increase in income.

While more and more sites are setting fees according to market principles based on the quality-price ratio for the service received, elasticity of demand and willingness to pay, political considerations also have to be taken into account. For instance, one of the policy aims may be to allow reasonably-priced access to the domestic population, for whom the attraction may be an important recreational facility. Alternatively, particularly where sites are more remote and expensive to reach, the policy may be to maximize revenue from overseas visitors. Differential fees can be a useful mechanism to balance these issues, for example, by charging nationals lower fees than those set for international tourists, or by charging reduced fees at times when resident nationals are most likely to visit, such as at weekends and on public holidays.

In many cases it is appropriate to generate income through user fees, either instead of or in addition to entrance fees. This entails getting visitors to WHS to pay, for example, for car parks, campsites, visitor centres, mountain huts, or canopy walkways, or for activities such as diving, hiking or mountain climbing. In some cases, these fees can be generated through commercial operation of businesses by the managing public authority, but in other cases, the legislative structures or human resources to permit this may not exist. This is one of the reasons why the partnership arrangements outlined earlier can be very successful, in that the public sector can formalize its links with private companies in order to channel funds into site management. In some cases, policy may be to allocate concessions in the form of permits, leases or licences which allow private companies, individuals, NGOs or community groups to run commercial operations while generating financial benefits for the site. Activities may include diving operations, provision of accommodation or catering facilities, souvenir shops, or the hire and sale of recreational and sports equipment. WHS can often also generate funds through merchandizing themed items such as clothing, books, or other souvenirs.

A further way in which protected areas can benefit from tourism is to encourage volunteer help and donations from companies or from individuals. Several organizations offer holidays where people pay to work on conservation projects, including helping at archaeological digs or with habitat management in national parks. An example of how these ventures can help WHS is a project which sends English-speaking volunteers to the Museum of the Terracotta Warriors, in China, where they help with signs in the museum, teach English to museum staff, and lead guided tours for visitors. More widespread is the trend for companies to express their corporate social responsibility through donations to charitable causes, often with aims linked to the company's holidays. For example, a UK-based tour operator running safaris to Zambian national parks supports a school in Zambia, while a walking holiday company funded the rebuilding of an ancient track to the Benedictine Abbey of Sant'Eutizio in Umbria. Most tour operators will expect some benefit in return for this type of action: for instance some may display the logo of the projects they support in their brochures, while a German tour operator, which provided funds for training Cambodians in restoration techniques at Angkor Wat, has special guided tours of the temple for its clients conducted by project staff.

Barnes and Eagles (2004) note the increasing tendency for companies to encourage philanthropic donations by their clients. Maximizing the opportunities for individual tourists to make donations to projects associated with WHS is another important way of ensuring that tourism supports conservation. An important aspect of promoting donations, and of revenue generation generally, is for sites to ensure that management of the funds raised is transparent and accountable, so that tourists and tourism companies, as well as local stakeholders, can see that funds are being used properly and effectively. A further way of supporting WHS is for tour operators to select accommodation and other services that emphasize conservation and community involvement and implement sustainability policies such as efficient use of water and energy.

An illustration of a successful partnership created around tourism to an important marine national park in a developing country is given below.

Case study: Bunaken Marine National Park, Indonesia

Bunaken Marine National Park, in North Sulawesi, Indonesia, was gazetted in 1991 because of its outstanding biodiversity, including coral reefs, mangrove forests and seagrass beds, and it has won several awards for its achievements in blending the needs of tourism and conservation. It is currently under consideration as a WHS.

Dive tourism in the area began in the early 1980s, and by the late 1980s there were at least four privately-owned dive centres handling around 4000 tourists per year. The founder of the first dive centre won the Indonesian Kalpataru conservation award for his actions in the mid-1980s, and it was partly due to local tourism entrepreneurs that the coral reefs were preserved from the destructive fishing methods which affect many other Indonesian reefs.

After the area's protected status was declared there were several management challenges. First, in common with other Indonesian national parks, Bunaken was managed by the Directorate General of Forest Protection and Nature Conservation (PHPA), which sits within the Ministry of Forestry. This was clearly an anomalous situation for a marine park. Secondly, the local government was reluctant to relinquish management of the area to PHPA because of the substantial returns from tourism. Thirdly, there was resentment from the then 20 000 or so residents of the park because they felt they had not been consulted over its formation or management, they were anxious about rumours that they would be moved from their homes, and because they gained little economic benefit from tourism. Although by 1992 at least 150 Indonesians were employed by the dive centres as dive guides and buddies, boat-drivers, maintenance men and hotel staff, most of these people were not actually residents of the park.

To some extent, local resentment was defused by entrepreneurial responses to the backpacker market, who began arriving by the early 1990s as the area became more widely known and appealed to wider markets as well as to divers. There was also considerable domestic interest in marine tourism by residents of the nearby city of Manado. Several 'homestays' were set up on islands within the marine national park, with around a dozen small establishments in existence by 1993. Although none of these had an official licence to operate, they were allowed to remain by the park authorities in order to allow some economic benefits to reach the wider community.

A management plan for the park was prepared under a Natural Resources Management Project funded by the United States Agency for International Development in the early 1990s, and WWF wrote guidelines for developing sustainable marine tourism at the park. As part of these initiatives a number of tourism-related activities were introduced, including the installation of mooring buoys to prevent dive boats anchoring on the reefs, training courses for dive guides to improve their awareness of reef conservation issues and their ability to look after clients safely, and conservation awareness materials aimed at tourists, dive operators, and residents of the park. The plan also allowed for the development of small, locally-owned tourism developments.

A significant eventual outcome of the plan, with supportive lobbying from the local dive industry and concerned individuals, was the establishment of a new national park management structure, which moved away from the 'sole responsibility' role of the PHPA in favour of a multi-stakeholder approach. This is Bunaken National Park Management Advisory Board (BNPMAB), which was formally established in 2001. Of the 15 seats on the board, members are drawn from dive operators, environmental organizations, universities, government departments and communities within the park.

The provincial government of North Sulawesi enacted legislation to allow the BNPMAB to collect income generated by the park and manage this. In most Indonesian national parks, entrance fees are not used directly to manage the park where they are generated, but are returned to provincial or national budgets. At Bunaken, however, only 20 per cent of the entrance fee revenue is split between local, provincial, and national government, which provides an incentive for the government to continue to support the scheme. The remaining 80 per cent is used specifically for conservation programmes at the park, including enforcement of regulations, conservation education, waste management, rehabilitation of coral reefs and mangroves, and environmentally-friendly village development projects. Thirty per cent of the entrance fee revenue goes directly to the community through a grants programme; there are now around 30 000 villagers living in 22 villages.

Entrance fee levels are based on surveys of visitor willingness to pay and in 2005 stood at US$6 for a daily fee and US$17 for an annual tag. The fee collection system has been designed in consultation with the local tourism sector, so that it is practical and efficient, with dive tags purchased through dive operators. Enforcement of the tag system is conducted via spot checks by park rangers on land and at sea. During the first three years of operation, the fee system raised US$420 000.

The BNPMAB was active in promoting the formation of the North Sulawesi Watersports Association (NSWA) which, in 2005, grouped 17 dive operators and resorts. The NSWA ensures that its members are properly trained in customer safety, reef protection techniques and general environmental awareness, and makes a specific point of encouraging visitors to support local enterprises, such as purchasing food and souvenirs, while discouraging practices such as 'over-bargaining', whereby prices are haggled down to unrealistic levels. Materials produced by both the BNPMAB and the NSWA stress the environmental and social responsibilities of the tourism industry, and both provide means whereby tourists can make donations to sponsor conservation and development activities, such as contributing to a fund which pays school fees for children from the park.

The BNPMAB has also diversified its revenue streams in order not to depend completely on user fees: other revenue is generated from national/international grants, merchandizing, and an international volunteer system.

In 2003, the park won the prestigious 'Tourism for Tomorrow' award, sponsored by British Airways, and in 2004 it won the Equator prize, sponsored by UNDP, in recognition of its efforts to ensure that tourism supports both conservation and development. It is largely due to the major contribution made by tourism to management of the park that it has been put forward for WHS status.

Conclusions

The techniques outlined in this chapter for enhancing the relationship between WHS and tourism provide an overview of the changing rationale of heritage management. In an era when sites can no longer rely on government support, other means have to be sought for ensuring the preservation of cultural and natural attractions. It is entirely reasonable to apply the 'user pays' principle by ensuring that the tourists who benefit from visits to the sites should pay for their upkeep. At the same time, there are many reasons why site managers cannot become over-reliant on this source of income. Tourism is a fickle industry, subject to fluctuations due to national or international political or economic factors and to trends in destination appeal. Some WHS are too small, too inaccessible or insufficiently robust to cope with the volume of tourists that would make a significant difference to their budget. Site managers therefore have to be realistic in their dealings with the industry, including gaining a good understanding of how tourism works.

Of course, closer links with the tourism industry can bring disadvantages in terms of over-crowding and damage to the fabric of the site, but there are well-known techniques for managing these issues. The focus on diversifying funding sources and in taking an entrepreneurial approach is likely to increase over the coming decades, and it is essential for conservation policy-makers and managers to appreciate that while the tourism industry needs them to provide a constant flow of attractions, they also need the tourism sector to provide not only funding, but also as part of a continued justification for the sites' survival as an accessible part of the global heritage.

References

Aas, C., Ladkin, A. and Fletcher, J. (2005) Stakeholder collaboration and heritage management. *Annals of Tourism Research,* 32, 128–148.

Barnes, M.L. and Eagles, P. (2004) Examining the relationship between ecotourists and philanthropic behaviour. *Tourism Recreation Research,* 29 (3), 35–38.

Howard, P. (2003) *Heritage: Management, Interpretation, Identity.* London: Continuum.

McKercher, B. and du Cros, H. (2002) *Cultural Tourism: The Partnership Between Tourism and Cultural Heritage Management.* Binghamton, New York: The Howarth Hospitality Press.

Nuryanti, W. (1997) *Tourism and Heritage Management.* Yogyakarta: Gadjah Mada University Press.

Pedersen, A. (2002) *Managing Tourism at World Heritage Sites: A Practical Manual for World Heritage Site Managers:* UNESCO.

Prentice, R. (1993) *Tourism and Heritage Attractions.* London and New York: Routledge.

Robinson, M., Evans, N., Long, P., Sharpley, R. and Swarbrooke, J. (eds). (2000) *Tourism and Heritage Relationships: Global, National and Local Perspectives.* Sunderland: Centre for Travel and Tourism in association with Business Education Publishers.

Scott, M. (2004) Building institutional capacity in rural Northern Ireland: The role of partnership governances in the Leader II programme. *Journal of Rural Studies,* 20 (1), 49–59.

Shackley, M. (1998) *Visitor Management: Case Studies from World Heritage Sites.* Oxford: Butterworth-Heinemann.

Tapper, R. and Cochrane, J. (2005) *Forging Links Between Protected Areas and the Tourism Sector: How Tourism Can Benefit Conservation.* Paris: UNEP.

WTO (2003) *Co-operation and Partnerships in Tourism: A Global Perspective.* Madrid: World Tourism Organization.

CHAPTER 8

Juxtaposing the timeless and the ephemeral: staging festivals and events at World Heritage Sites

Melanie Smith, Elizabeth Carnegie
and Martin Robertson

Aims

The aims of this chapter are to:

- Provide an overview of the conflicts inherent in organizing temporary events in heritage spaces and conservation areas
- Explore the relationship between global heritage, international tourism and local cultural provision in the context of World Heritage Sites
- Assess the degree of local engagement with festivals and events that have a national or international remit
- Provide analyses of two case studies of Edinburgh and Greenwich as a means of contextualizing some of the aforementioned issues.

Introduction

The aim of this chapter is to explore the complex relationship between World Heritage Sites (WHS) and temporary festivals and events, analysing some of the impacts and implications of staging 'ephemeral' arts projects in the context of 'timeless' heritage environments. While the physical impacts of visitation to both World Heritage Sites and festivals have been well documented in recent years, this chapter also seeks to consider some of the more intangible and symbolic aspects of management. Many of these relate to the often-dissonant juxtaposition of global status symbols (e.g. WHS), international tourism attractions (e.g. festivals and events), and local cultural provision. Cultural providers within urban environments are becoming more adept at programming a range of arts events for local communities, however, these are frequently delivered in isolation from heritage or tourism developments. In the contexts that have been chosen for analysis in this chapter (Edinburgh and Greenwich), the entire historic centres are designated WHS, and both were busy tourist attractions, even before designation. Thus, any analysis of cultural and arts developments – in this case, multi-venue festivals spanning several days – cannot be considered in isolation from heritage and tourism. It is the intersection of these elements that provide the key challenges for these and many other WHS: in short, how to conserve physical structures, while promoting tourism, at the same time as fostering local cultural engagement and understanding.

WHS management and cultural space

With the production of the compulsory WHS management plan, WHS are now obliged to set themselves the ambitious task of being all things to all people: beacons of conservation and sustainability; international tourist attractions; educational institutions encouraging local engagement; and catalysts for regeneration and business development. The reconciliation of all of these often conflicting elements is by no means easy. Most notably, restrictions on physical access for reasons of conservation are coupled with demands for greater symbolic engagement and access. The tools most frequently used to engender this are education, interpretation and marketing. Increasingly, attempts are being made to integrate the educational, experiential and symbolic to this end. Many agencies responsible for WHS (e.g. heritage steering groups, tourism offices and cultural organizations) are trying to animate the spaces and create greater local and visitor engagement. While conservation imperatives still tend to dominate in the majority of cases, this does not exclude more creative approaches to WHS management, including, for example, the hosting of festivals.

Nevertheless, in contrast to this, one could cite Shackley's (1998: 1) plea that 'visiting a World Heritage Site should be a major intellectual experience, on a different scale from visiting some theme park'. Accordingly, as festivals tend towards being experiential or jubilant performance rather than educational occurrence, questions may be raised as to their appropriateness for a WHS setting. Do they, for example, serve merely as an attractive backdrop and/or magnet for visitors? Moreover, where they provide the animation necessary to attract local people to sites that otherwise they would not visit, is the engagement of the audience at anything other than a superficial level? Is any depth in communication about the site and its history facilitated by the performance? So, while they offer a conscious and strategic platform for enlivening otherwise dead spaces or creating cultural access, festivals do not always sit comfortably with the conservation and education remit of WHS.

WHS that are whole cities or historic centres need to be viewed differently from individual monuments or sites. They are not only sites, they are also living places for communities, where the complexities of history, culture difference, local and national identity and the whole pulse of coexistence is necessarily served by pragmatic management. In Greenwich (inscribed in 1997) a number of historical buildings have been linked to create Maritime Greenwich. In Edinburgh the World Heritage Site (inscribed in 1995) embraces the entire historic city centre. Both WHS are vibrant, working areas as well as busy tourist destinations and cultural venues. Lippard (1997) suggests that place is a result of the union between space and lived culture, and that a sense of place is based on a combination of heritage and contemporary lifestyles. This is particularly relevant to WHS that are essentially whole towns or historic centres, and which are likely to have a multi-functional contemporary usage. Local populations may feel more affinity with contemporary cultural developments than they do with a history or heritage from which they feel alienated (e.g. imperial legacies or symbols of past oppression). Their tendency to visit attractions within the WHS may be limited as a result. As is the case of Greenwich, residents from the wider Borough tend to visit the historic centre rather infrequently. Tourists, on the other hand, may be drawn to the uniqueness of place that is offered by the existence of a site of universal value, i.e. a WHS.

The implications of this are that resident communities may be more drawn to experiential events such as festivals. Indeed, this may be the main way of encouraging visitation to the WHS if that is the specified aim of the WHS agencies in any particular locale. The staging of a culturally diverse festival in the same location may encourage attendance because local people feel that their cultures are somehow represented. Thus it may be the *animation* of space in the context of WHS that transforms it into a place where local people feel culturally connected, albeit for a short time. Longer-term engagement is more challenging, and may be achieved through both formal and informal educational channels, outreach programmes and interpretation.

WHS and festival venues

The bestowing of the World Heritage Site accolade can be seen as primarily of symbolic significance. It serves as a reminder that the site or area in question is of outstanding universal value. Of course, questions can (and should) be raised about who makes such value judgements and who are the main beneficiaries. World Heritage Status reflects the value of architectural space in terms 'of the important interchange of human values, over a span of time' but the evidence suggests that the inscription on the list, which creates a forum for the 'better protection and safeguarding of the site' (Edinburgh World Heritage Conservation Manifesto, www.edinburgh.gov.uk, 2005) is viewed as having planning implications rather than cultural ones. In addition, it should be remembered that, in many cases, the WHS inscription was awarded many years after the first tourist arrivals and the original programming of cultural events. Indeed the first Edinburgh Festival took place in 1947 while WHS inscription did not arrive until 1995.

World Heritage Site status is often perceived to offer advantages over other, non-inscribed, cities for the combined functions of destination marketing, promotion and branding and, ultimately, boosting tourist visitor numbers. Nevertheless, it should be remembered that tourists are usually non-expert audiences and may fail to spot or recognize a (WHS) logo. Even in cases where they do, it may not have any resonance for them unless they are knowledgeable about the true meaning of status (and on which there is no consensus anyway). More importantly, it could be argued that traditional heritage tourism has had its heyday and that there needs to be diversification of products in historic towns in order to meet changing consumer demands. The work of Pine and Gilmore (1999) implies that there has been a shift in leisure consumption towards more experiential activities, and Richards and Wilson (2005) suggest that, subsequently, cities need to take more creative approaches in order to compete in the international marketplace.

Clearly, the commercialization of heritage of universal value and its reduction to a form of entertainment is not advocated here. However, the observation is made that creativity can take many forms, moving even beyond the ubiquitous heritage trail to more innovative and inclusive engagement strategies. Some of these may involve festivals or special events. One of the problems for heritage is its static location and the need to encourage local engagement through geographical displacement. While heritage can be seen to be inanimate and impersonal, festivals are by contrast full of animation, vibrancy and spontaneity. They are to be found in multiple locations and can be taken to the people wherever they may reside. In addition, festivals can be more socially inclusive than other forms of culture and are often viewed by festival directors and residents alike as expressions of cultural diversity and identity.

Yet there are some problems with the favouring of festivals over heritage or the way in which – it is opined here – heritage may act as distant backdrop to the event itself. Unlike the permanent fabric of tangible heritage, festivals are usually temporary, fleeting or elusive experiences. They can fail to sustain or support cultural continuity if they are not repeated. Furthermore, as public events become increasingly internationalized, festivals may endanger their very own roots and connections to specific localities in the desire to have globally recognizable appeal factors. Small community festivals are often described as offering more for the local people than large megaevents. Nevertheless, without extensive public funding their longterm success is less sure and long-term funding more often than not requires evidence of commercial viability. Viability often means attracting more non-local, often international, visitors.

More significantly, stakeholder relationships in the context of WHS and festival management tend either to be rather complex or no more than embryonic. In the UK, there is no real tradition of local government departments working together, even if they are all somehow connected to the provision of culture elements. It is not uncommon for whatever WHS agencies exist (e.g. specifically appointed Committees, Steering Groups) to work entirely independently from cultural offices, which generally take responsibility for festivals, events and community arts projects. This complicates not only management and conservation but also the allocation of funding and issues of responsibility and security. In addition, these organizations are not necessarily adept at marketing and promotion (and almost certainly will not have the resources). Even where they do have appropriate resources promotion may be largely or entirely local (e.g. in the case of community-based festivals and events). Therefore the role of tourism offices and tourist information centres (TICs) may be crucial to the wider dissemination of information about both WHS and local festivals. This is not to say that there will be harmonious and symbiotic relationships between tourism, heritage and arts organizations. The philosophies governing the respective sectors are still rather different in orientation (as a historical generalization, heritage tends to be more conservation-orientated, tourism more commercial/economic, and the arts more socially/community focused). However, in some cases (e.g. the Millennium Year in Greenwich) strong synergies and complementarities can be explored and often retained. Since WHS management plans were made mandatory, this has also had positive impacts on the integration of different areas of function and operation.

What have been explored in less detail are the symbolic aspects of WHS status. Of course, these are intangible and difficult to measure. The creation of animation, engagement and a sense of place are all being cited as crucial to retaining the character of historic towns (e.g. English Historic Towns Forum, 2005). However, there is still very little guidance on how this should be achieved. The role of festivals may be pivotal to this process given that programming is fluid and flexible and can be adapted to the local environment, its communities and their cultures. The incorporation of aspects of the location's heritage is also imperative where a WHS is being used as a venue. This may be the tangible fabric of the built environment as well as the intangible narratives that are constructed around it. In some cases, festivals may be able to address issues of dissonance that frequently plague WHS of an imperial or politically sensitive nature. Whereas the physical structure of heritage buildings cannot be altered, associations, perceptions and interpretations can easily be explored through the arts, especially where local people are actively involved in modes of expression and representation. This can help to challenge historical patterns and emphasize the contemporary relevance of heritage. Although something similar can be achieved through exhibitions or interpretation panels, often there is less scope for interaction, animation and the use of multi-perspectives.

Case study: Edinburgh and Greenwich – WHS, festivals, culture, community and market forces

Using research based evidence the following case studies of Edinburgh and Greenwich attempt to exemplify and put in context some of the issues raised so far in this chapter.

The first Edinburgh Festival took place in 1947 in Edinburgh, in large part a conscious and active move to regenerate the city after the Second World War. WHS status was not achieved until 1995, some 48 years later. World Heritage status can therefore be said to have had little relationship with the history of festival audiences in Edinburgh. The World Heritage Site that is Edinburgh's Old and New Towns – distinct and clear elements of the city – are essentially functioning and pragmatic lived in spaces. They are also the focus for concentrated bursts of cultural activity throughout the year, especially in August when 'this essentially historic resource is transformed' (Prentice and Anderson, 2003: 9). Indeed, 80 per cent of visitors most recently surveyed for the city organizers stated that visiting the festival was either their sole reason for coming to Edinburgh or an important part of their decision-making (The Audience Business, www.eif.co.uk). While Prentice and Anderson (2003) argue that in 1996/1997, 51 per cent and 42 per cent of visitors to the city cited the WHS status as a reason for their visit, it should be remembered that these figures cover the period immediately after Edinburgh's inscription and as such can be viewed as a direct response of the immediate publicity machine rather than a deep rooted knowledge indicative of all subsequent visitors. Moreover, analysis of publicity materials (1999–2003) for the International Festival and Festival Fringe indicated that there has been very little advice or information offered to prospective festival visitors to the city as regards the WHS status. The same is true of the official Edinburgh tourism website (over the one year period it was studied). Correspondingly, it is unlikely that there would be knowledge of the status, at any level, at such a prevailing high rate as that in 1996/7.

In the case of Greenwich, the first Greenwich and Docklands International Festival did not take place until 1998, one year after WHS inscription. It could, however, still be argued that the two were largely independent of each other until relatively recently. Initially, WHS status created greater political and financial support, followed by measures to improve conservation and tourism development (Smith, 2002). Despite this, the issue of local engagement with heritage and culture has more recently become a key issue for the WHS Steering Groups. Questionnaire interviews with 158 local people in 2003 revealed that 74 per cent of people claimed to know that Greenwich was a WHS, but when probed further in a focus group, it transpired that they did not actually know what WHS status meant and seemed to view the status as merely being a label that was used to attract more tourists.

The WHS Steering Groups for Marketing and Education in Greenwich are working hard to promote the WHS brand – that is, the collective sites that form the WHS. This is starting to include more intangible and experiential aspects of the site (e.g. shopping opportunities, evening entertainment, and festivals and cultural events). As advocated in a branding review by MORI (2002), the brand image is increasingly marked by attempts to be 'trendy'. Although this review showed that visitors viewed Greenwich as one of the most beautiful sites in London because of the impressive architecture, the negative implication of this perception was that the buildings were seen as imposing and Greenwich was deemed to lack animation and vibrancy. The Tourist Information Centre (TIC) manager also stated in an interview in 2002 that Greenwich needed more animation in the streets, ideally through festivals. Research with local people showed clearly that, although they liked the WHS for its beauty and attractions, they also found it imposing and inanimate. Royal and military/naval connections were deemed interesting but of little local consequence. What is more, they were seen to represent the history and legacy of white aristocracy, rather than the 'true' heritage of local dockworkers, shipbuilders and sailors, not to mention the dissonant heritage of slavery.

In recent years, Edinburgh's festivals have grown beyond the WHS boundaries, and indeed have been encouraged to do so. This is part of local government agendas for regeneration of peripheral areas. A key example of this is the Edinburgh Mela, which is held in Pilrig Park in Leith, an area (once separate from the city) that suffered the highs and lows of life revolving round a once active vital port. The Mela has retained its significance to the local audience (who in 2004 were 79 per cent of the audience/participants), and has never functioned as a mainstream international festival, despite being by its very nature a multicultural event (Carnegie and Smith, 2005).

The Greenwich and Docklands International Festival (GDIF) is sited in multi-locations, that is, it uses different venues and spaces for artistic performance such as music, dance and other spectacles. The WHS spaces are only used for some of the events. This means that the impacts of the GDIF on the physical structure of the WHS are relatively limited and contained, but then so too are the economic benefits (e.g. contribution to local businesses). Nevertheless, restrictions are still placed on the Festival organizers by the estate owners regarding the use of the WHS as a venue, mainly for reasons of conservation. However, residents questioned in a focus group made it clear that they would only venture out locally for such events, especially at night. They would not cross the River Thames, despite its proximity, for example. Tourists may have even more restricted geographical definitions than the residents, as tourism tends to be concentrated in the historic centre of Greenwich, thus restricting them to see only those events that were in public spaces within the WHS. The WHS is therefore an ideally located venue for attracting audiences of both locals and tourists alike, despite the necessary restrictions imposed by conservationists.

A survey conducted on behalf of the Edinburgh Festival in 2002 highlighted that while 43 per cent of audiences were from Edinburgh and the Lothians (42 per cent in 2004, EIF Annual Review, 2004), 65 per cent of those surveyed were shown to be socioeconomic group A or B with a further 28 per cent being C1s. This overall figure of 93 per cent being ABC1 is higher than other cultural activities including art gallery and museum attendance (Hargreaves, 1997; Carnegie, 2003). All of which seems to suggest that cultural programming through festivals is geared more towards its economic value than its capacity for social regeneration.

Greenwich's heritage sites and museums tend to attract local visitors (as well as tourists) because of the dynamic nature of their outreach and the educational programmes that support and accompany them. Nonetheless, focus group participants made it clear that they were most fond of spectacles (e.g. arts events); 49 per cent of the 158 questionnaire respondents were also very positive about festivals and events compared to the 33 per cent who enthused about heritage. A content analysis of 90 copies of the local newspaper, *Greenwich Time*, over four years showed that arts and events featured most prominently, with 73 articles compared to 24 on heritage and only eight on tourism. Although many of these were promotional, it demonstrated clearly the Local Council's commitment to an ongoing local festival and event programme (as part of their social regeneration agenda).

A focus group in Greenwich – consisting of twenty local women – demonstrated that they were most interested in festivals and events that fostered an understanding of different cultures, claiming that the mixing of cultures was 'lovely' and 'the best thing'. The programming of the GDIF is rich and varied, combining global arts spectacles with local ethnic cultural performances (e.g. schoolchildren performing Bollywood dancing). Links are frequently made to Greenwich's heritage too, e.g. Elizabeth I was the focus of the 2003 Festival as it was the celebration of the 400th anniversary of her death (she was born at Greenwich Palace in 1533).

However, during a local discussion group in Greenwich entitled 'Who cares about Culture?', a comment was made that festivals and events were sometimes seen to be sucking resources away from ongoing cultural provision. In parallel, many of the criticisms directed against the local area were linked to the environment and conservation, with clear suggestion that its significance should not be neglected at the expense of cultural programming. Thus the original aims of WHS management plans were brought to the fore.

The GDIF continues to attract large numbers of local people despite growing in size. So, although it is branded as international, this label appears to refer to the quality of the programming and performance rather than audience numbers or profiles. The Festival Director states that it is a priority to bring cutting edge professional performances to people who would otherwise not have the opportunity to see them, and thus break down some of the psychological and physical barriers to the arts. However, a series of in-depth interviews with festival directors (Smith and Forrest, 2003) suggested that few tourists will visit Greenwich specifically for cultural events and festivals, including the GDIF, and are therefore not always economically viable. Many tourists attend incidentally, if they happen to be in the area. This is perhaps not surprising given the significantly lower profile of the GDIF compared to the Edinburgh Festival. It can also be seen as a result of limitations in any attempts in marketing strategically. Similarly, economic impact research is limited. The latter undoubtedly due to lack of funding, and both actions affected by the fact that many of the events are either free or allow special access. As a result exact implications for tourism have been historically difficult to measure.

Unlike Greenwich, which aims to animate the global through the local, Edinburgh aims to be as international as possible, both in terms of its cultural products but also in terms of the audience attracted to it. The current aims of the International Festival include displaying arts of the highest possible standard to the widest possible audience, and thereby reflecting international culture to Scottish audiences and Scottish culture to international audiences (EIF Annual Review, 2004). Much is made of the number of repeat visits to the various festivals, with the 2002 survey showing that 50 per cent of the audience surveyed had attended at least nine previous festivals (www.eif.co.uk/about). Prentice and Anderson's research also suggests that there is a 'core of repeaters whose imagery of Scotland (is) as an arts rather than a historical destination...' (Prentice and Anderson, 2003: 11). As such it can be argued that to a festival audience events are the core expression of culture and not the historic fabric of the city. This has clear implications for the perceived role of Edinburgh's World Heritage Status. The city is clearly enlivened and animated as a cultural space by the addition of festivals, but the actual contribution to WHS status in real terms can be questioned.

Case study: Edinburgh and Greenwich – paths towards reconciliation of WHS and festivals

Robertson and Wardrop (2004: 124–5) hypothesize that Edinburgh's recognition has as its satellites 'Edinburgh the festival city; Edinburgh the world heritage city and Edinburgh the contemporary city'. They suggest that any profound assimilation of festivals with the values of being a world heritage city are compromised by the strategic function of the city's festivals to 'have a community – host resident – responsibility' (125) maintained through repeated public sector subsidy as well as commercial partnership. Interviews with key players in the City of Edinburgh Council (CEC), with direct responsibility for the festivals (2004–5), reflect clear awareness of the WHS status and great show is made, privately, of explaining how festivals are not impinging on this. However, no mention is ever made in the documentation relating to the city's festivals of how one can aid or support the other. In fact no public reference to the WHS status is present in the strategic documents for Edinburgh's festivals. This includes the two main strategic plan documents: *Events in Edinburgh* (2002) and *The Edinburgh Festival Strategy* (2001). Similarly, the City of Edinburgh Council's more recent evaluation of the impacts of Edinburgh's summer festivals (2004), undertaken by respected Edinburgh based consultants and thus, one would imagine, conversant with Edinburgh's WHS status, give no reference to the city's special status despite looking at many events within the boundaries set in that special area. The research by Prentice and Andersen (2003) and, more recently, in the first phase of its study, *Interbrand* (2004) – the consultancy appointed by the Edinburgh City Region Brand Project (a public and private sector partnership steering group) to develop the identity of the city – conclude that in the mind of visitors and prospective visitors the city does create a sense of being a cultural place but not a history-specific one.

While its festivals appear to have little synergy with the built and cultural history in Edinburgh, the strategic purpose that holds it together can nonetheless be positive. It does have potential benefits for the community and can bring together, as Derrett (2003; 2004) suggests, a sense of community and place within the overlapping desires to market the destination, attract visitors, and create a differentiated cultural tourism product (Figure 8.1). The fact that World Heritage Site status has not, as yet, been seen as an important aspect of this does not necessarily mean it will not become so in the future. Conversely, in Greenwich, World Heritage status is stated as being something on which tourism and hospitality visitor and business interest can be further developed (Greenwich Council, 2002) as well as support the more clearly associated aims of economic regeneration, conservation and pride.

Edinburgh World Heritage (the trust set up in 1999 to manage Edinburgh's status) acknowledge that Edinburgh's festivals are significant, vital and rewarding to the city, but it also warns that 'the pressure on the physical capacity of the Site at Festival times is immense' and states that the challenge is to 'maintain harmonious balance between the needs of the city's Festivals and other communities' (2005: 60). Accordingly, it sets policy 55 and 56, respectively, to seek the maintenance of the Festivals within the city centre, and support policies aimed at stimulating festival activities in less used areas

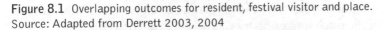

Figure 8.1 Overlapping outcomes for resident, festival visitor and place.
Source: Adapted from Derrett 2003, 2004

outside the world heritage area. These suggest that the strategic managers of Edinburgh's festivals, principally the City of Edinburgh Council, may have myopic views towards culture as capital. However, diverting their gaze from the historic significance of the city and the value of being a WH designated area, the Edinburgh World Heritage Trust similarly indicate in their most recent management plan a complicit agreement not to intervene with the festival and its operation.

This illustrates some of the major conflicts and dilemmas for all WHS that host festivals. What should be the relationship between the festival organizers and the WHS Committees, if any? How can local and tourist audiences be reached simultaneously? Should there be a one-brand image or is segmentation required for different products (i.e. pure heritage versus heritage as a backdrop for cultural events?). Conservation dilemmas also abound, especially where visitation is heavily concentrated (e.g. in the case of seasonal festivals). One obvious question is who should foot the bill for increased wear and tear?

Conclusions

It is the conjecture of the authors that the existence of WHS status for any town or city that hosts a festival or festivals is significant but that it is often under-stated. As backdrops to the performance of festivals, the built heritage is seen as pleasing, but its significance as moderator of that pleasure is most often nominal. That is to say that its aesthetic appeal is generally valued above its intrinsic historic importance. Although attempts are sometimes made to highlight the historical relevance of location in festival themes or performances, this could be seen as tokenistic. Only where more intangible aspects of heritage interpretation are explored (e.g. local perceptions, associations and narratives) could the role of festivals be said to be truly transformational.

Some of the research in Edinburgh suggests that the city wishes to be a world phenomenon – for visitors, business and its residents. It is competing with many cities sharing similar aspirations. A precise historical backdrop, rightly or wrongly, does not seem to catch people's imagination as much as other forms of entertainment. The same could not necessarily be said of Greenwich as its scale is so different, often being perceived as an appendage to London rather than a cultural destination in its own right. However, marketing efforts there are also shifting away from 'traditional' heritage marketing towards the promotion of more contemporary and experiential activities. The role of WHS clearly cannot be extrapolated from market forces. In the case of Edinburgh this appears on one hand to threaten it and on another to ensure that the Festival is not dependent on it (a result no doubt of its much longer history as a visitor destination).

What makes the events in Greenwich stand out from those of Edinburgh is that the events are consciously set within, and in relation to, the identified WHS. While the knowledge of the festival interviewees in Greenwich suggest that there is only a limited knowledge of what WHS means, this is still in contrast to those in Edinburgh where festival revellers partake in the Festival with no knowledge of either WHS status or, indeed, that it has significance to Edinburgh as a festival performance area at all.

World Heritage status arguably has a symbiotic function for the festivals of both Greenwich and Edinburgh. In the former it announces a more organic role than in the latter. In neither can it be said that the status is central to the festival performance offered. In Greenwich the WH status offers an additional spotlight. For Edinburgh, it may be a barely noticed backdrop. The real performance – the magic and the vitality – are the events themselves. Despite this, it is the view of the authors that noticed or not, the spell of the festivals would never be so effective were it not for the fantasy that the heritage-scape allows.

To close, a number of lessons are forthcoming from this study for WHS in general. Ostensibly these are related to potential for the singularity of the spectacle and activities of a festival or festivals to encroach on the needs of the WHS in which they are being held. Accordingly, while the festivals in Greenwich and Edinburgh have different relationships with their respective audiences – the first more localized and the second more international – the retention, preservation and understanding of the significance of WHS appears to be obscured by the function of the event itself. It is concluded that the needs would be better served if they were composite to the enjoyment and respect of the festival and its location. The history and allocation of control and power in those (people and organizations) with influence over heritage, conservation, the arts, tourism, and the local community, is the dynamic. Change may be conducted through alternative or complementary promotion, and greater understanding by festival-goers and incidental WHS visitors may arise.

Put simply, the WHS risks becoming an appendage to the market forces and social functions of any given number of festivals if the WHS management plan fails to address all elements of its responsibility in a clear and measurable way. However, with exacting management, the overlapping benefits of a festival could in fact ensure that the WHS is both a core part and a specific beneficiary of its activities. It is to this end that the authors ascribe their hope.

References

Carnegie, E. (2003) It wasn't all bad: Representations of Working Class cultures within social history museums in Edinburgh and Glasgow and their impacts on audiences. IEFA, Vienna, March (forthcoming in Picard et al. (2005) *Tourism, Festivals and Social Change: Nodes and Transitions,* Clevedon: Channel View).

Carnegie, E. and Smith, M. (2005) It Takes Two to Bangra!: The Mela in Edinburgh or Edinburgh in the Mela? Partnership building and audience development within the festival city. Amsterdam: IFEA.

City of Edinburgh Council (2002) *An Events Strategy for Edinburgh – the biggest and the best?* Edinburgh: The City of Edinburgh Council.

City of Edinburgh Council (2001) *Festivals and the City: The Edinburgh Festivals Strategy 2001.* Edinburgh: Edinburgh City Council.

City of Edinburgh Council (2004) *Edinburgh Festivals 2004–2005 Economic Impact Survey Stage 1 Results.* Edinburgh: The City of Edinburgh Council.

Derrett, R. (2003) Making sense of how festivals demonstrate a community's sense of place. *Event Management,* 8, 49–58.

Derrett, R. (2004) Festival, events and the destination. In Yeoman, I., Robertson, M., Ali-Knight, J., Drummond, S. and McMahon-Beattie, U. (eds) *Festival and Events Management – An International Arts and Culture Perspective.* Oxford: Butterworth-Heinemann, pp. 32–50.

Edinburgh International Festival Society (2004) *Edinburgh International Festival Review 2004.* Edinburgh: Edinburgh International Festival Society.

Edinburgh World Heritage (2005) *Management Plan for Old and New Towns of Edinburgh World Heritage Site.* Final Draft April. Edinburgh: Edinburgh World Heritage.

English Historic Towns Forum (2005) *Using heritage and cultural assets in regeneration,* Gateshead & Newcastle, 8–9 June.

Greenwich Council (2002) *Economic Development Strategy.* April. Greenwich: Greenwich Council.

Hargreaves, R. (1997) Developing New Audiences. In Hooper-Greenhill, E. (ed.) *Cultural Diversity: Developing Museum Audiences in Britain*. London: Leicester University Press.

Interbrand (2004) *Live Invest Visit – Creating the brand for the future of Edinburgh* – project update, November. (www.edinburghbrand.com accessed 18 April 2005).

Lippard, L.R. (1997) *The Lure of the Local: Senses of Place in a Multicentred Society*. New York: The New Press.

MORI (2002) *Visitor/User Perceptions of Greenwich – Summary of MORI Findings, May 2002*. London: MORI.

Pine, B.J. and Gilmore, J.H. (1999) *The Experience Economy*. Harvard: Harvard University Press.

Prentice, R. and Anderson, V. (2003) Festivals as creative destination. *Annals of Tourism Research*, 30 (1), 7–30.

Richards, R. and Wilson, J. (2005) Developing creativity in tourist experiences: A solution to the serial reproduction of culture? *Tourism Management* (in press, available online 22 August 2005).

Robertson, M. and Wardrop, K. (2004) Events and the destination dynamic: Edinburgh festivals, Entrepreneurship and Strategic Marketing. In Yeoman, I., Robertson, M., Ali-Knight, J., Drummond, S. and McMahon-Beattie, U. (eds) *Festival and Events Management – An International Arts and Culture Perspective*. Oxford: Butterworth-Heinemann.

Shackley, M. (1998) *Visitor Management: Case Studies from World Heritage Sites*. Oxford: Butterworth-Heinemann.

Smith, M.K. (2002) A critical evaluation of the global accolade: The significance of World Heritage Site status for Maritime Greenwich. *International Journal of Heritage Studies*, 8 (2), 137–151.

Smith, M.K. and Forrest, K. (2003) *Enhancing Vitality or Compromising Integrity? Festivals, Tourism and the Complexities of Performing Culture*, IEFA, Vienna, March (forthcoming in Picard et al. (2005) *Tourism, Festivals and Social Change: Nodes and Transitions*, Clevedon: Channel View).

World Heritage Conservation Manifesto www.edinburgh.gov.uk/heritagem (accessed 20 April 2005).

Web sites

www.eif.co.uk/about (accessed 17 April 2005)
www.edfringe.com (accessed 16 April 2005)
www.gildedballoon.co.uk (accessed 16 April 2005)
www.theunderbelly.co.uk/about/index.html (accessed 16 April 2005)
www.edinburgh.org/conference (accessed 15 April 2005)
www.edinburgh.gov.uk/heritage (accessed 13 April 2005)
www.greenwichwhs.org.uk (accessed 18 April 2005)

CHAPTER 9

Information communication technology applications for World Heritage Site management

Dimitrios Buhalis, Ruth Owen and
Daniël Pletinckx

Aims

The aims of this chapter are to:

- Examine the concept of information communication technology (ICT) and how it could be applied to World Heritage Sites (WHS)
- Present uses of ICTs at heritage sites
- Determine the extent to which ICTs can be applied to WHS.

Introduction

Information Communication Technologies (ICTs) present new opportunities for WHS to enhance the service that they currently provide. ICTs can support site management; add to interpretation approaches; and promote site conservation. This chapter focuses on built World Heritage Sites and concentrates on heritage management within a single site. This is in contrast to more complex World Heritage Sites, such as the City of Bath, where management strategies are likely to vary in accordance to the context.

The chapter begins by exploring the concept of ICTs within a heritage management context. The main duties within cultural heritage management are discussed and ICTs that can assist them are identified and explored. Each ICT is evaluated in terms of suitability for the site. Finally, the implications of ICTs regarding visitor expectations are presented.

Information communications technologies (ICTs)

ICT (information and communications technology – or technologies) can be defined as :

> an umbrella term that includes any communication device or application, encompassing: radio, television, cellular phones, computer and network hardware and software, satellite systems and so on, as well as the various services and applications associated with them, such as videoconferencing and distance learning (www.whatis.com, 2005).

ICTs and heritage management

In order to examine how ICTs can assist in the management of a WHS, the main functions involved in heritage management have been

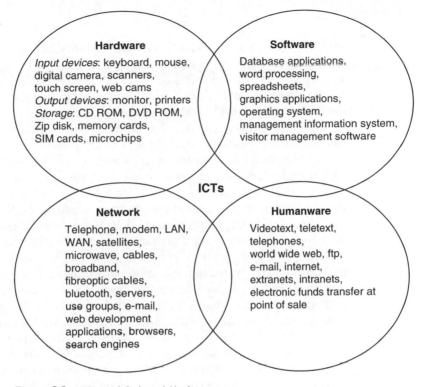

Figure 9.1 ICTs and Cultural Heritage.
Source: Adapted from Buhalis 2003

identified. These can be classified into three categories: conservation, education and site management (Ambrose and Pain, 1998; McKercher and du Cros, 2002).

Conservation

The purpose of conservation in heritage management is to preserve cultural heritage resources for current and future generations to enjoy (McKercher and du Cros, 2002). Conservation duties in heritage management involve documentation, environmental monitoring, treatment and preventative care (Ambrose and Pain, 1998). People visit WHS to view the extraordinary (Rojek, 1997) as they have a right to do (http://whc.unesco.org). They are often motivated by educational, cultural, sociological and psychological reasons and may be local, domestic or international visitors. The most popular and significant sites may attract up to several million visitors a year. However, visitation can cause damage to, or wear out irreplaceable resources (Millar, 2004). This chapter examines how ICTs can assist conservation in heritage management.

Education

Interpretation is an important aspect of education because it explains the significance of the exhibit within the context of the site and its wider historical and cultural context. Interpretation can be defined as 'the act or process of explaining or clarifying, translating, or presenting a personal understanding about a subject or an object' (Dean, 1996). Interpretation can also demonstrate how heritage is relevant to people's everyday lives (Edson and Dean, 2000).

Interpretation is a complex process because visitors differ in their age groups, cultural background, motivations and desire to learn. Visitors also vary from those who know little about the site before they arrive, to knowledgeable experts or enthusiasts (McKercher and du Cros, 2002). Interpretation must address the different needs of visitors and enable each market segment to find sufficient information to enhance their visit. Traditional interpretation media (such as posters and leaflets) are limited in terms of the information they can provide due to constraints of space. Therefore, marketers must decide on which audience segments to focus the marketing material. ICTs offer unlimited space and can use a wide range of multimedia formats such as photographs, diagrams, videos and virtual reality representations. The use of hypertext facilitates inter-linkages between interrelated themes, exhibits and artefacts enabling visitors to explore Cultural Heritage sites in greater depth. Hypertext links also allow audience segments to be targeted simultaneously and in different depths. For example, children may learn from animated cartoons, while historians from expert researchers.

Site management

Pre-visit

Publishing information that is designed to be used prior to visiting a site allows the visitor to plan in advance. They can decide whether or not to visit, or to narrow down the exhibits/areas within a site to those that they specifically wish to view. In addition, they can use this information to place the WHS into context and relate it to other areas or sites visited before. From the visitor's perspective gathering information in advance allows them to make the most effective use of their time. But from site management's view, this information may result in more accurate visitor expectations, thus reducing the likelihood of disappointing visitors and preventing negative word of mouth from spreading. Using multilingual information and interpretation techniques staff can provide different perspectives of the same exhibit. For example, the Auschwitz experience may require different interpretation for German and Jewish visitors to reflect their different motivations for the visit. Similarly, a Buddhist visiting Indonesia could have different information needs compared to fringe tourists.

Due to the nature of visitation the public decide for themselves when to visit a site. This results in demand fluctuations (Barlow, 1999). ICTs and Internet sites in particular can assist this situation by publishing demand patterns so visitors can make informed decisions about the time of their visit. Visitors can choose whether or not to book in advance to avoid queues. This increases visitor satisfaction. The information that can be captured from an electronic ticketing system enables site managers to analyse visitor behaviour and target resources accordingly. For example, employing more guides and cashiers to work during peak periods or creating special attractions in less busy areas of the WHS.

During the visit

To manage visitor flow around the site and reduce bottlenecks traditional navigational aids such as signs and audio guides can be complemented by interactive mobile multimedia communications. These devices can provide contextual based information facilitating the visit through announcements and guidance that is dynamically adapted to reflect the current location at the site. Personal Digital Assistants (PDAs), for example, can assist site interpretation by guiding visitors according to their needs, available time, cultural background, linguistic ability and cultural segments. Not only can this provide information according to location but it can also relate dynamically interrelated areas, artefacts and stories. Also virtual visits can replace physical visits to areas of a site that are fragile, in order to prevent further erosion.

Post-visit

The information provided at a site is intended to generate interest rather than provide every minute detail on a subject (Ambrose and Paine, 1998). Therefore post-visit, the site can provide additional information, encouraging visitors to develop their knowledge in areas of interest. Photos, videos, digital souvenirs, blogs, electronic games and references to scientific articles are all potential electronic aids that can enhance the post-visit experience (they can also be used pre-visit if required). This may generate repeat visits to the WHS to study a subject of interest in more detail.

How technology can assist heritage management

Figure 9.2 presents a summary of how ICTs can be used to assist the heritage management process. The technologies were selected on the

TECHNOLOGY	SITUATION	CONSERVATION	EDUCATION	SITE MANAGEMENT
TICKETING AND RESERVATION SYSTEMS	Walk-ins	Monitor attendance levels to prevent possible damage to site	For internal use to get closer to the customer	Avoids overcrowding
	Advanced bookings	Avoid site overcrowding and possible damage to site as restrictions are applied	Visitors learn booking in advance guarantees a visit at time specified and avoids queuing	Sites can prepare for groups/events in advance
	Site awareness	Educates visitors about conservation issues and increases awareness as to what to do to reduce impact	Websites can be used before, during and after the visit to supplement knowledge	Generates realistic visitor expectations as well as reduce the needs giving orientation and other information at the time of visit
WEB SITE	Information provision	Opportunity to present conservation message	Allows museum visitors to access the information they choose according to market segments	Reduces staff's time answering the publics' questions
	Inventory awareness	Fragile artefact need not be displayed. A digital image can be used instead	Showcase entire inventory range and interrelate with relevant context, artefacts, sites, stories	Site managers restrict access to fragile areas and artefacts
	Virtual tours	Restrict public from fragile areas. Improve understanding of conservation issues	Virtual tours provide 'edutainment' that is entertainment and education combined	Addresses accessibility issues and provides better capacity management
	Augmented Reality	Shows the effect of the environment/visitors	Visitors can compare what was once on the site to what there is today	Ensures every visitor sees the same reconstruction
MOBILE MULTIMEDIA GUIDE	Orientation	May reduce some impacts by monitoring visitor's location ensuring they follow the appropriate path	Information is fed to visitor in accordance to location on site	Navigation assistance and dynamic updates enable a more responsive site management to market segments, demand levels, weather, etc.
COLLECTION MANAGEMENT DATABASE	Remote access to database	Reuse of digital content	Greater access to information for private study and professional use	Connect to other research institutions and exchange of information
	Record information	Record condition of the artefact use to compare artefact in the future	Collate information for use in interpretation and research	Information stored in one place

Figure 9.2 ICTs functional for WHS

basis that they are particularly beneficial to heritage management. WHS vary considerably and technologies will be more applicable to some sites than others. The remainder of this chapter explores these technologies and how they can be used at WHS.

Ticketing and reservation systems

Traditionally, site visitation was monitored manually to record the number of visitors entering the site. Long queues often form at popular sites and, to address this issue, the concept of booking in advance was developed. To begin with customers were able to reserve tickets over the telephone, speaking to a member of staff who input their details into the computer reservation system. Some larger sites, such as the Science Museum in London, use an interactive voice response system which is connected to their computer reservation system. Thus the booking system is automated. Today it is feasible for each com-munication channel (telephone, Internet, walk-in) to be connected to the site's booking system (www.btconsulting.com). A computerized system allows additional visitor information to be captured without slowing down the entry process. This information can be used for vis-itor management analysis. Marketing could use visitor attendance information to identify their audience composition and then translate the findings into developing suitable products or paths for appropri-ate market segments, advertising campaigns, guiding systems, souvenirs and relationships with intermediaries. Finance use attend-ance figures to calculate income generated and predict future income from tracking historical trends. In addition, invoicing systems can be put into place to facilitate billing with tour companies and other partners.

A computerized ticketing system can be installed for onsite use only. This allows cashiers to have instant access to availability infor-mation. Incorporating bar code readers allows membership cards to be scanned and discounts are allocated automatically (http://www.expsoft.com). Once the payment has been made, a ticket is printed and handed to the visitor as a record of the transaction. Timed tours, displays and shows can also be driven by this technology.

Advanced booking gives visitors peace of mind. They can avoid spending time in queues and are guaranteed entrance at the time specified. From a site management perspective, providing advanced booking facilities effectively devolves the decision to the visitor who has the choice of booking in advance or on the day. Thus it becomes the visitor's responsibility if they choose not to book in advance and they arrive at the site to find a long queue.

Ticketing and advanced reservation systems are particularly use-ful if the site attracts large numbers of visitors or if the site organizes

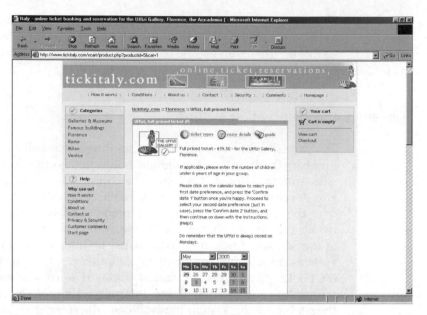

Figure 9.3 Online booking for the Uffizi, Italy.
Source: http://www.tickitaly.com/ (reproduced with permission)

special events, where reservations must be processed quickly and advanced bookings can ease the administrative burden. Also, advanced bookings can help the site maximize income generated from events and exhibitions (www.btconsulting.com).

Automating the reservation and ticketing process not only reduces labour cost but also enables better capturing of visitor patterns and profile information facilitating WHS management.

Website

The World Wide Web's global reach enables more extensive site promotion. A WHS may have limited space to present exhibits. In this situation, heritage managers have to select objects to go on display. Websites have virtually limitless space (Janal, 1998) and can be used to exhibit objects not on display at the WHS (Tsekeleves and Cosmas, 2003). Unlike print production, the incremental cost of adding extra pages to a website is minimal (Janal, 1998). Therefore web content developers are not restricted in terms of the numbers of web pages they develop. This means that, unlike other marketing communications media, the choice of audience segments to target is more flexible. Hypertext links can channel different audience groups to different parts of a website site. For example children visiting the National Trust's website may select the link to 'Trusty' the hedgehog's web pages that are designed primarily for this audience group (www. nationaltrust.org.uk/).

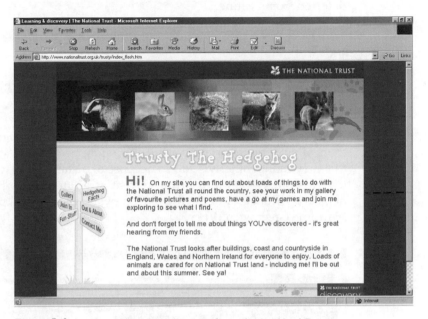

Figure 9.4 Trusty children's web pages from the National Trust.
Source: http://www.nationaltrust.org.uk/ (reproduced with permission)

A web presence extends opening hours to 24 hours a day, 7 days a week, enabling more people to use the services of a WHS, at a time that suits them. Also, people using a website effectively serve themselves searching for answers to their own questions, as opposed to speaking to a member of staff which incurs costs to the site in the process of answering the question (Keene, 1998). The website can provide suitable themes for a wide range of market segments offering information in different languages, styles and depth according to visitor requirements.

The general public are beginning to expect establishments of all sizes to have a web presence at the very least. The difference between a web presence and a website is that the website is designed solely for that establishment. A web presence involves limited information published on a special interest site. For example, Fishbourne Roman Palace, which houses the largest collection of *in-situ* mosaics in Britain, does not have a website of its own. Instead it features on other websites, such as Sussex Past website (www.sussexpast.co.uk/), which was designed by the Sussex Archaeological Society in the UK.

It is recognized that a web presence may encourage visitation to sites that are already overcrowded. To combat this, the site can suggest the best times to visit such as during off-peak periods. Nevertheless, it cannot be assumed that the website always encourages visitation, with competitors only a click away, some people are likely to be deterred from visiting.

Virtual reality

Virtual reality (VR) is defined by Beekman (2005: 580) as 'Technology that creates the illusion that the user is immersed in a world that exists only inside the computer …'

VR can also be employed in a virtual tour of the WHS. Virtual tours allow remote access to a site. Therefore people can 'visit' a site that they cannot otherwise do so because of distance, cost, or disability. This often leads to a physical visit at a later stage. Figure 9.5 depicts a virtual tour of the Royal Observatory in the UK, part of the Maritime Greenwich WHS.

Figure 9.5 Virtual tour of the Royal Observatory.
Source: http://www.nmm.ac.uk/ (reproduced with permission)

To an extent the virtual tour allows the site to fulfil its aim of providing access to all. Virtual tours can also be used within a site allowing visitors to 'virtually' visit, rather than physically visit areas of sites that are fragile (McKercher and du Cros, 2002) and also to provide 'edutainment', which is a combination of education and entertainment (Buhalis, 2003).

VR can be used to enable new experiences such as the temporary exhibition at the British Museum entitled 'Mummy: the Inside Story' (www.thebritishmuseum.ac.uk). A CT scanner was used for digital image acquisition without removing the mummy's wrappings. A virtual tour in 3D takes the viewer inside the mummy's body and also provides information about life in ancient Egypt as well as the mummification process and rituals.

Avatars are computer-generated images that have the appearance of a human being. An Avatar can represent the user in a virtual environment (Beekman, 2005) or can take on the guise of a virtual tour guide. Avatars can be static in a video sequence, or dynamic where they interact with users. The use of Avatars ranges from a simple figure used to point to an image or to introduce a presentation to fully interactive guides and presenters.

Figure 9.6 Avatar example.
Source: Ryder et al., 2004 (reproduced with permission)

Figure 9.6 depicts an application that recreates the city of Wolfenbüttel, Germany. The user manoeuvres the Avatar shown in the bottom right hand corner of the image. When the Avatar arrives at a building, the user can ask questions, such as its historical significance and the Avatar supplies the answer. This form of virtual tour is expected to appeal to children who are used to playing computer games. This application was developed as a museum installation but could be made available on a website for use at home.

From a heritage management perspective, VR movies can show the exact appearance of the site at the time the movie was taken. They are quicker to produce and require less development costs than computer-generated reconstructions. The latter are suitable when a scene has to be re-created, for example to show the appearance of a city several hundred years ago and to contrast it with the existing ruins.

In terms of use at a WHS, a movie or a simple use of Avatars may be well within the financial reach of many WHS. Avatars using complex computer-generated reconstructed environments would probably require corporate sponsorship.

Augmented reality

Augmented reality (AR) involves taking a 'real world' image, usually from photographs or video, and then overlaying this with a computer-generated reconstruction. The key difference between VR and AR is that VR aims to *immerse* the user into a computer-generated world (Laudon and Laudon, 2000; Beekman, 2005) while AR uses technology to enhance and interpret reality.

AR does not always require the use of a dedicated computer system. One image of a photo overlaid onto a computer reconstruction is all that is required. AR can be used in posters, leaflets etc., thus widening the number of WHS sites that could use this application.

Figure 9.7 AR in use at ENAME, Belgium.
Source: http://www.ename974.org/

AR can help visitors compare before and after scenarios. For example, visitors to the archaeological site depicted in Figure 9.7 use the touch screen (shown in the hut) to compare how the site looks today with how it once looked. By pressing the appropriate area of the touch screen, a computer-generated reconstruction of the abbey that once stood at the site is depicted. Computer reconstructions can help visitors to visualize a subject and will ensure that visitors see the subject in the same way (Roussou and Drettakis, 2003). Computer reconstructions can also assist in the provision of contextual information and storytelling through representations, videos and other reconstructions.

Mobile multimedia guides

A mobile multimedia guide is essentially a handheld device, such as a PDA, which visitors carry around the site and use to access information on the exhibits. The multimedia capability of these devices allows movies, AR reconstructions, direct links to the website and other interpretation methods to be shown. Information can be sent wirelessly to the visitor according to their location on the site, or visitors can access information manually by pressing the appropriate buttons. The multimedia device assists the user in orientation and navigation around the site, while providing additional information and interrelationships with other sites or locations. Thus there is less need for signs which detract from the authenticity of the site. Questions asked to the visitor at the beginning of the presentation, such as age or country of origin, as well as time available for the visit and level of expertise or interest allows a degree of personalized content to be fed to the user. This makes interpretation much more relevant to the user and to their particular needs and context.

In terms of suitability for a WHS, wireless devices require hardware located on the site in order to deliver the information to the multimedia guide. This can detract from the authenticity of the site and therefore the infrastructure would have to be hidden, perhaps behind an exhibit and so on. The costs incurred in developing such systems would make this device only feasible in a site with high visitation levels to justify usage, but would be particularly appropriate at WHS which contain a wealth of heritage information such as Olympia, Greece (see case study). Nevertheless, the proliferation of WiFi recently is reducing both costs and size of antennas making this restriction minimal.

Case study: ARCHEOGUIDE – Olympia, Greece

This case study was written by Vassilios Vlahakis, Project Co-ordinator, INTRACOM and describes the ARCHEOGUIDE system: an advanced processing and mobile guiding system addressing the needs of cultural sites. It provides navigation information, 3D virtual reconstructions of ruined monuments and re-enactment of ancient life with synchronized narration and on-line access to digital cultural collections. The system was originally developed and used at the archaeological site of Olympia, in Greece, the birthplace of the Olympic Games and one of the most important WHS.

ARCHEOGUIDE description

The ARCHEOGUIDE system is a modular system making use of the latest ICTs. It has been designed according to the client-server model allowing a centralized infrastructure to be shared by a number of mobile user devices, while the latter can also operate as standalone entities. The heart of the system is a standard PC server incorporating a multimedia database where all relevant data (textual descriptions, narration, photographs and drawings, 3D models, animations, and video) are archived. These data are stored along with metadata elements, that is descriptions identifying key scientific information like dating of the original physical item, creator, material, etc., and other information relating to the potential exploitation of the multi-media objects. For instance, the geographic coordinates of a building where a particular artefact was excavated may be used to describe where a 3D model of the artefact will be presented in a virtual or augmented tour of the site. The server incorporates a suite of windows-based tools for creating the digital content, documenting it, and editing the relevant metadata elements. As a result, archaeologists can easily identify and group relevant objects into meaningful tours in the site to be used with the mobile clients or virtual tours to be delivered over the Internet.

The clients are a set of mobile devices, which visitors can carry with them for the duration of their visit. According to their preferences, they may choose between a PDA, a tablet-PC, or an augmented reality (AR) device. All devices are equipped with GPS receivers and feature fully automatic operation. They continuously track the user's position and launch the presentation of the appropriate synchronized audiovisual content once they approach a point of interest. For instance, when the visitor approaches the Temple of Zeus, they are automatically presented with a virtual reconstruction and other information on the PDA's screen. An advanced version of the same information can be viewed on the more powerful tablet-PC where an A4-sized screen offers higher visual quality. The user can also see augmented panoramas that automatically align with his natural view and which are augmented with reconstructed monument, annotations, and events like the lighting of the Olympic Flame. Similarly, he may walk to navigate through a virtual 3D site as it was in antiquity.

To increase realism and provide a more intuitive and immersive experience, the visitor may be provided with a mobile AR device. As opposed to the e-book concept of the PDA and tablet guides, their AR counterpart employs a pair of special glasses or binoculars equipped with a digital compass and camera. These devices allow users to experience reality as seen with their eyes, while at the same time virtual buildings are rendered in their field-of-view in a seamless way, creating the illusion of a 2500-year travel back in time. They can enjoy this captivating experience simply by approaching and staring at the ruins in their vicinity. The device uses position and orientation data and combines them with a sophisticated real-time video tracking algorithm to calculate accurately the user's field-of-view. It then adapts the rendered graphics so as to avoid virtual buildings flying over the physical ruins or getting out of alignment every time the visitor turns his head.

A particular case occurs in the stadium where disciplines of the ancient Olympic Games are re-enacted in the same venue as in antiquity with the help of virtual athletes. The visitor may watch them come into life through his glasses or binoculars and mingle with today's visitors.

Tackling practical problems in a WHS

The use of ARCHEOGUIDE at Olympia posed several constraints on its installation. Zero invasiveness on the site itself and interference with its normal operation imposed such a difficult access that communication hardware had to be installed outside the site.

Another serious problem when dealing with such a site is the creation of scientifically accurate content. Despite the use of the data supplied by the Hellenic Ministry of Culture, ARCHEOGUIDE supports the presentation of multiple interpretations making it suitable for scientific use, education and edutainment.

ARCHEOGUIDE targets the satisfaction of the site administrators who want to use such an ICT system for promoting their site's visibility, visitor satisfaction, and use it as a development lever. Besides being an attraction in itself, the system offers its users the opportunity to experience information in an intuitive way, and to visit areas with restricted access such as the interior of temples. Access to museum exhibits and information from other historical sources provides an integrated presentation. Furthermore, visitor satisfaction can also be achieved through content personalization. The information that is presented during the visit is automatically adapted in real time to the user's profile and behaviour. Different levels of detail are presented to a child as opposed to an adult, and according to their language of preference.

Future prospects

These features resulted in very positive comments from system users. The realism of the AR device was praised, although size and weight of the processing device makes the implementation more challenging. The e-book concept proved very familiar as visitors found it easy to use with the PDA scoring highest due to its pocket size. The intuitive use of all devices was appreciated and computer-literate users enjoyed the optional interaction with their devices.

The positive comments from ARCHEOGUIDE users led INTRA-COM to develop and market intCulture. This system also provides centralized monitoring and control of the operation of all devices, as well as support for inventory monitoring, and statistics collection and processing. It can support content reuse and services, such as web and multimedia publishing, and educational applications.

Figure 9.8 Users of the ARCHEOGUIDE mobile devices at Olympia.
Source: Vlahakis et al., 2002

Collection management databases

Databases can be viewed as repositories for storing cultural heritage knowledge. Traditionally, collections information was stored in many different places: on paper, in books, journals and even in the heads of staff (Keene, 1998; Fahay, 1999). Databases have the capability of storing collections information in a variety of formats such as images, movies, audio etc. Therefore, all the information about collections can be stored in one place to facilitate easy access for researchers, historians and interested visitors.

Some cultural heritage sites, such as the National Maritime Museum in the UK, allow access to their catalogue over the Internet (Figure 9.9). This benefits different types of users from casuals, to enthusiasts, to experts, all who have access to a wider body of knowledge. Password protection must be installed and users given different access rights. For example, the public would have permission to view the collection, but would be restricted from adding, editing or deleting records which authorized experts would have the ability to do (Keene, 1998).

The costs involved in digitizing images alone can be an expensive and time-consuming process. However once digitized, content is reusable. There is much discussion in the literature concerning the speed at which technology gets replaced and whether digital images will be accessible in the future. The underlying question is 'will this investment in digitization be wasted?' The current advice is to invest in technology that meets agreed standards (Keene, 1998) and gradually interoperability and standardization will prevail. In terms of

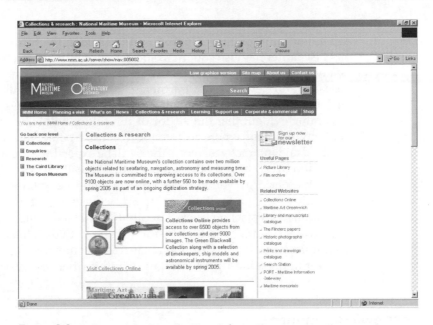

Figure 9.9 Online access to collections information.
Source: National Maritime Museum http://www.nmm.ac.uk

suitability, a WHS with a small budget may consider purchasing a Collections Management Database off the shelf, which is usually considerably less expensive than a proprietary system, but at the expense of functionality. A WHS that invests in a proprietary system will be able to choose the functionality they require.

The heritage sector is effectively embarking on a recording programme en masse. Future generations will benefit from this flurry of recording activity undertaken at present.

Conclusions

This chapter demonstrates how ICTs can be used to support heritage management. In terms of site management, visitors have been given the tools to serve themselves; to make advanced bookings; search for answers to their questions; or take a virtual tour. Technology now presents the WHS with new ways of presenting information to educate visitors in terms of augmented reality and mobile multimedia guides. The conservation message can be transmitted through the Internet content as well as mobile guides on location. Augmented reality can show a contrast between what used to be at a site and what is there now and provide comprehensive contextual information to improve interpretation. The technologies highlighted in this chapter are technologies that are being developed today. Only time will tell what new ways of interpretation will be used in the future.

The chapter has also sought to show that ICTs need not be prohibitively expensive for the WHS. Collaboration between sites and with research and development partners can provide substantial savings in developing and maintaining ICT solutions. However, it is gradually becoming evident that the visitor of the future will be used to a virtual environment where information will be personalized, contextualized and interactive. Hence, they will be expecting similar levels of provision by WHS and other cultural heritage attractions. Organizations that perform well in these aspects therefore will increase their competitiveness and will be able to attract visitors, while others will offer limited satisfaction levels. Equally ICT enabled WHS will encourage further scientific research by interacting with the global scientific community and by networking resources for maximizing opportunities for understanding interpretation and further discovery.

Acknowledgements

This study forms part of the European Commission, FP6 Network of Excellence IST-2002-507382 EPOCH. The authors would like to thank the EPOCH partners for contributing and the European Union for their substantial financial support, without which this project would not have been possible. In addition, they wish to thank Fraunhofer IGD, ZGDV, A&C2000, Post Reality, CCG, and the Hellenic Ministry of Culture for their contributions to the ARCHEOGUIDE case study.

References

Ambrose, T. and Paine, C. (1998) *Museum Basics*. London: Routledge.

Barlow, G. (1999) Managing demand and supply. In Leask, A. and Yeoman, I. (eds) *Heritage Visitor Attractions*. London: Thomson Learning.

Beekman (2005) *Computer Confluence*. London: Pearson Education Limited.

Buhalis, D. (2003) *eTourism Information Technology for Strategic Tourism Management*. London: Pearson Education Limited.

Dean, D. (1996) *Museum Exhibition Theory and Practice*. London: Routledge.

Edson, G. and Dean, D. (2000) *The Handbook for Museums*. London: Routledge.

Fahy, A. (1999) *Collections Management*. London: Routledge.

Janal, D.S. (1998) *Online Marketing Handbook*. Chichester: John Wiley & Sons Ltd.

Keene, S. (1998) *Digital Collections, Museums and the Information Age*. Oxford: Butterworth-Heinemann.

Laudon, K.C. and Laudon, J.P. (2000) *Management Information Systems*. New Jersey: Prentice Hall.

McKercher, B. and du Cros, H. (2002) *Cultural Tourism: The Partnership Between Tourism and Cultural Heritage Management*. Binghamton, New York: The Haworth Hospitality Press.

Millar, S. (2004) An overview of the sector. In Leask, A. and Yeoman, I. (eds) *Heritage Visitor Attractions*. London: Thomson Learning.

Rojek, C. (1997) Indexing, dragging and the social construction of tourist sights. In Rojek, C. and Urry, J. (eds) *Touring Cultures: Transformations of Travel and Theory*. London: Routledge.

Roussou, M. and Drettakis, G. (2003) Photorealism and non-photorealism in virtual heritage representation. VAST 2003 Conference Proceedings.

Ryder, G., Flack, P. and Day, A.M. (2004) Adaptive crowd behaviour to aid real-time rendering of a cultural heritage environment. VAST 2004 Conference Proceedings.

Tsekleves, E. and Cosmas, J. (2003) The dissemination and promotion of cultural heritage sites to people on the move employing digital TV. VAST 2003 Conference Proceedings.

Vlahakis, V., Ioannidis, N. and Karigiannis, J. (2002) ARCHEOGUIDE: Challenges and solutions of a personalized augmented reality guide for archaeological sites. *Computer Graphics in Art, History and Archaeology Special Issue of the IEEE Computer Graphics and Applications Magazine*, September–October, 52–60.

Websites

BT consulting, 2005, Consulting & Systems Integration services from BT, accessed 18 April 2005
http://www.btconsulting.com/mediacentre/pressreleases/corporate/corporate_press_release_2003_03_17.htm

ENAME, 2005, Untitled Document, accessed 25 April 2005
http://www.ename974.org/

Explorer Systems Inc, 2005, Overview, accessed 25 April 2005
http://www.expsoft.com/overview.htm

INTRACOM, 2005, Archeoguide, accessed 20 April 2005
http://archeoguide.intranet.gr

Sussexpast, 2005, Museums & Properties – OFFICIAL SITE – Fishbourne Roman Palace, accessed 20 April 2005
http://www.sussexpast.co.uk/property/site.php?site_id=11

The British Museum, Mummy: the inside story – homepage, accessed 10 April 2005
http://www.thebritishmuseum.ac.uk/mummy/index.html

The National Maritime Museum, Collections and Research, accessed 3 May 2005
http://www.nmm.ac.uk/server/show/nav.005002

The National Trust, 2005, Learning & discovery; The National Trust, accessed 20 April 2005
http://www.nationaltrust.org.uk/trusty/index_flash.htm

The Royal Observatory, 2005, ROG virtual tour – Meridian Line, accessed 25 April 2005
http://www.nmm.ac.uk/server/show/nav.00500000d

Tickitaly.com, 2005, Italy – online ticket booking and reservation for the Uffizi Gallery, Florence, the Accademia (David) and other Italian museums and galleries, accessed 3 May 2005
http://www.tickitaly.com/xcart/product.php?productid=5&cat=1

UNESCO, 2005, UNESCO World Heritage Centre – Home, accessed 10 February 2005
http://whc.unesco.org

WHATIS.COM. 2005, Whatis.com, the computer and Internet dictionary and encyclopaedia, accessed 27 April, 2005
http://www.whatis.com

Strategy

Part Four focuses on the strategic management of the World Heritage List (WHL) with particular emphasis on the fundamental issues, such as how many is practical, appropriate and feasible in the long term. The chapters consider how effective current strategies are in balancing the representation of the WHL and what can be done in the future to ensure the successful achievement of the overall aims.

In Chapter 10, Greg Ashworth and Bart van der Aa critically review the strategy and policy of the World Heritage Convention, elucidating the differences in practice between various national decision-making structures and investigating how the dominance of national interests often exceeds those of international interests in WHS selection. They then go on to raise some of the possible future solutions that would increase the viability of site selection within the WHConvention. These include consideration of options such as reassessment of the whole concept of WHS, reassessment of resources appropriate for the status or reassessment of the instruments used to determine this.

The final chapter in Part Four is written by Alan Fyall and Tijana Rakic and considers the broader context within which WHS operate. They start by reviewing the current relationship between World Heritage and tourism and re-examines the relationship between tourism and World Heritage Sites with particular regard to visitor trends at sites. Current issues pertaining to the 'sustainability' of the WHL are then explored with particular reference being made to a study by Tijana Rakic into the future of the WHL and the views of WHS managers, managers in the advisory bodies and heritage organizations across the globe. The chapter concludes with the identification of some future issues for World Heritage Sites with regard to the development of tourism in States Parties and some of the measures necessary to meet the needs and demands of visitors. This chapter marks the completion of the issue-specific chapters within this textbook and includes some conclusions gleaned from the authors preceding it. The following section moves to consider specific sites rather than broader issues.

CHAPTER 10

Strategy and policy for the World Heritage Convention: goals, practices and future solutions

G. J. Ashworth and
Bart J. M. van der Aa

Aims

The aims of this chapter are to:

- Demonstrate the dominance of the national over the international interest in World Heritage Site selection
- Elucidate the differences in practice between various national decision-making structures
- Discuss some possible future solutions to the consequent practices which would increase the viability of site selection within the WH Convention.

Introduction

The goals

The 1972 UNESCO WHConvention was introduced to preserve the world's 'most outstanding' heritage sites in the built or natural environment for the benefit of all humanity now and into an undetermined future. A World Heritage List should thus comprise the best heritage sites, selected on their intrinsic merit, conserved and managed in a way that satisfies the aims of both preservation for future generations and presentation to the very humanity in whose name they have been designated. The argument of this chapter is simply that a dangerous gap is increasingly evident between the goal and the evolving reality stemming from its implementation. Such a discrepancy is structurally embedded in the convention and inherent in the processes of its application. It can thus only increase to the detriment of the original goals, leading to an unsatisfactory list, inadequate management and lost opportunities unless quite radical revision of the approaches, restructuring of the organization and strengthening of the measures takes place.

The practices

The core of the problem lies in the simple and not unexpected dominance of the national over the international interest. The rhetoric is global: the practice is national. WHS are, of course, nominated not by UNESCO or its agencies, such as ICOMOS (International Council on Monuments and Sites), but by the national governments in whose territories they are currently to be found. The only notable exception to this was the listing of Jerusalem as a WHS in 1981, despite it being nominated by Jordan, which neither occupied nor managed it.

Despite the fact that the world heritage list should contain the world's 'best' natural and cultural heritage sites, it largely depends on each State Party's ability and willingness to nominate sites and, although such nominations are assessed by ICOMOS or the IUCN (World Conservation Union), 82 per cent of the 'cultural' sites and 68 per cent of the 'natural' sites nominated have ultimately been designated (van der Aa, 2005a: 20). Thus WHS inscription is a compromise reaction among national governments to national nominations and interests. It is not a challenge to national sovereignty by a supranational valuation.

As each nomination has to be initiated at the national level, States Parties that do not actively participate in the WHConvention will not have any listed WHS, even though they may possess sites likely to fulfil the selection criterion of 'outstanding universal value'. Saudi Arabia, for example, has not nominated the cities of Mecca or Medina, even though they can be regarded as the 'heart' of Islam. Conversely, States Parties that actively participate in the WHConvention nominate more sites. A total of 21 of the 178 participating States Parties have seats on the WHC but this 12 per cent of members has actually nominated more than 30 per cent of listed sites between 1978 and 2004 (van der Aa, 2005a: 81).

It can be argued that UNESCO has tended to support the national rather than the international dimension through a number of its policies. For example, it asserts the paramount right of the national claim to ownership of cultural property, favouring the present occupiers of territory, which in practice means their governments, over any other claim on heritage artefacts and sites. UNESCO, understandably given its membership structure, has rarely contested the sovereign rights of governments to determine their own priorities and act accordingly, even if this resulted in damage or displacement of cultural property. UNESCO may warn of the consequences of government actions, provide advice and finance to mitigate their effects, but it has not contested the rights of government to take them. Even the currently discussed convention on cultural diversity is in practice little more than support for national cultural protectionism which does little for national cultural minorities nor for the consumption of culturally diverse products (van der Ploeg, 2004).

The search for global balances (UNESCO, 1994: 3) and the implementation of the Global Strategy in 1994 (Fontein, 2000: 41) is likely to prove not only a chimera but, in practice, is little more than a bargaining counter in national competition. There is a claimed 'over-representation' of historic towns, religious (notably Christian) buildings, and European sites and 'under-representation' of sites from prehistory, the twentieth century, non-Christian and 'living cultures'. The harder UNESCO has tried to redress these 'imbalances', however, the more they have grown, at least in terms of spatial distribution. This is because, first, thirty-one States Parties, including many in central and eastern Europe, have ratified the convention between 1994 and 2003. The new European States Parties have designated four sites each on average, new States Parties in other continents about two. The new States Parties have had seventy-five sites listed during this period, of which only three concern prehistory or archaeology. Secondly, European States Parties make the best use of the opportunities offered by the Global Strategy. Regardless of whether one looks at cultural landscapes, modern twentieth century heritage, industrial heritage, or prehistoric heritage, Europe has taken most advantage of the opportunity to nominate sites in these categories. Between 1995 and 2003, 29 of the 44 cultural landscapes (Fowler, 2003: 24), 13 of the 14 industrial heritage sites, seven of the 10 modern heritage sites and four of the 11 prehistoric sites are located in Europe. Not only does practice contradict intent, the very use of 'balance' as a criterion fundamentally contradicts the criterion of intrinsic quality: the choice can be of the best or of the fairest but not both.

It has become increasingly evident in the past few years that the current domination of national interests is at the expense of not only the international but also the local dimension. There is a growing resistance in many States Parties to local disinheritance by national and international interests who may be represented by international or national designations and by tourists manifesting the global claim by exercising their rights of access to their heritage. Local inhabitants are likely to select, interpret and use heritage differently from outsiders and locally determined authenticity and identity is frequently just different. Local rejection of world heritage inscription, as in the Wadden Sea nomination by Denmark, Germany and the Netherlands (van der Aa et al., 2004: 298) is no longer exceptional.

Finally, States Parties nominate for different reasons, in pursuit of different national strategies, using different criteria as will be illustrated from the cases briefly introduced below.

These problems are manifest in three characteristics of the World Heritage List. First, there has been an increasing inflation of the lists in total and in diversity. Admittedly the 2004 figure of 788 does not seem in itself an unduly excessive representation of the productivity of a world population through many millennia. However, there are, in addition, 1325 tentative sites under consideration and 75 per cent of all member states are preparing nominations within the next 5 to 10 years (World Heritage Newsletter 2001/2: 5). Secondly, and consequently, the composition of the list and the quality of the sites is increasingly difficult to reconcile with the adjectives 'outstanding' and 'best' as required by the convention. Thirdly, there are manifest deficiencies in the management and funding of many sites, as exemplified in many of the cases discussed at length elsewhere in this book, which threaten both the preservation for future and experience by present generations.

Case study: Cases of national decision-making

In some States Parties, such as the Netherlands and Poland, the decisions are made at the national level with the intent of using WHS as 'national flag carriers, symbols in some way of national culture and character' (Shackley, 1998: 1) so that world heritage becomes a list of 'national icons' (Lowenthal, 1998: 228). Selection is made of sites that reflect the 'golden age' or historical theme chosen as characteristic of national qualities (van der Aa, 2005a: 41–48). The sites that were nominated by Poland, for example, before the end of Communism in 1990 focused on that part of the State Party that had long been part of Poland and which reinforced Polish national identity by focusing upon a 'Golden', largely Jagellonian, age of Polish culture and expansion. Heritage sites related to the parts of contemporary Poland settled dominantly by Germans, such as the Castle of the Teutonic Order in Malbork (previously Marienburg), the cities of Toruń (Thorn) and Gdańsk (Danzig), the Church of Peace in Jawor (Jauer) and Swidnica (Schweidnitz), were initially ignored and only nominated from 1997 onwards. In the Netherlands, most WHS are located in the western part of the States Party, which lies below sea level, and are intended to illustrate the selected theme of the Dutch 'battle against the water', an important aspect of Dutch self-identity and externally projected image (Kinderdijk, Beemster Polder, Schokland and the Wouda steam pumping station).

Many States Parties treat WHS nominations as one instrument in their creation of a distinctive recognized national identity. Mexico, for example, attempts to balance pre-colonial, colonial and post-colonial heritages in search of some distinctive Mexican identity (van der Aa, 2005b). These heritages represent the Indígenas, the pre-conquest inhabitants (now constituting 14 per cent of the population), colonists from Spain (10 per cent) and a mixture of these two groups, the Mestizo (who constitute about three-quarters of the population) (Fischer Weltalmanach, 2001). The idea that, 'only the Mestizos were true Mexicans, since creole (that is, descendents of Spanish colonists) landowners were European in cultural affiliation and Indians were bound by the parochial loyalties of their pueblos ...' (Brading, 2001: 525), encourages a search for a Mexican identity through an increasing nomination of post-colonial Mestizo heritage sites (van der Aa, 2005a: 52) such as Hospicio Cabañas and the works of Luis Barragán or WHS expressing a combination of periods and cultures (such as Mexico City and the floating gardens of Xochimilco as well as the amalgamation of the colonial city of Oaxaca and the archaeological site of Monte Albán).

Figure 10.1 Home Study Museum of Diego Rivera and Frida Kahlo, Mexico

Figure 10.2 Castle of the Teutonic Order, Malbork, Poland

States Parties with federal governmental systems, such as Spain and Germany, will often place a higher priority in selection upon balance between political units than any absolute values. In Spain, although sites are nominated by the central government's office in Madrid, the goal of fair spatial distribution is an established policy and by April 2005, all of Spain's seventeen autonomous regions as well as the two African enclaves of Ceuta and Melilla had a site on the tentative list. Similarly, the UK, as a multi-national entity has nominated sites in England, Northern Ireland, Scotland and Wales since 1986 (van der Aa, 2005a: 55–61).

In some States Parties the local level has played a major role in nomination and there has been a trend in many more States Parties for the initiative to be increasingly delegated to sub-national jurisdictions. The more decentralized the nominations the more dominant become local considerations over national ones. Issues of local preservation, encouraging tourism, local economic regeneration and restoration of local self-esteem take precedence over national pride and national identity. Blaenavon, for example, in the coal valleys of South Wales has quite consciously attempted to use world heritage status as an instrument in a programme of local economic regeneration.

Future solutions

A reassessment of the concept

If the idea of world heritage is a set of rights and obligations of humanity as a whole towards what it regards as its heritage, there should be a redefinition, or at least restatement of these international rights and duties. The rights can be translated into a series of demands of humanity upon this heritage. These may be only the knowledge that the heritage continues to exist to satisfy an unspecified and possibly never exercised future demand (option demands); recognizing the right to bequeath to futures (bequest demands), and direct participation or consumption demands (Ashworth, 1998: 12). The first two demands are satisfied just by knowing the heritage continues to exist but the third is manifested in the most powerfully visible claim of humanity upon its heritage, namely tourism. If a cultural property or site is designated as being world heritage then it is difficult to understand how the world can be excluded from experiencing it. Yet this frequently occurs partially or wholly (see the discussion of tourism management and even tourist exclusion in Shackley, 1998). The familiar dilemma is that the preservation of the heritage is frequently seen by its curators to be dependent upon restraining the exercise of a tourist claim. However, the original designation is dependent upon the building of a consensus valuation of the site and the publicity that this allows is then used to generate support for its preservation and maintenance. The creation of such a global consensus and the concomitant publicity inevitably increases world consciousness of the existence of the site, authenticates the quality of the heritage experience and thus increases the demands to experience it.

Rights are necessarily accompanied by obligations and thus the world is presumably responsible in some way for its own heritage. Such responsibilities may be exercised through concern, monitoring, and the donation of expertise and financial subsidy. However, at what point does the exercise of these global obligations necessarily impose upon the sovereignty of the nation-state? First, the protection of the site by national legislation has to be assured before it can be listed as World Heritage. Furthermore, the acceptance of international concern, expertise and aid implies the acceptance of international priorities, values, methods, and behaviours, which are not inevitably the same as national or local ones. Indeed, it is likely in many poorer States Parties that national economic priorities may take precedence over global priorities for heritage protection. World heritage designation is often treated by national planning agencies as if it were an extra category or class of heritage to be added to those that already exist at national or local level. However, it is not, for the same site can have local, national and international significance. If these different scales conflict there is little doubt that the national scale uses and interpretations will take priority.

In most Western States Parties the differences are generally small and the problem rarely arises: World Heritage Status is generally just added marginal value to sites already valued and possibly some extra leverage upon national funding. However, in less economically advanced States Parties and especially those with a different cultural background and economic priorities to the dominant value consensus represented by the world organizations, problems are likely to arise.

A reassessment of resources

The financial contribution to the world heritage fund is currently 1 per cent of the national contribution to UNESCO. This amount is small (US$ 4105000 in 2002, falling to US$ 3995000 in 2003) and becomes derisory if calculated per designated WHS. The options would seem to be more money or fewer commitments. More money would allow more inspection, research, and help with maintenance and the management of users. If the world is becoming more interested in its heritage, and rapidly increasing its quantity and variety through the ever lengthening lists of natural and built environmental WHS, then it seems opportune to ask it to pay more for them. In such an argument the growth of tourism interest may be seen as an opportunity to garner economic and political support rather than as a threat. Ideas for new long-term financial partnerships with private institutions or the use of UNESCO funds as 'seed money' which will help generate funds from elsewhere are all under discussion but the greatest need occurs in the areas least likely to generate such funding.

The alternative would be to exercise more selectivity and parsimony in listing so that resources would not be spread so thinly. The increase in sites designated is not matched by an anticipated increase in resources and an increasing number of sites are likely to be nominated in States Parties with limited technical and financial resources of their own. List inflation with thin subsidies and with little guarantee of local or international protection, is likely to result in damage and deterioration by accident and indifference as much as by design.

List inflation could be met by stricter pre-listing conditions or a pre-selection process but these would tend to favour the richer States Parties and not offer protection to vulnerable sites in poorer States Parties where such protection is most needed. The list could in theory be capped at a number of sites supportable with the current resources and new sites only accepted as replacement for existing sites. This would be financially prudent and allow the list to reflect changing tastes and standards for why should listing be permanent and eternal when ideas may change and even new discoveries made? Less radically new inscriptions could be limited to one or two rather than the current limit of thirty annually. Stricter criteria would not only improve quality, increase the status of inscribed sites, but also allow the WHC more opportunities to monitor the management of listed sites. A quality graded listing is also a solution that is adopted in most national lists of monuments. A division into 'A' and 'B' lists or awarding stars to a limited number of sites would allow scarce resources to be concentrated. None of these solutions would however be acceptable to the States Parties.

A reassessment of instruments

The power of UNESCO is both considerable and severely limited. It is in a powerful position to influence and mobilize world opinion and thus to persuade and put pressure upon national governments. Its World Heritage declarations, as well as its conventions and pronouncements are influential. However, if this moral and largely indirect influence is insufficient then UNESCO has few instruments or sanctions.

The most effective solutions should confront the central problem argued above, namely the balance of international and national interests needs to be reassessed. The nomination of sites could become a responsibility of cultural organizations and even individuals rather than states. Nomination would then no longer be dependent upon the willingness, ability and political influence of States Parties nor their internal jurisdictional structures or cultural and political tensions.

It is currently not clear what can be done when global concerns diverge from national ones. The concept of world heritage implies some obligation for intervention if a national government will not, or cannot, maintain a WHS, or is in danger of damaging it through war or neglect, or perhaps just has different and more pressing immediate priorities for its attention and finance. There is a post-listing right to inspection and regular monitoring but this is not only costly, it is also unclear what sanctions would result from unsatisfactory reports. UNESCO can in theory 'de-designate' a WHS. The political, economic and promotional consequences of this possibility give considerable leverage on governments failing to maintain, or threatening to damage, World Heritage. This would have some direct financial implications, not least on the flow of international subsidies and World Bank loans and be a clear signal to managers at listed sites that they have to fulfil a wider responsibility. However, the international community would also lose its influence over the future of the site.

It has even been mooted (World Heritage Newsletter, 2001/2) that damage to World Heritage could become a legally indictable 'crime against culture' that ought to be prosecuted by some international tribunal. However, threats of sanctions, de-listing and even inscription on the 'List of World Heritage in Danger' are unlikely to be politically acceptable within the present states dominated structure of UNESCO (van der Aa and Ashworth, 2002: 8). World heritage depends upon a 'consensual approach' (King, 2001) but the political reality is that this consensus is between States Parties, which ultimately explains the powerlessness of the international agencies.

Conclusions

It is understandable and commendable that there is a growing sentiment in favour of recognizing and protecting a World Heritage expressed through the best of human creativity. So also is the search for diversity, for balances, for fairness, for equities among the different regions, eras, philosophies, and cultures of the world. The World Heritage List should reflect all of these ideas. The current list is far from perfect, predominantly because of the role played by the States Parties in how the list is constructed. There is an institutional and conceptual contradiction within the idea of a World Heritage nominated and managed by national entities. This becomes apparent once the questions, 'who decides what is significant?' and, 'who acts to make it manifest?' are posed. UNESCO is not a world government but a forum for the interaction of national governments. It can only operate within the powers allowed it and these are severely constrained. There is, in addition, a growing and perhaps inevitable mismatch between commitments and resources. States Parties are more eager to be included on lists than to pay for them. Consequently, more is promised with less ability to fulfil such promises. This is just one element in the much wider question of the necessity for a world order managed by a world community. Clearly, there is no consensus about what either term could mean but, equally clearly, there is a growing consensus about the desirability of paralleling the increasing globalization of economic power, population mobility, social and consumer behaviour with some exercise of global responsibility. The idea of World Heritage at sites with a global significance is an obvious and important part of such a world order.

Acknowledgements

The authors would like to acknowledge the significant role in the research programme from which this chapter is drawn of our faculty colleagues, Peter Groote and Paulus Huigen.

References

Ashworth, G.J. (1998) Is there a world heritage? *The Urban Age*, 4 (4), 12.

Brading, D.A. (2001) Monuments and nationalism in modern Mexico. *Nations and Nationalism*, 7 (4), 521–531.

Fischer Weltalmanach (2000) *Der Fischer Weltalmanach: Zahlen, Daten, Fakten*. Frankfurt am Main: Fischer Taschenbuch Verlag.

Fontein, J. (2000) *UNESCO, Heritage and Africa: An Anthropological Critique of World Heritage*. Edinburgh: Edinburgh University.

Fowler, P. (2003) World heritage cultural landscapes, 1992–2002: A review and prospect. In Caccarelli, P. and Rössler, M. (eds) (2003) *Cultural Landscapes: The Challenges of Conservation*. Paris: UNESCO, pp. 16–31.

King, P. (2001) Interview. *World Heritage Newsletter*, 30 (May/June), p. 2.

Lowenthal, D. (1998) *The Heritage Crusade and the Spoils of History*. Cambridge: Cambridge University Press.

Shackley, M.L. (1998) *Visitor Management: Case Studies from World Heritage Sites*. Oxford: Butterworth-Heinemann.

UNESCO (1994) *Expert meeting on the 'global strategy' and thematic studies for a representative world heritage list*, 20–22 June. Paris: UNESCO.

van der Aa, B.J.M. (2005a) *Preserving the Heritage of Humanity? Obtaining World Heritage Status and the Impacts of Listing*. Enschede: Febodruk.

van der Aa, B.J.M. (2005b) World heritage as a means of marking Mexican identity. In Ashworth, G.J. and Graham, B. (eds) *Senses of Place, Senses of Time*. Aldershot: Ashgate, pp. 133–148.

van der Aa, B.J.M. and Ashworth, G.J. (2002) Dertig jaar werelderfgoedconventie: Een loze lijst? *Geografie*, 11 (10), 6–9.

van der Aa, B.J.M., Groote, P.D. and Huigen, P.P.P. (2004) World heritage as NIMBY: The case of the Dutch part of the Wadden Sea. *Current Issues in Tourism*, 7 (4–5), 291–302.

van der Ploeg, F. (2004) Comment. *Journal of Cultural Economics*, 28 (4), 257–261.

World Heritage Newsletter (2001/2) 33 (December/January).

CHAPTER 11

The future market for World Heritage Sites

Alan Fyall and Tijana Rakic

Aims

The aims of this chapter are to:

- Outline the current relationship between World Heritage and tourism
- Explore the relationship between tourism and World Heritage Sites with particular regard to visitor trends at sites
- Examine some of the current issues pertaining to the 'sustainability' of the World Heritage List and explore some of the corresponding likely impacts on visitor trends
- Identify some of the future issues for World Heritage Sites with regard to the development of tourism in States Parties and some of the measures necessary to meet the needs and demands of visitors.

Introduction

Although unique in its own right, this chapter brings together many of the visitor-related issues discussed in a number of the preceding chapters in order to assess the future market for World Heritage Sites (WHS). With 812 sites currently inscribed on the World Heritage List (WHL) of which 628 are cultural, 160 natural and 24 mixed, sites are as plentiful as they are diverse and spread widely among 137 States Parties. Although there is widespread recognition of the inherent imbalance within the WHL vis-à-vis site type and location (see Chapter 1), the Global Strategy (World Heritage Committee, 1994) has sought to redress the imbalance by encouraging nominations that meet other criteria and originate from less well represented States Parties and themes. However, irrespective of the nomination process and the additional hurdles put in place to make the WHL more rigorous, fair and balanced geographically, the majority are likely to have to deal with the issue of tourism and the likelihood of changing visitation patterns.

With such a mix of sites located around the world it is nearly impossible to forecast the future market for WHS in their entirety. What is possible, however, is to clarify many of the current trends at WHS and in view of the future sustainability of the WHL, explore some of the likely impacts on visitor trends. This chapter begins with an overview of the sometimes conflicting relationship between World Heritage and tourism and goes on to explore specifically the relationship between World Heritage status and levels of visitation at sites. The chapter then examines some of the issues impacting on the future sustainability of the WHL before synthesizing a number of issues likely to impact on the future development of WHS for purposes of tourism.

World Heritage and tourism

Rationale for inscription

As evidenced throughout this book so far, and in the case studies that follow, irrespective of the site in question, motivations for inscription are traditionally mixed. Although conservation, preservation and protection may have historically been the principal drivers for inscription, more recent trends suggest that the entire process is becoming more political with motivations for nation building, identity, and an eagerness to tap into the economic benefits to be derived from tourism at sites becoming more prominent (Bonnette, 2005). It is accepted that despite the laudable intentions of the Global Strategy, nominations are in fact very difficult to stop in that the political drivers are simply becoming too strong a force. In an interview conducted with Bonnette (2005) in her study of the future of the World Heritage List, Rakic (2005) concluded that, whereas nominations used to be managed by experts and professionals, now that countries have discovered the WHL's significant tourism potential, greater political involvement is apparent with the real purpose of many nominations being tourism, with States Parties often seeking to influence the opinions of the experts! In the same study, there was also a reported unwillingness of the heritage sector to work with the tourism industry and an ingrained reluctance to adopt visitor-oriented practices.

Although deemed problematic and troublesome in some quarters, the growth of tourism as a driver for inscription is understandable in that the reasons why so many sites are proposed for inscription are, in most instances, the same reasons why visitors find such sites attractive and worthy of visitation in the first place. Depending on one's view of heritage generally, and World Heritage in particular, if a site is inscribed on the WHL then it is difficult to understand how the world at large can be excluded from experiencing it; tourism representing the most powerfully visible claim of humanity upon its heritage.

Interestingly, in the study conducted by Rakic (2005), in terms of WHS status, stakeholders within the tourism industry, more than in any other sector, deemed inscription to be most significant in that the enhanced profile and opportunities for marketing were just too good for sites to miss. In the same study, just under two-thirds of respondents thought that increased visitation and overall attractiveness of the site to visitors was a motivation for pursuing inscription with benefits from tourism considered to be a principal advantage of listing.

Maintaining the balance

Clearly, one of the underlying problems with sites gaining WHS status and the consequent economic benefits that may accrue, are the means by which the two activities – conservation and tourism – are managed. As identified in a number of chapters already, the large number of stakeholders involved, conflicting agendas and priorities, and funding mechanisms to name but a few, serve as impediments to the achievement of consensus. McKercher et al. (2005) identified the need for a holistic viewpoint to be adopted in that all parties in this 'awkward relationship' need to recognize 'realistic appreciation of the tourism value of the asset, the need to conserve core cultural values and clearly defined roles' (McKercher et al., 2005). Above all, those managing sites require a wider appreciation of the implications for visitation levels once inscription has been achieved and those factors underpinning visitor levels in the first instance. Heritage and tourism are ultimately mutually dependent where operators and destinations can use them to add value to their products and local services which, in turn, generates greater income from tourists while the heritage sites achieve higher revenues and profile that help when seeking assistance/funding for preservation from authorities.

In the context of World Heritage, one of the issues is the extent to which WHS status does in fact lead to increasing visitor levels. As a number of chapters have already identified, insufficient research has been conducted throughout the world that explores fully this issue – the relationship between inscription and levels and types of visitation. The diversity of sites and varying resource levels, their location in developing or developed countries, expertise of staff and the local political context all contribute to making general findings inappropriate to many sites.

Heritage as an attraction

Irrespective of type, size, nature or ease of access, heritage represents just one component of the attractions' sector and competes for visitors with a whole myriad of privately and publicly-funded attractions. Although maybe not the original intention of the founders of the WHL, World Heritage Sites are in the marketplace for visitors, albeit somewhat reluctantly in some quarters. In recent years, the world has seen an unprecedented growth in the number of attractions, with particular growth recorded in the commercial attractions' sector. Stevens (2003) goes as far to predict that the future attractions' landscape is to experience a 'new geography and typology of visitor attractions' that require different forms of management and organizational structures. Stevens also forecasts growth in multi-faceted and multi-occupier type attractions and suggests that the future lies with destination-style attractions where visitors can experience shopping, eating and other aspects of leisure at the one location. Clearly, this leads to a growth in corporate-style 'all-inclusive' attractions where shopping and entertainment come together.

At first glance, it is difficult to appreciate where heritage fits into this future scenario, especially smaller heritage attractions. However, although not instantly recognizable as a 'corporate' attraction, the benefits to be gained from World Heritage 'branding' suggest that the future for the majority of sites inscribed on the WHL is likely to be positive vis-à-vis tourism. Listing provides a suitable magnet for visitors and provides an effective 'differential advantage' for sites when 'competing' for visitors with other attractions. Although the use of such language may appear offensive to some, heritage *per se* is a significant catalyst for travel; Boyd (2003) commenting that 40 per cent of all travel includes a heritage component, albeit partly due to increasing grey markets within key origin markets.

Heritage and tourism

The growing demand for 'heritage based' tourism is best depicted by Lowenthal (1979) and Hannabuss (1999). Lowenthal (1979) argues that people's nostalgia for the past is deepened by the contemporary destruction of historic relics. The proof for that, as he describes it, is the search by people for their roots and identity as well as the increased appreciation of community culture and family legacy. Hannabuss (1999) similarly claims that people consuming heritage (visitors) are in search for coherence in their increasingly fragmented (post-modern) lives. The phenomenon of heritage consumption (through tourism) tends to portray tourism as a negative phenomenon which contributes considerably to the utilization of heritage rather than conservation. However, tourism can also be seen as being the only valid reason for its preservation, especially in places where other economic developments would imply its destruction (Hall, 2001).

The never ending discussion trying to find the fragile balance between tourism consumption and heritage conservation, frequently engaging historians and tourism practitioners, further emphasizes the indestructible connection between heritage and tourism. This relationship is further explored by Robinson et al. (2000: v) who note that it would be hard to imagine tourism without heritage. Heritage is seen as an 'exhibit' used for the purposes of tourism, where the past is '... continually being restored, and reconstructed, packaged, interpreted and displayed ...' and where '... tourists are offered a wide range of heritage products ...' (Robinson et al., 2000: v). It is agreed that heritage has increasingly been commodified for touristic consumption where, through further processing and packaging, it is now more accessible, popular, entertaining and educational than ever. Robinson et al. (2000) suggest that there are two different views of the tourism and heritage interaction; one by which such actions are re-enforcing the significance of the past and the other by which we are challenging our link with the past.

Timothy (1997) argues that heritage is the essence of tourism. Accordingly, he divides heritage and heritage tourism experiences, while acknowledging category overlapping, to personal, local, national and world heritage. The world heritage, he argues, are the heritage attractions drawing large masses of international tourists and producing little personal affection, while the national are the historical monuments representing national ideals and pride, the local are the landmarks of cities, towns and villages used by the community as a connection to their collective past and the personal are places of emotional importance for a person or a group of people. Clearly, World Heritage Sites, although evident among all categories highlighted by Timothy (1997) predominate in the 'world' category.

Returning to the future scenario advocated by Stevens (2003), the question to be asked in the context of World Heritage is the extent to which such sites represent an appeal that can compete with other attractions and that can engender increasing levels of visitation afforded by the endorsement by UNESCO of the World Heritage brand?

Visitation at World Heritage

The preceding discussion is clear in that World Heritage Sites, although originally listed on the WHL for the purpose of protection and preservation, have for the most part increasingly become visitor attractions, with the WHL immensely important not only for heritage preservation but also for the tourism industry (Bandarin, 2005). Tourism is an attendant phenomenon as inscription to the World Heritage List 'not only confers recognition in terms of conservation, but also raises a site's profile and stimulates tourism demand' (Bandarin, 2005: v).

One question that is repeatedly asked but fails continually to be answered fully is the extent to which inscription does actually contribute to higher visitor numbers at sites previously not on the WHL. It is the view of Bandarin (2005: v) that for internationally well known sites, such as the Tower of London, World Heritage status may have little impact on visitor numbers. However, in less established destinations inscription is usually accompanied by an upsurge in tourism.

Venice is also highlighted as an internationally well known example, although the sheer volume of visitors to this unique city is in danger of destroying the very assets that have attracted visitors over past decades. What is difficult to ascertain is the extent to which World Heritage Site status has contributed to this problem. Although there are obvious pressures caused by visitor levels at many sites around the world, Boyd and Timothy (2001) argue that tourism really is not the great evil it is often made out to be. Lack of suitable resources to implement management plans, poverty and civil unrest, war, deprivation and a lack of political will are responsible for more sites being recorded on the List of World Heritage in Danger than the negative impacts of tourism. Another point worth repeating is that raised by Buckley (2004) in that it is the nature of the WHL and the work undertaken by conservationists that have actually given tourism professionals a significant hand in preserving their key resource – and advertising it!

One of the outcomes of inscription is that many sites, once on the WHL, are elevated to the 'status of global icon' (Shackley, 1998: 205). The 'icon' was also mentioned by Young (2001) who noted the strong relationship between tourism and WHS status, and had additionally described how such 'icons' are incorporating the values of World Heritage which are looked for both by visitors and the tourism industry. Hall and Piggin (2001: 204) emphasize that inscription on the WHL endorses the site with an extremely strong brand, while Evans (2001: 81) adds that '… WHS and "wonders" have become just that, "must see" symbolic attractions in cultural tours and national tourist board marketing, and the WHS award equivalent of a Michelin guide 5-star rating'.

Although there is a paucity of research that validates the views of Bandarin (2005), it would appear at the outset that one can distinguish between international destinations, such as London, where visitor numbers have always been significant, and less well-established destinations, especially in the developing world, where World Heritage status is particularly viewed as a catalyst to drive the local, regional or even national tourism economy. Bandarin (2005) argues that problems often arise with relatively new World Heritage Sites in lesser developed economies anxious to acquire the developmental benefits of tourism. For such countries the fact that tourism can be an environmental or cultural threat is far outweighed by its perceived advantages. Furthermore, 'even though there are positive impacts from tourism, it is not invariably the people who live in World Heritage Sites who benefit' (Bandarin, 2005: v).

The assumption that inscription on the WHL automatically results in increased visitation levels is, however, naïve and overly simplifies the nature of visitor trends at World Heritage Sites. Despite a growing body of literature in the field of World Heritage vis-à-vis actual economic impacts of listing and increased visitation and income levels as a result of listing, findings remain inconclusive. In part this can be attributed to the lack of quality research in the field. However, it can also be accounted for by the considerable diversity of sites and range of developed and developing States Parties 'playing the game'.

One study, which explores the implications of listing, is that conducted by English Heritage (2005). Understandably, international recognition and accountability feature, as does the requirement for improved protection and management, implications for planning, and a number of opportunities afforded for new partnerships. It also highlights the 'potential' increase in visitation which depends upon existing visitor levels, location, theme and level of marketing and promotion. Many of these issues have in fact been introduced in some of the preceding chapters. For example, in Chapter 2, the inadequate monitoring and evaluation of visitor numbers was highlighted as a principal impediment to researchers wishing to gauge the impact of WHS status on visitor numbers. This point was emphasized by Buckley (2004) who stated that even in Australia, which benefits from a strong research culture and infrastructure, past data on visitor numbers and origins are generally poor with only broad trends being recognized. Hence, evidence to suggest that increased visitation occurs is often incomplete. In the context of the UK, work by Rodwell (2004) found no proven relationship between WHS status and visitor numbers at cultural sites, while in a study conducted across OECD countries, Hall and Piggin (2001) found that increases in visitor levels were predominantly in the range of 1 to 5 per cent and merely represented average rates of growth in the States Parties surveyed. In a further study by Wall (2004), a very small minority (less than 5 per cent) of respondents suggested that a visit would not have taken place at all if the site had not carried WHS status. This does actually raise the question as to whether visitors, and the trade, actually understand what WHS status is and means, either pre- or during the visit!

In addition to the above, Chapter 6 introduced the issues of easier access to sites, the growth of 'no frills' airlines and the more diverse use of discretionary leisure time by origin markets as some of those factors contributing to the popularity of some WHS. Shackley (1998) also refers to the extensive publicity given to WHS, not available to the majority of sites of a heritage genre around the world not inscribed on the WHL, as a catalyst for visitation. More generally, for many mature markets around the world more sophisticated experiences are required while expectations at sites are rising in that sites in the developing world are expected to meet the 'high' standards anticipated at home. Site location is a key issue in that safety and security is now a key threat at some WHS, such as in Egypt, where tourists are clearly a target for some extremist groups.

Drawing on statements from ICOMOS (1999), Leask and Fyall (2001) argue that WHS status increases a site's attractiveness to visitors with both positive and negative impacts with a number of visitors demonstrating very little genuine interest in culture and who frequently display cultural insensitivities at sites. Returning to familiar themes, visitors display a full variety of motivations in the first instance while Boyd and Timothy (2001) claim that designation does not always result in increased visitor numbers with marketing and accessibility possibly even more significant. In Chapter 4, the same authors state that natural sites, which tend to be less accessible and are often parts of national parks and protected areas, experience less dramatic increases in visitor numbers with issues of peripherality, sensitivity, and threshold use levels taking on greater importance at such sites. Peripheral attractions do, however, often rely on tourism even more as there are so few alternative options available with their remoteness also being very appealing to some markets. Clearly, peripherality will self-select certain markets and cut out others. This was raised in Chapter 4 where the national parks in the USA are often peripheral but are visited by large numbers of tourists due to the sheer quality of the product on offer. In contrast, urban sites have traditionally recorded good visitor levels due to sites often appearing on established tourist routes already.

Interestingly, Chapter 17 introduces the contrasting fortunes between Canada and the USA in that, whereas the overall effect of Canada's WHS designations on tourism was a positive one, relatively few sites in the USA have experienced tourism growth that may be attributed to WHS designation. Most sites in the USA have experienced a neutral effect or only slightly positive due to a unique understanding of the convention by the US authorities. This contrasts strongly with the example of the Neolithic Temples in Malta (Chapter 19) where tourism success on the island is driven by volume with very little consultation with the appropriate heritage organizations taking place as the negative impacts on such sites.

One example of a dramatic increase in visitation as a result of inscription is that identified in Chapter 14 in Lijiang, China where the opening of a new airport served as a further catalyst for a 20-fold increase in the number of visitors. What is evident from the preceding discussion is that those managing World Heritage Sites will have to come to terms with techniques of visitor management and the need to improve the visitor experience and manage visitor numbers at the same time as balance the need for conservation and protection. In short, a more strategic outlook is required as was advocated in Chapter 4 with the example of the Giant's Causeway in Northern Ireland, UK. Chapter 3 introduced similar themes to the above in that historically there have been problems at some WHS with visitor expectation levels being too high. The World Heritage 'brand' clearly brings with it responsibilities as visitor expectations are naturally likely to rise once inscription is achieved; despite the fact that very few people appear to understand what it means and what it represents.

Sustainability of the World Heritage List

One of UNESCO's significant achievements is that it marked the international turning point in heritage protection and preservation by ratifying the WHConvention (UNESCO, 2004). The Convention introduced the World Heritage concept for the first time while States Parties were to engage in identification, protection and preservation of natural and cultural heritage of 'outstanding universal value' for present and future generations. However, although the WHL has achieved a significant global success and the WHS status is perceived to be a highly appreciated accolade (Smith, 2002), the future of the WHL is uncertain due to numerous problems that have emerged, as partly introduced in the preceding chapter.

The first challenge to the List is that it is neither complete nor representative, while the second challenge is that it has an inherent long-standing bias towards cultural sites in Europe. The previous chapter highlighted the fact that a dangerous gap is increasingly evident between the goal and the evolving reality stemming from the WHL's implementation with the national agenda tending to dominate the wider international domain. In Chapter 10 Ashworth and van der Aa rightly stated that while the rhetoric is global, the action is local with inscription now a compromise reaction among national governments to national nominations and interests. In reality the spatial imbalance has also grown, particularly in Europe, in that ratification of the Convention by a number of Central and Eastern European States Parties from the mid-1990s has led to many European nations particularly proactive in seeking new opportunities.

Although gradual change in the balance of the WHL is evident via implementation of the Global Strategy (World Heritage Committee, 1994), worries remain over the third challenge, the potential negative consequences of its indefinite expansion. With an annual growth in new sites being inscribed standing at approximately 25–30 per annum, the sustainability of the WHL is threatened. Fears that it is likely to become unmanageable exist, while one can argue that more emphasis ought to be applied to the management of existing sites, so guaranteeing their protection rather than continuing to add yet more to the WHL. One could argue that the whole system is committed to creating more sites with a genuine potential for the dilution of the overall value of the WHL caused by saturation of sites carrying the endorsement of UNESCO.

In trying to manage the future of the WHL, clearly one has to acknowledge the role played by the inclusion of Cultural Landscape in 1992 (World Heritage Committee, 1994) and the adoption of the Global Strategy in 1994 (World Heritage Committee, 1994) which were designed to assist filling in the existing gaps on the WHL. More recently, ICOMOS published *ICOMOS: The World Heritage List: Filling the Gaps – an action plan for the future*, which was produced to 'contribute to the further development of the Global Strategy for a credible, representative and balanced World Heritage List' (ICOMOS, 2004: 2). The ICOMOS analysis was based on three frameworks: typological, chronological – regional and thematic, while the reasons for gaps in the WHL were divided in two: structural (nomination process, management and protection) and qualitative (identification, assessment and evaluation of properties). The five principal aims of the plan were to:

- achieve a credible Tentative List for every States Party which has ratified the Convention
- optimize the success of World Heritage nominations
- make the new Operational Guidelines operational
- achieve sustainable World Heritage properties in the sense of constant protection and conservation
- raise awareness of the World Heritage Convention.

Similar proposals were also advanced by IUCN in their document *The World Heritage List: future priorities for a credible and complete list of natural and mixed sites*, published in April 2004. It is the view of the chapter author that, in all reality, the most likely future of the WHL is that it will continue expanding, never to be 'complete' and that more sophisticated and rigorous measures to get sites listed are needed to ensure its credibility and representativeness. This was alluded to in Chapter 1 where Leask highlighted that agreement was needed between the two key parties, IUCN and ICOMOS, as ICOMOS (2004) state that there should be no limit on the number of properties inscribed and IUCN state that there must be a finite number of existing and potential properties for inclusion on the List. According to IUCN, the WHL was never intended to ensure complete representativity of all the earth's ecosystems and habitats. However, from a visitor perspective, it is clearly the one that they generally recognize and the one that represents the brand that in many cases is most likely to serve as a catalyst for increased visitation.

Future issues for World Heritage Sites

In view of the above, the market implications for future patterns of visitation at World Heritage Sites are difficult to gauge. If anything this chapter has raised more questions than it has provided answers. Certainly, those interested in pursuing further research on World Heritage Sites are far from short of questions that need addressing! For now, a few key issues have been identified by the author that require specific attention in the years to come.

Balancing heritage with tourism

Increasingly, it is believed that tourism will acquire greater significance in the process of inscription with an even greater need for those managing the process to maintain the balance between heritage conservation and the development of tourism opportunities. This will especially be the case in the developing world and those countries not yet members, such as Korea. The planning for tourism and management of visitors ought to be a central feature of future plans with suitable visitor management techniques proposed that maintain a suitable balance between guaranteeing accessibility and preserving authenticity.

Impact on visitation, visitor type and patterns of behaviour

It is important to emphasize that, although tourism is often the 'accompanying phenomenon' (Bandarin, 2005: v) of the WHS status, it is not seen as a direct consequence but is often believed to be 'assisted' by stakeholders in the economic development of the area in which the site is located. This belief is justified both by the fact that not all WHS developed into tourism attractions, while some others (i.e. Venice) were popular tourist attractions prior to inscription.

Notwithstanding, those managing WHS need to understand fully what visitor groups frequent the site, their patterns of behaviour and the trends in that market that are likely to make visitation to such sites more or less popular in the years ahead. One also needs to keep abreast of the varying, and often continuing expansion of motivations for visiting sites. Inappropriate visitor activity and behaviour that may endanger the brand image of WHS status needs to be managed (as highlighted by Hall and Piggin, 2003), while visitors and the trade need to be educated as to what inscription means and how – if at all – it is to impact on future patterns of visitor behaviour. With regard to different visitor types, work by McKercher and du Cross (2001) identified five categories of cultural tourists. These ranged from the 'purposeful cultural tourist' who enjoys a 'deep cultural experience' to the 'incidental cultural tourist' who enjoys some cultural experiences (all be it they are somewhat shallow) despite the fact that culture failed to serve as a trip motivator in the first instance. Such typologies need to be understood further by those managing WHS, while further typologies need to be explored.

WHS as a means of differentiation

For many sites, endorsement by UNESCO represents a significant means by which differentiation can be achieved. Tourism is a highly

competitive phenomenon locally, regionally, nationally and internationally, so any means by which individual sites or destinations
are able to seek additional points of differentiation are welcomed
with open arms. Inscription brings with it a mark of externally recognized quality which is increasingly becoming an integral part of
site or destination marketing campaigns.

Market saturation and dilution of brand values

One of the problems of the continued expansion of the WHL is that
saturation is likely to occur at some point in the future. Overexposure
of the World Heritage 'brand' is likely to dilute the benefits to be
derived from such a quality 'trademark' with the source of differentiation achieved through brand recognition no longer carrying influence in the market. As with many other sectors, there is always the
danger that the heritage marketplace becomes commodified, apart
from the most significant 'icons' around the world. This may in turn
lead to the creation of another 'elite' list, which will start the entire
process of inscription all over again.

Brand control

As is the case when developing brands for destinations, the sheer
volume and diversity of stakeholders at WHS ensures that any attempt
to manage and/or control the 'brand' is beset with difficulties. One
of the problems to date is that use of World Heritage status is not
consistent around the world – even within regions – so the market
is confused as to what it really represents. To date, there are too
many instances of misuse and misinterpretation of the brand despite
operational guidelines provided by UNESCO. For consistent use of
the brand to be achieved, significant resources need to be made
available – an unlikely event in many parts of the world.

Managing stakeholders

The previous issue leads directly for the need to manage better stakeholders at sites and minimize the potential for stakeholder conflict.
When referring to attractions more generally, Henderson (2003) stated
that seldom are they driven by economic forces alone. Attractions are
employed by national governments and their agencies exploring, dis-
covering and expressing various dimensions of their national and cultural identities. This is clearly true also of WHS so sites and wider

destinations inscribed on the WHL require effective strategies to manage their numerous and often conflicting stakeholder groups.

World Heritage Sites as literary and travel icons

Publications in the area that strengthen further the view that WHS status is a stamp of authentication or 'brand' are increasing in number. Evans (2001: 81) drew a parallel between WHS and the 'Michelin guide 5-star rating', while more generally a large number of books continue to be published which raise the overall level of awareness of the World Heritage List, both directly and indirectly. Publications to date include: *50 Places of a Lifetime*, published by National Geographic (National Geographic, 2005); *1000 places to See Before You Die: The World's Wonders On and Off the Beaten Track* by Patricia Shultz (2003); *Unforgettable Things to See Before You Die*, by Steven Davey (2004); and *The Traveller's Atlas: A Global Guide to Places You Must See in Your Lifetime* by Man et al. (1999). All these publications include a wide range of World Heritage Sites, with particular emphasis being placed on the status of WHS.

Economic benefits

It is fair to say that a number of sites have yet to capture fully the economic benefits to be derived from tourism. Accepting that tourism is to remain a central component of World Heritage more directed efforts are required in the future for sites to reduce leakages and improve economic benefits to be derived from tourism and to the local community.

Broad attraction trends

Fyall et al. (2003) identified a number of issues to be addressed in the future by attractions of all shapes and sizes. Managing security and gauging the impact of security on travel patterns is fundamental to all attractions but particularly WHS where they are a magnet for visitors. Sites need to be fully aware of changing patterns of demography and leisure trends among their key markets and the principal sources of competition. The migration to 'destination' style attractions advocated by Stevens (2003) is significant in that those WHS that have around them a critical mass of tourist provision are likely to be those that succeed in the longer term. Clearly, the wider destination needs to be considered in its entirety; the level of facilities available to accommodate large numbers of tourists at Uluru, Australia for example serving as the catalyst for the development of a tourism industry and making the

WHS a destination in its own right. Finally, those managing World Heritage need to be fully conversant with developments in information communication technologies (ICTs) (as highlighted in Chapter 9), while all parties need to develop a more visitor-focused approach to their management of the heritage product where appropriate to the resource.

Marketing

Not only do many World Heritage Sites require more effective packaging but more innovative approaches to the development of World Heritage trails, cross-border initiatives and collaboration with other destination stakeholders need to be developed to maximize the benefits to be derived from tourism.

Conclusions

Despite the initial intentions of the WHL, it is difficult to foresee a time when there is less pressure on States Parties to nominate sites for inscription for purposes of tourism. The widely acknowledged increasing politicization of the process of inscription appears to be here to stay with the desire by States Parties to propose sites for inclusion on the Tentative List reaching 'arms race' proportions on a global scale. Tourism is clearly beneficial to a large number of sites carrying World Heritage status, but two themes underpin this chapter and many of those that precede it: the extent to which the WHS 'brand' really does contribute to increased levels of visitation and greater economic benefits to be derived from tourism. Although no firm conclusions can be drawn, the chapter does bring together many of the issues that impact on visitation levels and a number of strategies that can impact on the development of sites for purposes of tourism. Clearly, more research, and especially the collection, analysis and reporting of data at the micro 'Site' level, is necessary if sound judgements are to be made and effective strategies developed and implemented. With the constant expansion of the WHL the need for more research output becomes critical if the management of World Heritage is to move forward and make the most of the tourism potential that exists – both now and in the future.

References

Bandarin, F. (2005) Foreword. In Harrison, D. and Hitchcock, M. (eds) *The Politics of World Heritage: Negotiating Tourism and Conservation.* Clevedon: Channel View Publications.

Bonnette, M. (2005) Personal communication. In Rakic, T. (2005) *The Future of UNESCO's World Heritage List*. Unpublished thesis, Napier University, Edinburgh.

Boyd, S. (2003) Marketing challenges and opportunities for heritage tourism. In Fyall, A., Garrod, B. and Leask, A. (eds) *Managing Visitor Attractions: New Directions*. Oxford: Butterworth-Heinemann.

Boyd, S. and Timothy, D. (2001) Developing partnerships: tools for interpretation and management at World Heritage Sites. *Tourism Recreation Research*, 26 (1), 47–53.

Buckley, R. (2004) The effects of World Heritage Listing on tourism to Australian national parks. *Journal of Sustainable Tourism*, 12 (1), 70–84.

English Heritage (2005) What are World Heritage Sites? Available at http://www.english-heritage.org.uk/server/show/conWebDoc.4194 (accessed 10 December 2005).

Evans, G. (2001) World heritage at World Heritage bank: culture and sustainable development. *Tourism Recreation Research*, 26 (1), 81–84.

Fyall, A., Garrod, B. and Leask, A. (eds) (2003). Conclusion. In *Managing Visitor Attractions: New Directions*. Oxford: Butterworth-Heinemann.

Hall, C.M. (2001) Editorial. *Tourism Recreation Research*, 26 (1), 1–3.

Hall, C.M. and Piggin, R. (2001) Tourism and World heritage in OECD countries. *Tourism Recreation Research*, 26 (1), 103–105.

Hall, C.M. and Piggin, R. (2003) World Heritage Sites: managing the brand. In Fyall, A., Garrod, B. and Leask, A. (eds) *Managing Visitor Attractions: New Directions*. Oxford: Butterworth-Heinemann.

Hannabuss, S. (1999) Postmodernism and the heritage experience. *Library Management*, 20 (5), 295–302.

Henderson, J. (2003) Visitor attraction development in East Asia. In Fyall, A., Garrod, B. and Leask, A. (eds) *Managing Visitor Attractions: New Directions*. Oxford: Butterworth-Heinemann, pp. 73–85.

ICOMOS (1999) *Tourism at World Heritage Cultural Sites*. Washington: World Tourism Organisation.

ICOMOS (2004) *The World Heritage List: Filling The Gaps – An Action Plan for the Future*. Paris: ICOMOS.

Leask, A. and Fyall, A. (2001) World Heritage Site designation: future implications from a UK perspective. *Tourism Recreation Research*, 26 (1), 55–63.

Lowenthal, D. (1979) Environmental perception: preserving the past. *Progress in Human Geography*, 3, 549–559.

McKercher, B. and du Cross, H. (2001) Cultural tourism: the partnership between tourism and cultural heritage management. Binghamton, New York: The Haworth Press.

McKercher, B., Ho, P. and du Cross, H. (2005) Relationship between tourism and cultural heritage management: evidence from Hong Kong. *Tourism Management*, 26 (4), 539–548.

Peard, G. (2005) Personal communication. In Rakic, T. (2005) *The Future of UNESCO's World Heritage List*. Unpublished thesis, Napier University, Edinburgh.

Rakic, T. (2005) *The Future of UNESCO's World Heritage List*. Unpublished thesis, Napier University, Edinburgh.

Robinson, M., Evans, N., Long, P., Sharpley, R. and Swarbrooke, J. (2000) *Tourism and Heritage Relationships: Global, National and Local Perspectives*. Gateshead: Athenaeum Press.

Rodwell, D. (2004) The World Heritage Convention and the exemplary management of complex heritage sites. *Journal of Architectural Conservation*, 3, 40–60.

Shackley, M. (1998) *Visitor Management: Case Studies from World Heritage Sites*. Oxford: Butterworth-Heinemann.

Smith, M.K. (2002) A critical evaluation of the Global Accolade: the significance of World Heritage Status for Maritime Greenwich. *International Journal of Heritage Studies*, 8 (2), 137–151.

Stevens, T. (2003) The future of visitor attractions. In Fyall, A., Garrod, B. and Leask, A. (eds) *Managing Visitor Attractions: New Directions*. Oxford: Butterworth-Heinemann.

Timothy, D. (1997) Tourism and the personal heritage experience. *Annals of Tourism Research*, 24 (3), 751–754.

UNESCO (2004) Convention concerning the protection of the World Natural and Cultural Heritage, also known as the World Heritage Convention. http://whc.unesco.org/nwhc/pages/doc/mainf3.htm (accessed 26 December 2004).

Wall, G. (2004) Protected areas as tourist attractions. Paper presented at *Tourism Crossroads – Global Influences, Local Responses*, 13th Nordic Symposium in Tourism and Hospitality Research, Aalborg, 4–7 September.

World Heritage Committee (1994) Expert meeting on the Global Strategy and thematic studies for a representative World Heritage List, UNESCO Headquarters, 20–22 June 1994. http://whc.unesco.org/archive/global94.htm (accessed 14 March 2005).

Young, I. (2001) The influence of fundamental values on the relationship between World Heritage Sites and tourism. *Tourism Recreation Research*, 26(1), 109–112.

PART 5

Case studies

Part Five relates directly to case studies from around the world, demonstrating the issues raised in the previous chapters and providing examples of management techniques in practice. Each individual case links with the relevant chapters in Parts One to Four, including consideration of the relevant themes where appropriate. While a brief amount of description is included in each case to set the context and location, the case studies deal with issues and themes, rather than simply describing the management of the particular WHS. Each case study chapter also includes three questions at the end for the purpose of further discussion and reflection on the key issues raised.

Part Five starts with Peter Mason and I-Ling Kuo tackling the issue of visitor management with reference to Stonehenge, UK. The key issues in this area are raised with reference to Stonehenge, followed by research findings relating to the attitudes of visitors to the WHS vis-à-vis motivations for visiting, management issues, visitor experience and the future of the site. The debate over the future of Stonehenge is very topical and aspects of the site were raised in Chapters 3 and 6, though Chapter 12 is more applied. The findings of this case study are interesting in that they largely contradict the results of government reports pertaining to Stonehenge and suggest that the majority of visitors do in fact have an enjoyable visitor experience. This therefore does question the need to spend in excess of £160 million in the development of the site, as currently proposed by English Heritage!

Moving across the continents to Peru, Chapter 13 considers the opportunities afforded by sustainable tourism development at Machupicchu WHS. This chapter, written by Otto Regalado-Pezúa and Jesús Arias-Valencia, seeks to provide reflective considerations to contribute to solving the difficulties currently faced by Machupicchu Historical Sanctuary. An outline proposal for the sustainable management of the WHS is suggested, promoting an integrated management structure including elements of land management, tourist development and education.

Chapter 14 by Hilary du Cros continues the theme of visitor management and investigates the management of visitor impacts at Lijiang WHS, China. The chapter starts with an appraisal of the key issues, the development of tourism activity on the site and draws from a range of studies undertaken at the site by interested stakeholders. This case study develops the theme of stakeholder participation, concluding that tourism at the site may go into decline if the social impacts of the activities are not addressed.

László Puczkó and Tamara Rátz tackle the issues of managing urban WHS with specific regard to the Cultural Avenue project in Budapest. They develop the key challenges in managing complex urban environments and present an overview of the project in offering some solutions to the challenges. Again the issue of the large number of stakeholders interested in the management of the WHS is raised, arguing that it is virtually impossible to find an effective resource management approach that is able to satisfy all kinds of interests. While not offering a complete solution, the Cultural Avenue project is suggested as a mechanism to assist in combining some of these interests by joint interpretation of the WHS resources.

The issue of local community participation is considered as part of Li Fung Mei Sarah's chapter relating to tourism development, empowerment and the Tibetan minority in Jiuzhaigou National Nature Reserve in China. A brief statement on the development of tourism in the Reserve is provided prior to examination of the effects of this development on the Tibetan minority residents. Empowerment is used as a framework to assess how tourism has changed the economic, social and cultural environments of such communities. The overall outcome of the research is positive and this WHS provides an example of how mass tourism and the economies of scale that accompany it can be harnessed.

Chapter 17 by Dallen Timothy and Stephen Boyd moves from site-specific issues to broader States Party ones, and explores the WHS situation in the Americas. This concise chapter examines the growth and distribution of WHS and the opportunities and challenges faced by them. A great variety of views and values are reported as existing across the countries of the Caribbean and North, Central and South America, hardly surprising when consideration is given to the differing political, economic and social situations. However, in most States Parties the desire to achieve WHS status is strong and offers great opportunities for cross-border and international cooperation – one of the main aims of the World Heritage Convention. Perhaps surprisingly though, the USA are reported as lacking in the political will to engage further with the WHConvention, most notably following disagreements between UNESCO and US Foreign Policy, though their recent re-joining with the organization might aid the recovery of this link.

Trevor Sofield and Li Fung Mei Sarah's case study on Huangshan (Yellow Mountain) in China considers some of the aspects of World Heritage listing raised in Chapters 10 and 11. It explores the concept of world view and examines the predominantly western paradigms that determine World Heritage listing. The case of Huangshan is utilized to show how the Chinese world view sees cultural and natural heritage as a single unitary construct in contrast to the Western, positivist, scientific approach. The issues raised by this contradiction are discussed and offer a valuable insight into the differences that exist between the States Parties and how these are incorporated (or not) in the UNESCO World Heritage Convention.

Returning to the issue of integrating WHS management within existing stakeholder settings, Chapter 19 refers to the situation experiences in Malta with regard to the Megalithic Temples. Nadia Theuma and Reuben Grima explore the impacts of WHS listing on local communities and highlight the often conflicting views that appear between heritage and tourism organizations. This chapter concludes that the role of the site specific management plan is a crucial element of WHS management and the accommodation of the variety of stakeholder needs.

The final chapter in the book is written by Jo Mackellar and Ros Derrett, with reference to managing tourism in the Central Eastern Rainforest Reserves of Australia. Chapter 20 completes the discussion of balancing stakeholder needs and the need for a strategic approach in managing WHS. The case considers the facilitators and barriers to progress in the development of the Rainforest Way and how there is a need to progress through a series of phases, addressing the issues in each phase, in order to achieve the overall aims and needs of the variety of stakeholders.

CHAPTER 12

Visitor management at Stonehenge, UK

Peter Mason and I-Ling Kuo

Aims

The aims of this case study are to:

- Discuss visitor management issues at Stonehenge
- Present research findings on attitudes of visitors to Stonehenge vis-à-vis motivations for visiting; management issues, including interpretation and regulation; visitor experience; and, the future of the site.

Introduction

Managing visitors is one of the important ways of attempting to control the impacts of tourism at a World Heritage Site (WHS) and particularly to reduce negative impacts (Pearce, 1989; Hall and McArthur, 1996; Mason, 2003). Three approaches are commonly used: diverting tourists from the so-called 'honey pots', which are locations with large volumes of visitors; 'hardening' (e.g. resurfacing paths and footpaths); modifying visitor behaviour (Hall and McArthur, 1996; Mason, 2003). This third approach usually involves attempts to regulate visitors, although such tourism regulations are unlikely to have legal standing and are more likely to be voluntary and of a self-regulatory nature (Mason and Mowfoth, 1996). However, as well as regulation, managing visitors can involve education, often via the process of interpretation (Mason, 2003). In certain situations, a combination of education and regulation has been used in an attempt to manage visitors (Kuo, 2002).

This chapter discusses visitor management at a major WHS in the UK, the prehistoric monument of Stonehenge. It focuses on the particular management issues of Stonehenge and reports on research conducted via a questionnaire survey of visitor attitudes conducted at the monument. The chapter initially discusses the specific management issues of Stonehenge, then presents results from a survey conducted there, and this is followed by a discussion of these findings. This case study clearly complements elements of Chapters 3 and 6 by offering some interesting insights into some valuable primary research conducted recently by the two authors.

Visitor management at Stonehenge

Stonehenge is located in the county of Wiltshire in England. It is a stone monument dating back at least 4000 years and possibly as far back as 4000 BC. Stonehenge is one of the world's most important archaeological remains. What the monument was used for has caused controversy over a period of several hundred years. This controversy has generated much literature, which has acted as marketing to potential tourists. Mason (2003) indicated a number of theories exist in relation to Stonehenge's purpose:

- it is a prehistoric temple or religious site
- it is a prehistoric calendar
- it has astronomical significance helping to mark the position of stars
- more fancifully, it is part of an earlier landscape which helped alien beings locate themselves from space.

It seems likely that it was a combination of the first three above, with compelling evidence that it was a calendar as the stones mark the position of the sun at different times of the year, with mid-summer's day (June 21) and mid-winter's day (December 21) given particular prominence.

Stonehenge is one of the relatively few WHS that draws large numbers of both international and domestic visitors (Timothy and Boyd, 2003). According to English Heritage (EH) (Wilson, personal communication), it had approximately 850 000 paying visitors in 2003 (plus at least 200 000 who looked from the road but did not pay). It is the most visited prehistoric site in the UK and has consistently been in the top ten UK visitor attractions since 1990. In 2001, as many as 73 per cent of visitors were from overseas (41 per cent from the USA) and 98 per cent of visitors arrived by car/coach (Mason, 2003). Most visitors stay for only 20–30 minutes and about half do not get beyond the visitor centre/car park, so they do not actually go to the stones. It has been estimated that up to 500 visitors per hour could be accommodated in the stone circle, if access was allowed, but there are up to 2000 visitors per hour in the peak summer season of July and August. The facilities include a visitor kiosk, a souvenir shop, a take away café/restaurant, toilets and a car park.

Stonehenge is owned by EH, an independent body set up in 1984 by Parliament to protect England's archaeological heritage. It is marketed globally, but particularly in the USA, by EH and VisitBritian (previously the British Tourist Authority). The interpretation of Stonehenge is almost exclusively by mobile phone-sized electronic devices, known as audio-wands. These provide a basic interpretation of the site, but also have the option of more detailed commentary. There are numbered stopping off points with a linked commentary in English, five different European languages and also Japanese.

There are a number of key management issues. These are as follows:

- The number of visitors (there is likely to be an increase to over 1 million paying visitors by 2007), which contributes to problems of crowding at Stonehenge itself, as well as related car-parking problems, as the site is almost inaccessible by any means other than road.

- There is the problem of damage to the monument. Stonehenge has suffered major deterioration as a result of past tourists who have clambered over the stones (Timothy and Boyd, 2003). Although visitor numbers vary throughout the year, 1000 per day is not uncommon in winter and can reach as high as 2000/hour in the peak summer season. Many of the stones show evidence of this, in terms of their smooth surfaces. Of greater significance is that the earthworks surrounding and supporting the stones have been weakened, so some stones have fallen over. When it became clear that Stonehenge was suffering irreversible damage, the Department of Environment erected a perimeter fence in the spring of 1978 (Timothy and Boyd, 2003). Since then, to prevent damage the stones are normally roped off. In addition to the rationale of potential damage caused by paying tourists, another reason is that alternative groups, those who claim to be Celtic priests (Druids) and others, including so-called 'hippies' and travellers, have tried to use Stonehenge for festivals and quasi-religious ceremonies. In the early part of the 21st century, access was granted for the use by 'Druids' on the summer solstice (June 21st), but as most visitors cannot get this type of access they may feel cheated.
- Entrance costs were relatively low – £5.20 for adults and £3.20 for children in 2004 – at the time the fieldwork research was conducted. With concessionary fares for groups and senior citizens, and free entry for students in full-time education, this may encourage large numbers of visitors.
- Authenticity of the experience and related tourist satisfaction is a key factor. The large numbers of visitors coupled with the use of roped off areas and the inability of visitors actually to touch the stones may contribute to a less than satisfactory experience. Bender and Edmonds (1992) actually suggested that visitors would feel that they had not fully experienced Stonehenge unless they could get close to the stones. They argued for greater access, though on a limited basis. The visitor experience is also likely to be affected by the current use of the landscape. The site is between two relatively major roads, one linking London with South West England. The traffic noise, particularly in summer, can be disruptive to the experience of Stonehenge. In December 2002, after many years of discussion, plans were finally accepted to divert, to the south, the main A303 trunk road that passes close to the site, and build a tunnel to house it (Mason, 2003). This will remove the road from the site of Stonehenge, with the added benefit of reducing noise levels.
- The Visitor Centre is currently underground and there is an under-road by-pass to get to Stonehenge. This is for safety reasons as there were road accidents in the past. The Visitor Centre was called 'a national disgrace' by the House of Commons Select Committee on Heritage in 1994 (Mason, 2003). A new visitor centre is planned

near Amesbury, approximately 2.5 km away. This centre will provide an interpretation of the site over a 10 000-year period. Visitors
who wish to will then be able to walk to Stonehenge from this visitor centre. However, siting a visitor centre away from Stonehenge
has raised authenticity issues.

- Who actually owns the site and for what purposes it should be
used, is a major area of controversy (Bender and Edmonds, 1992;
Mason, 2003). Stonehenge is in a curious position of being on a
small area of land owned by EH, which is set in a much larger area
owned by the National Trust (NT). The attitude of the NT to management is linked to the concept of estate management. This has
meant that the site of Stonehenge is viewed by the NT as one of its
many, albeit very significant, archaeological sites within its large
estate (Fowler, 1992) which should be managed as an area of land
and not solely because of its archaeological value. Since the early
1980s at least, various groups have claimed that they should have
access to the site, including 'hippies' for festivals and 'Druids' for
religious purposes. As these groups were viewed, until recently, as
outside mainstream society, it was relatively easy for the police and
authorities to get the support of locals to restrict access. However, in
the mid-1980s, a number of clashes between police and 'hippies/
travellers' led to serious injuries, resulting in compensation claims
against the police and access then returned to the agenda. Bender
and Edwards (1992) argued that there should be greater, although
regulated, access for a variety of both tourists and non-tourist
groups, including academics, Druids and international visitors, as
Stonehenge should be recognized as a place of enjoyment, research
and religious worship. However, in the early part of the 21st century, Stonehenge remains roped off most of the time, although there
have been occasions, such as mid-summer's day, when access has
been allowed. Increasingly, private access is being allowed outside normal opening hours, particularly for educational purposes,
but this raises the issue of who should be allowed regular access.
Is it fair, for example that scientists/archaeologists can gain easy
access, but not those who claim they want to use the site for religious purposes?

Methodology

A questionnaire was designed asking respondents to provide demographic information, as well as responding to some Likert scale questions. The questions were developed from issues raised in academic
literature, comments derived from media statements on Stonehenge,
and research on attitudes to tourism (see Mason and Cheyne, 2000;
Mason and Beaumont-Kerridge, 2003; Raybould et al., 1999). Prior to

its use, a draft copy of the questionnaire was sent to EH staff involved in the management of Stonehenge. As a result the questionnaire was slightly modified and EH staff also indicated there were likely to be some differences between weekend and weekday visitors (Carson, personal communication). Research, therefore took place over two days; one in September and the other in November, 2004.

Results

The demographic characteristics of respondents are summarized in Table 12.1. Figure 12.1 shows a more detailed breakdown of respondents' normal place of residence by geographical region.

Visitors responded to a series of Likert scale questions to indicate their reasons for visiting Stonehenge. Table 12.2 shows the mean and

Table 12.1 Demographic characteristics of the sampled visitors

Demographic characteristics	Number of visitors	Percentage
Gender		
Male	101	43.2
Female	133	56.8
Total	234	100.0
Age		
20 or younger	24	10.3
21–30	79	33.8
31–40	46	19.7
41–50	30	12.8
51–60	38	16.2
Above 61	17	7.3
Total	234	100.0
Place of residence[*]		
UK	87	38.5
Overseas	139	61.5
Total	226	100.0
Type of visits[†]		
First-time visit to Stonehenge	176	75.5
Repeat visits	57	24.5
Total	233	100.0
Level of education[‡]		
Less than Polytechnic/first degree	65	28.9
Polytechnic/University degree	106	47.1
Postgraduate qualification	54	24
Total	225	100.0

[*]8 invalid cases; [†]1 invalid case; [‡]9 invalid cases.

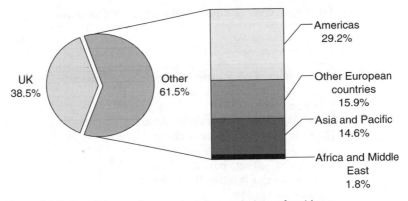

Figure 12.1 Breakdown of respondents' normal place of residence

Table 12.2 Major motivations for visiting Stonehenge

Motivator	Mean	Standard deviation
Stonehenge is unique	4.49	0.814
To expand my knowledge	4.07	0.954
I am interested in prehistoric monuments	4.03	0.94
Stonehenge is a World Heritage Site	3.72	1.265
I am interested in archaeology	3.55	1.261

Table 12.3 Visitors' views on their visit to Stonehenge

Visitors' perceptions on the following descriptions of the site	Mean	Standard deviation
Overall my visit was enjoyable	4.31	0.783
The handheld audio guides (wands) are useful	4.26	0.97
Visitors behave well	4.12	0.756
Not allowing visitors to touch the stones is necessary to conserve Stonehenge	4.11	1.147
Signs and signage are clear and easy to understand	4.09	0.985
Stonehenge exceeded my expectations	3.65	1.007
Stonehenge is overcrowded with visitors	2.86	1.069

standard deviation for the five most important motivational factors indicated by respondents for visiting Stonehenge.

A series of statements involving a Likert scale were used to prompt visitors to indicate their views immediately post-visit. Selected responses, showing mean scores and the standard deviation, are shown in Table 12.3.

Table 12.4 Visitors' views on the future of Stonehenge

Visitors' views on the future of Stonehenge	Mean	Standard deviation
Visitors who disobey instructions on behaviour at the site should be fined on the spot	3.5	1.180
Stonehenge needs a new visitor centre	3.42	1.179
There should be no entrance charge to Stonehenge, visit should be free	3.16	1.23
It would be better to have a real person to act as a guide rather than a hand-held audio guide	2.69	1.17
All visitors should be allowed to touch Stonehenge	2.43	1.41
Access to Stonehenge should only be for archaeologists, historians or those with special permission, such as religious groups	1.64	1.015
Visitors should be encouraged to go to a visitor centre rather than Stonehenge itself	1.9	1.13

The final section of the survey involving Likert scale questions asked respondents to give views on the future of Stonehenge. Table 12.4 provides selected responses, showing mean scores and the standard deviation, on the future of Stonehenge.

In an attempt to reveal any differences within the sample to question responses such as that related to, for example, age or gender, the student's t-test was conducted. Table 12.5 shows results from the student's t-test, where there was a statistically significant difference.

Discussion

In terms of demographics, the age breakdown of the sample was compared with that obtained in EH research and found to be very similar, except there was a slightly higher proportion in the 21–30 age group and a slightly lower one in the 41–50 age group, than EH research (Carson, personal communication). The sample was also similar to comparable EH research in terms of respondents' origin, with a high proportion from overseas (62 per cent) and, as with this EH research, respondents from the USA were the single most important overseas visitor group. As with comparable EH research, visitors were well educated and a very high proportion (75 per cent) were first time visitors (Carson, personal communication).

Table 12.5 t-test results for Stonehenge questionnaire survey

Likert scale statement and t-test factor	Mean	Standard deviation
Stonehenge is unique		
• Female visitor	4.64	0.762
• Male visitor	4.37	0.902
Not allowing visitors to touch the stones is necessary to conserve the site		
• Female visitor	4.32	1.170
• Male visitor	3.90	1.758
Current entrance charges are acceptable		
• International visitors	3.53	1.298
• British visitors	3.16	1.170
The entrance charges should be increased, with the extra money raised used to help conserve the site		
• International visitors	2.78	2.37
• British visitors	1.693	1.212
Access to Stonehenge should only be for archaeologists, historians or those with special permission such as religious groups		
• First-time visitors	2.02	1.498
• Repeat visitors	1.49	1.120
Current entrance charges are acceptable		
• First-time visitors	3.47	1.273
• Repeat visitors	3.05	1.301
Visitors should be encouraged to go to a visitor centre rather than Stonehenge itself		
• First-time visitors	2.27	1.543
• Repeat visitors	1.65	0.991

Stonehenge is regarded as one of the most significant prehistoric monuments in the UK and it inspires various motivational factors. The apparent uniqueness of the site plays an important role in attracting visitors. Given that a high proportion of visitors are well educated, perhaps it is not surprising that 'expanding knowledge', and being interested in archaeology and prehistoric monuments are important motivational factors. Interestingly, visitors indicated that the fact that Stonehenge is a WHS is an important motivational factor. This implies that designating it as a WHS may have increased its status in the mind of visitors, and may help to explain why Stonehenge attracts significant numbers of both domestic and international tourists (see Timothy and Boyd, 2003).

Much of the controversy surrounding the visitor experience of Stonehenge has centred on its presentation and interpretation. Although guided tours are provided, the great majority of visitors are offered the free usage (in 2004) of an audio wand. The results indicate that visitors find these particularly useful. There are numbered way-markers and signs at the site (which mainly request visitors to stay behind the rope barrier) as well as signs immediately off-site and in the car park, providing information on Stonehenge and the surrounding area. Visitors generally indicated that these signs were clear and easy to understand. The results suggest that visitors responded positively to both the use of the audio wand and the on-site signs and signage, with 80 per cent and 79 per cent of the visitors, respectively, indicating the audio wands were useful and signs were easy to understand. Further confirmation that visitors have a positive reaction to the audio wands comes from response to a Likert scale statement on the future of Stonehenge, where approximately half of the visitors indicated that they would not support the use of a real person in preference to the audio wand. At other heritage sites, interpretative activity involving a guided tour has the constraints of timing, lack of flexibility and potential language issues. When participating in a guided tour, a visitor needs to follow the pre-planned timing, routes and the pace of the tour. However, visitors' average stay at Stonehenge is less than 30 minutes (Mason, 2003). The audio wands allow visitors to skip unwanted information, rewind, restart and repeat as they wish, and proceed at their own pace. Also, observational evidence during the research revealed the audio wands are not only free, but offered to visitors upon entry to the site. It seems likely that they are perceived as convenient, as there is no need to wait for the tour to start or to be at a certain location on time.

Since 1978, partly as a result of excessive wear, but also because of 'illegal' entry, almost all visitors have been prevented from entering the stone circle. It has been argued (Bender and Edmonds, 1992) that this could lead to visitors feeling they had not fully experienced Stonehenge. However, as many as three-quarters of the visitors in this research indicated that not allowing visitors to touch the stone is necessary for conservation. Responses to a related statement suggesting that all visitors should be allowed to touch Stonehenge support this view of 'conservation by restricting access', as here just over half of those questioned disagreed with allowing access. There is further confirmation of this belief of restricting access in responses to the statement that visitors who disobey instructions on behaviour at the site should be fined on the spot, as here a majority of respondents agreed with this view. However, some care should be taken with this particular response, as the visitors surveyed 'strongly agreed' that Stonehenge visitors behave well, and by implication it is likely that they considered their own behaviour here!

There have been suggestions that the access to the site should be reserved to selective groups such as archaeologists, historians and special permit holders such as religious groups (see Mason, 2003). However, the great majority of the sample (86 per cent) disagreed that access should only be for such groups. These findings suggest that although visitors feel they should have access, they are also aware that Stonehenge is of such significant historical and cultural importance that their on-site behaviour and activity needs to be managed and restricted. These findings also raise the issue of ownership of Stonehenge. Visitors appear to believe that the site does not belong to a specific group, but all peoples.

Less than 30 per cent of the samples felt the site was overcrowded with visitors. However, this could be explained by the fact that the survey was conducted on two occasions towards the end of the main tourism season (in mid-September and mid-November). Therefore, the visitor volume was not as large as it would have been during the summer months where there are up to 2000 visitors per hour (Mason, 2003).

A staffed visitor centre usually plays a major role in visitor management at tourism destinations. Its function includes providing information and assistance at the site. Some form of interpretation is frequently delivered at a visitor centre. Currently, Stonehenge lacks a true visitor centre, due in part to spatial constraints. One of the major proposals is for a new visitor centre to be built at 2.5 km distance from Stonehenge at Amesbury. However, this survey suggests that visitors' experience of Stonehenge is less likely to be 'complete' if they are encouraged to go to only a visitor centre, rather than the site itself. Only 13 per cent of respondents agreed that visitors should be encouraged to go to the visitor centre instead of visiting the stone circle, while over 75 per cent of the visitors disagreed with such a suggestion. Just over 50 per cent of the visitors felt there is a need for a new visitor centre at the site itself, while approximately a quarter of the sample felt a new visitor centre is unnecessary. However, it is possible to argue that these responses do not provide strong support for the Parliamentary Committee view of the site being 'a national disgrace' (see Mason, 2003).

Opinion was almost equally divided on whether entrance to Stonehenge should be free. However, the entrance charge in 2004 of £5.20 for adults was deemed acceptable by nearly half of the visitors. In addition, only 15 per cent of the visitors felt that the entrance charges should be increased, with the extra income used for conservation of Stonehenge. This suggests that although the 'user-pays' concept was accepted by visitors, they were likely to object to increases on entrance charges, even if the money raised was for conservation. In general, visitors seemed fairly satisfied with their visit, with a small majority indicating that Stonehenge exceeded their expectations and very strong agreement with the statement 'overall my visit was enjoyable'.

Although, in general, the t-test results revealed little difference between male and female visitors' responses, they did show that female visitors felt more strongly about the uniqueness of the site and also felt more strongly than the males that not allowing visitors to touch the stones is necessary to conserve Stonehenge. There were differences between British and international visitors in relation to views on entrance charges. International visitors supported more strongly than British visitors the entrance charge of £5.20 for adults, and also showed a higher acceptance of increasing entrance charges and using the extra income for resource protection. The frequency of visits to the site may play a significant part in this finding. British visitors are more likely to be repeat visitors and this seems likely to affect what they consider to be value for money – repeat visitors are less in agreement than first time visitors that 'current charges are acceptable'. Also, international visitors to the UK may spend a large proportion of their budgets on transportation and accommodation and the entrance charge may seem a relatively small amount within this overall budget. In addition, as overseas visitors believe strongly that Stonehenge is a unique attraction and since they have come some distance to visit it, their perception of what constitutes a fair entrance fee may be relative to this 'uniqueness' factor. Such visitors may also be less likely to object to the idea of increased fees, particularly if they do not intend to return to Stonehenge!

Repeat and first-time visitors also show some differences in their views on the future of Stonehenge. The results show statistically significant differences in relation to two particular issues: 'access to the site should be reserved for specialist groups' and 'visitors should be encouraged to go to a visitor centre rather than Stonehenge itself'. Repeat visitors are less in agreement on access restriction. They have visited the site before, hence they are likely to feel that their access to Stonehenge should not be restricted either now or in the future. Repeat visitors disagree more with the idea of 'visiting a visitor centre only', rather than Stonehenge itself. This seems most likely to stem from their consideration that, if they can visit the site now, they would want to be able visit it in the future.

Conclusions

In the mid-1990s a British Government Report described Stonehenge as a 'national disgrace' (Mason, 2003). Since then, there have been plans to improve the experience for visitors at what is the major prehistoric tourism attraction in Britain. However, what was criticized previously – the proximity of major roads, the access via an underground tunnel, the almost continual roping of the actual stones, the temporary nature of the toilets and the limited scale of the food/refreshment and souvenir facilities and the lack of a real visitor centre – still existed in late 2004 when the fieldwork was conducted. The reaction of the visitors to the survey conducted as part of this research reveals a variety of views, and a rather more complex picture than the outright damnation of the British Government Report. Hence, overseas visitors are more positive in their reaction than British visitors, first time visitors (who made up 75 per cent of this survey) are more satisfied than repeat visitors and women, as with other tourism issues have different views to men, with female visitors somewhat more positive in their reaction than men. Largely contradicting the Government Report claims, the majority of visitors indicated that Stonehenge is a unique site, with good interpretation, a fair entrance charge, generally good value for money and, overall, is an enjoyable experience.

Acknowledgement

The authors would like to thank English Heritage staff for their information, advice and support. However, the research was solely that of the authors and was not financially supported in anyway by English Heritage.

References

Bender, B. and Edmonds, M. (1992) Whose past? What past? *Tourism Management*, 13, 355–357.

Fowler, P. (1992) *The Past in Contemporary Society: Then, Now*. London: Routledge.

Hall, C.M. and McArthur, S. (eds) (1996) Visitor management: principles and practice. In *Heritage Management in Australia and New Zealand*. Melbourne: Oxford University Press, pp. 37–54.

Kuo, I-Ling (2002) The effectiveness of environmental interpretation at resource-sensitive tourism destinations. *International Journal of Tourism Research*, 4 (2), 87–101.

Mason, P. (2003) *Tourism Impacts, Planning and Management*. Oxford: Butterworth-Heinemann.

Mason, P. and Beaumont Kerridge, J. (2003) Attitudes of visitors and residents to the Sidmouth International Festival. In Yeoman, I., Robertson, M., Ali-Knight, J., Drummond, S. and McMahon-Beattie, U. (eds) *Festival and Events Management*. Oxford: Elsevier, pp. 311–328.

Mason, P. and Cheyne, J. (2000) Resident attitudes to tourism. *Annals of Tourism Research*, 27 (2), 391–411.

Mason, P. and Mowforth, M. (1996) Codes of conduct in tourism. *Progress in Tourism and Hospitality Research*, 2 (2), 151–167.

Pearce, D. (1989) *Tourist Development*. London: Longman.

Raybould, M., Digance, J. and McCullough, C. (1999) Fire and festival: authenticity and visitor motivation at an Australian folk festival. *Pacific Tourism Review*, 3, 201–212.

Timothy, D. and Boyd, S. (2003) *Heritage Tourism*. London: Prentice Hall.

Questions

1 Unlike some World Heritage Sites, Stonehenge attracts significant numbers of both domestic and international visitors, why do you think this is so?

2 In the mid-1990s, a UK Government committee described the site of, and experience at, Stonehenge as a 'national disgrace'. What reasons would you suggest for this claim?

3 The visitor survey discussed in the chapter produced results that do not fit with the claim that Stonehenge is a 'national disgrace'. What reasons would you give for this?

CHAPTER 13

Sustainable development in tourism: a proposition for Machupicchu, Peru

Otto Regalado-Pezúa and
Jesús Arias-Valencia

Aims

The aims of this case study are to:

- Create awareness of the environmental risks that endanger Machupicchu Historical Sanctuary
- Provide reflective considerations to contribute to solving the difficulties Machupicchu Historical Sanctuary is facing
- Contribute to current debate regarding the sustainable management of Machupicchu Historical Sanctuary.

Introduction

Peru, in spite of its vast geography and great variety of tourist practice, continues to be a unipolar tourist destination. Visitors concentrate on the city of Cusco, and in the so-called 'southern circuit' which contains the major attraction of Machupicchu Historical Sanctuary (MHS). Thus, it is economically and socially important to preserve, conserve and plan the development of such a cultural and natural World Heritage Site (WHS). Despite this fact, the current external factors involving tourist activity to the MHS are not the best, with recent studies having shown a number of risks endangering the ruins and their surroundings. This situation reflects how important the government's role is with regard to tourism development. On the one hand, adequate policies may provide great advantages and benefits in economic, educational and sociocultural conditions but, on the other hand, deficient policies may contribute to environmental degradation, and the loss of the local people's identity, among other negative effects at the WHS.

This case study is aimed initially to guide the reader through the importance of tourism in Peru, and its main attraction. Secondly, it describes the difficulties – causes and consequences – of MHS being a natural and cultural tourist destination. Finally, it offers a likely solution based on the key principles of sustainable development.

Peru's tourism statistics

Various studies agree with Peru being shown as a historical, archaeological and cultural tourist destination. Peru's Promotion Tourism Board (PromPerú, 2000) points out that Cusco, the MHS, and/or the 'southern circuit' are considered worth visiting by 50 per cent of tourists who arrive in the country, while the Monitor Company's report (1995) points out that between 70 and 75 per cent of the tourists arriving in Peru visit Cusco and the MHS. Although the figures on the tourist flow may be initially confusing, it is evident that Peru has a very important position as a unipolar tourist destination in accordance with Leiper's Tourist Pattern (Leiper, 2004) where the city of Lima constitutes a transit route (Regalado-Pezúa and Arias-Valencia, 2004).

Diverse sources point out the great variation evident in visitor statistics, even among information provided by the official organizations. For example, the World Tourism Organisation Barometer shows that 931 000 international tourists arrived in Peru in 2003. However, the Ministry of External Trade and Tourism (MINCETUR) points out that 242 105 out of 587 112 tourists visiting Cusco and their main tourist attractions in 2003 were national and 345 007 foreign visitors.

In accordance with the registered statistical records of the Inca City and the Inca Trail in Machupicchu, managed by Cusco Culture National Institute and by Machupicchu's Management Unit, the amount of tourists welcomed during the year 2003 surpassed 500 000 people, including both domestic and international visitors.

Figure 13.1 shows the main destinations across Peru during 2003 and the visitor breakdown obtained by each one. In accordance with PromPerú (2004), although tourists visited Lima, most of them mainly

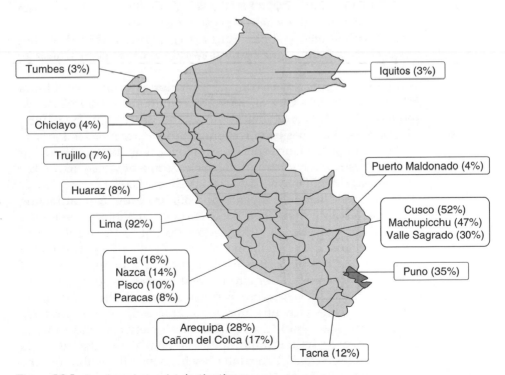

Figure 13.1 Peru's main tourist destinations.
Source: PromPerú (2004: 9) (reproduced with permission)

197

travelled around Cusco, the MHS and the Sacred Valley (located 60 km northwest of Cusco), and subsequently went on visiting other southern destinations such as Puno, Arequipa, Ica and Tacna.

These figures are sufficiently clear to comprehend MHS's important role as Peru's principal attraction and the concerning interest in its maintenance and preservation. In the following section, MHS is introduced while the natural and cultural wealth it possesses and the difficulties the tourist and agricultural activities cause without any adequate management unit are discussed.

Machupicchu Historical Sanctuary (MHS)

The Inca city was rediscovered in 1911, and exposed to science by the North American historian and explorer Hyram Bingham. However, it was not until 1950 that tourist activities began and, therefore, the development of infrastructure as well as the necessary tourist support services. At the beginning of the 1980s, rapid tourism growth was observed; however, due to terrorist forces and the economic crisis Peru was facing at the time, it declined considerably and it was not reactivated until 1992, when the social situation stabilized. From then on, tourism activity has been growing consistently.

The MHS, located in a Natural Preserve Area of 32 592 hectares, was declared a Cultural and Natural World Heritage Site by UNESCO in 1983.

This exceptional area is worth attention due to its multiple cultural values: the Old Inca City of Machupicchu, the Inca Trail Network, and more than 35 archaeological sites within an outstanding natural environment. Peru has been recognized to be a rich States Party in relation to flora and fauna species. Moreover, it has been noticed that there are restrictively-distributed species, some of which are highly endangered (PROFONANPE 2002a, 2002b and 2002c).

The world's 'nature and culture' tourism growth is attracting major interest in visiting the MHS. As stated previously, the tourist registrations surpassed 500 000 visitors during 2003, and it is estimated that more than 10 million visitors have already been attracted by this mysterious place. It is evident that the growing number of visitors has increased the environmental impact: bigger production of solid wastes; development processes; uncontrolled and direct influences on the evidently major cultural and natural attractive sites, mostly at the Inca City, the Inca Trail Network, and some of their primary forests. It is important to emphasize that the Vilcanota River basin (also called Urubamba River), which flows through the MHS, is a catchment for the residuals and the polluted water flows of the region's biggest human conglomerate.

This situation, as well as the ecosystem's natural vulnerability, has unleashed detrimental processes that threaten the MHS's natural and cultural values in relation to its long-term attractiveness. Under this threat, UNESCO, in agreement with the Peruvian authorities, has asked for a diverse evaluation and monitoring studies on the current conditions of resources within this Preserve Area.

It is not only the tourist activities that endanger Machupicchu's ecosystem, but also the agricultural practices carried out within the sanctuary have caused forest fires, deforestation and soil degradation because of over-shepherding, among other harmful effects.

Figure 13.2 shows the concerns about the MHS after analysis and checking of the reports from different UNESCO 'Evaluating Missions', and the records of other diverse public and private organizations that have been working on the area.

Now that these concerns have been stated, as well as their causes and effects, it is vital for their solution that the national government takes part in the strategic consideration, and the local participants in the operative one. For once there is a political will with priority being given to preserving the MHS and when the local community actively takes part, it will be possible to think about sustainable tourist development for the MHS.

The design of these strategies and their applications must be compatible with the three fundamental sustainable development principles: long-term profitability, the rational use and conservation of natural resources, and the local community's taking part.

Proposed solution

The main critical factor to success is related to participation mechanisms within strategic planning and programme execution processes. These mechanisms are designed to set guidelines and limitations to the development process, and not just negotiations by 'consensus' that only satisfy the interests of individual and particular institutions leaving out the goals of the MHS preservation.

Moreover, the multiple participation of public organizations within the MHS hinders the managerial activities and, inadvertently, worsens its concerns.

Therefore, this proposal, aimed at the sustainable development of the MHS, requires a management unit to be created in order to speed up the 'legal reorganization' of this heritage, and to start the 'environmental services evaluation' process. Everything is thus to be integrated within regional development considerations.

To achieve this, the state authorities are to create an autonomous organization (technical, economic, and administrative) that consists of an international 'World Heritage Committee' which will serve as

Concerns	Causes	Effects
Concerns produced by tourism activities	• The 'carrying capacity management' concept is not understood so that it has not been included in the planning process	• Tourist overcharging on the Inca's City and Inca Trail Network tours; especially in high season, producing detrimental effects • Unplanned tourist growth (large seasonal number of visitors)
	• Great tourist service demand (transportation, lodging, catering, among others)	• Disorderly urban growth at the MHS various entrances and at mid-stops within the natural area • Land invasion where poor service infrastructure is developed • Lack of adequate solid waste and polluted water flow management systems • Very poor tourist services • Hostelling services development • Urban growth • Public transportation service development (railroads, helicopters, and buses) • Over-demand on animals (horses, mules and donkeys)
	• Lack of adequate strategic and operational planning processes (Master Plan, Site Plan, Annual Plan) to the diverse attractions	• Superimposing of jurisdictional and institutional responsibilities • Institutional chaos and disorganization when implementing individual operational plans • Irrational soil use and lack of zone discrimination (lack of micro-zoning) • Lack of conformity with in-force laws
Concerns produced by farming activities	• Incompatible farming activities with the MHS • Authorities' limited monitoring ability of the activities developed within the MHS	• Forest fires • Decrease in tree varieties and deforestation • Fuel demand (firewood) • Introduction of diverse exotic species, competing against and displacing native ones • Domestic raising of exotic animals • Shepherding fields erosion and degradation (carrying capacity exceeded up to five times) • Poaching and taking out of flora species • Biodiversity loss
	• Lack of planning in farming development	• Limited implementation
Concerns produced by public services	• Lack of planning in public services activities development • Limiting environmental laws to regulating public services within the MHS • Limited monitoring ability at executing complementary economic and social activities within and outside the MHS	• Hydroelectric power station enlargement and renovation without adequate environmental impact studies • Non-existent environmental monitoring of public transportation services within and outside the MHS • Lack of Operational Environmental Protocol • Fuel spillage, polluting noises and incomplete combustion gases emission • Poor mastery and repair workshops (inadequate infrastructure) • Lack of Environmental Impact Studies (EIS) and Environmental Impact Evaluations (EIE) relating to social and economic activities

Figure 13.2 Current concerns about Machupicchu

the highest decision-making authority to handle the MHS. This Committee is to be directed by an executive director, and integrated by public state officers, preservation organizations, delegates from national private companies and specialists from international organizations.

As a support unit the directorate is to have a 'World Heritage Convention' integrated with national and international people from diverse scientific and technological areas that are to cooperate with the sustainable development of the MHS on behalf of their different specialities.

As the principal unit for implementation there is a proposal to create a 'Management Committee', bringing together the different public and private organizations and delegates working at the MHS. Their main objective will be to expedite and to support the identified the MHS strategy risk management and planning processes.

Thus, six general strategies have been identified to achieve the goals established by the MHS Master Plan, approved in 1998, which will be updated and methodologically adapted to strategic planning based upon a risk management focus. An outline proposal for the sustainable management of MHS is highlighted in Figure 13.3.

As stated above, the MHS Master Plan will be permanently updated and will benefit from the implementation of such a structure. The main goal will be to set guidelines aimed at the site's tourist

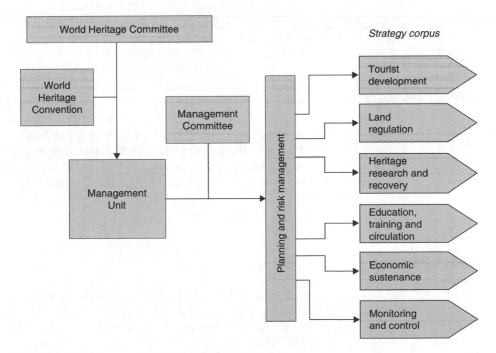

Figure 13.3 MHS management proposal structure

use and regulation, improvement in the quality of life of local people, the ecological carrying capacity of the site, and the need to obtain more benefits that will attainably assure the handling of the MHS's natural and cultural heritage.

The strategy relating to the area's tourist development will allow for activities planning. It will consist of: forecasting tourist-consumers' level of comfort and satisfaction; guaranteeing service quality in accordance with set standards; controlling tourist entry in accordance with maximum visitor carrying capacity levels; diversifying service offers; and foreseeing future needs in accordance with the environment sustenance of the site.

With regard to the land regulation strategy, the MHS structure and legal reorganization will facilitate its implementation. Moreover, it will be possible to evaluate the boundary's area and extension. On the other hand, this strategy will be useful to set up specific rural and urban guidelines for the MHS's economic and sociocultural activities.

The strategy concerning heritage research and recovery will allow the evaluation, planning and implementation of natural and cultural heritage renovation and preservation of the MHS. This planning is to be based on scientific research and approved by the corresponding organizations.

The education, training and circulation strategy is to pass the environmental vulnerability of the MHS on to all stakeholders, direct and indirect. Thus, the implementation of this strategy will make the local people actively take part in the MHS preservation programmes, and it will make the visitors feel committed to the preservation of the MHS.

The economic sustenance strategy, as plainly stated, will aim at economically benefiting the local people, creating employment opportunities and increasing the workers' salaries and everything will be carried out with respect for the carrying capacity indicators relating to investment, adequate infrastructure, and the necessary equipment.

Finally, the monitoring and control strategy is to propose a monitoring system that permits the pre-emptive control and lessening of the negative environmental impacts around the MHS, which were produced by economic and sociocultural activities performed within the sanctuary. These strategies interact with one another so that they are to be taken as a whole (Regalado-Pezúa, 2005).

Conclusions

Various studies concur that Peru is seen as a historical, archaeological and cultural tourist destination. Diverse sources for figures point out that between 50 and 75 per cent of all foreign tourists visit Cusco and the MHS, which describes the States Party as a unipolar tourist destination (Regalado-Pezúa and Arias-Valencia, 2004;

Lozato-Giotart, 2003). However, the current conditions of tourist activity and development around the MHS are likely to endanger the World Heritage Site.

Despite the fact that the MHS is Peru's main tourist destination, it is not managed with regard to sustainable warranty procedures. On the contrary, the separately adopted steps only contribute to its environmental degradation. Not only do excessive tourist activities cause environmental degradation to the MHS, local farming practices also contribute to degradation as do inadequate infrastructure or unplanned housing.

This proposal to sustain the MHS is based on the key principles of sustainable development. In fact, it is proposed that there is a management structure in charge of the MHS strategic planning, supported by both an international committee and a scientific consultant convention, each one of them consisting of capable personnel.

Alongside, it is proposed that there is a management committee in charge of expediting the implementation of the strategy: tourist development; land regulation; heritage research and recovery; education, training and circulation; economic sustenance; and monitoring and control. These strategies are to be taken as a whole because they are closely related to and interact with one another.

If the negative environmental impacts continue to increase, it will decrease the number of visits to the MHS. At this juncture, the authorities would be compelled to close the MHS down, partially or completely, for some time in order to facilitate its recovery and relaunch.

References

Leiper, N. (2004) *Tourism Management*, 3rd edn. Frenchs Forest: Pearson Education.

Lozato-Giotart, J-P. (2003) *Géographie du tourisme: De l'espace consommé à l'espace maîtrisé*. Collection tourisme. Paris: Pearson Education.

Monitor Company (1995) Construyendo las ventajas competitivas del Perú. El Turismo.

PROFONANPE (2002a) Ampliación de la base de datos sobre diversidad boilógica del Santuario Histórico de Machu Picchu: Diversidad botánica. Informe final. Instituto de Investigaciones en Ciencias Biológicas de la Universidad San Antonio Abad del Cusco.

PROFONANPE (2002b) Ampliación de la base de datos sobre diversidad boilógica del Santuario Histórico de Machu Picchu: Diversidad zoológica. Informe final. Asociación para la conservación de la selva sur y del Museo de historia natural de la Universidad San Antonio Abad del Cusco.

PROFONANPE (2002c) Biodiversidad del Santuario Histórico de Machu Picchu: Estado actual del conocimiento. Centro de datos para la conservación de la Universidad Nacional Agraria La Molina, Lima.

PromPerú (2004) *Perfil del Turista Extranjero 2003*.

Regalado-Pezúa, O. (2005) Hacia un desarrollo sostenible de la industria turística en el Perú. Leadership, Magazine for Managers. CLADEA, Lima, pp. 10–11.

Regalado-Pezúa, O. and Arias-Valencia, J. (2004) Posicionamiento de Machu Picchu en el sistema turístico del Perú: ¿Riesgo u oportunidad?. Seminario: Between Sustainable Tourism and Local Development: Prospects and Paradoxes. Centro de Estudios y Documentación Latinoamericanos – CEDLA, Amsterdam, 8–10 de diciembre.

Questions

1 What would happen to Peru's tourist activity and how would the region's economy be affected if the MHS were to be closed?
2 Would other tourist destinations be able to replace the MHS tourist offer? Would such tourist destinations be in great demand?
3 How long can the MHS continue to bear its current management policies? What policies should be adopted in order to avoid scientifically and technically irreversible degradation?

CHAPTER 14

Managing visitor impacts at Lijiang, China

Hilary du Cros

Aims

The aims of this case study are to outline:

- The main characteristics of Lijiang that have relevance for understanding the nature of visitor impacts and initiatives employed so far to mitigate them
- Its tourism development through the 1990s with specific regard to the legislation, policies and strategies that seek to retain these unique characteristics
- The impact of the 1996 earthquake and UNESCO World Heritage inscription on the heritage asset
- A growing number of studies undertaken on visitor impacts by anthropologists and other analysts, because of their potential to provide lessons for authorities elsewhere in China concerned about their heritage assets and for the management World Heritage Sites generally.

Introduction

The rationale behind exploring this case study is primarily that it is one of the best managed and most studied World Heritage Sites in the People's Republic of China. This is due to the partnerships and initiatives that have provided major advances in conserving tangible and intangible heritage. However, some problems still remain requiring on-going attention, particularly with regard to minimizing visitor impacts on the local community, which are common to many such sites around the world.

Key historical and cultural characteristics

Lijiang lies in Northwest Yunnan, a province in the Southwest of China. It is currently divided into Lijiang New Town and Ancient Town (also known as Dayan Ancient Town). The latter was first recognized as an administrative unit by the imperial authorities in 1253 AD during the Yuan Dynasty. However, Lijiang had served as a meeting place for Chinese and Tibetan groups before this date, being a market town and trading post on the Tea and Horse Trade Route that was in operation from before the Tang Dynasty until the 1950s. The town is chiefly inhabited by the Naxi, a Tibetan derived cultural group.

The Naxi have their own rich intangible heritage comprising writing, art, craft, music, festivals, and customs known as Dongba culture. Other aspects of non-Dongba culture were also retained in the town's urban design, architecture and music (e.g. Ancient Han music is still performed by a separate group from those that perform Dongba music). Alternatively, the Naxi people combined elements of their own traditional style of architecture with that of the Han Chinese and ethnic Bai people to make up the vernacular architecture of Lijiang Ancient Town (Duang, 2000). Most remarkably, the town still draws its water supply in open culverts from the scenic Black Dragon Lake and the catchment of Jade Dragon Snow Mountain nearby. The city also has several 'three eyed' wells with separate pools for collecting drinking water, cleaning vegetables and washing clothes. The water supply can be adjusted upstream to allow sufficient water through to cleanse the streets, a unique feature in China (Ebbe and Hankey, 2000).

Early planning for tourism

The cultural value of the town was formally recognized in 1986, when it was made a Historical and Culturally Famous City under the National Cultural Relics Protection Act, 1982 by the State Administration for Cultural Heritage (SACH). A plan to make Lijiang an 'international level tourism city' was devised in 1994 by the Yunnan Provincial Tourism Administration. It included measures for increasing transportation services, tourism infrastructure and services. Measures were also proposed to enhance tourism product development and to 'strengthen propaganda[1] to the outside world' (Duang, 2000: 11). No specific measures were included to minimize or mitigate visitor impacts.

In 1995 a new airport was opened, capable of taking some international flights from the region. A five star hotel was also constructed, one of only two in Yunnan until 2001. Other mostly three star and low budget hotels followed. Domestic tourism to the town doubled and international tour operators started to discover Lijiang.

1996 Earthquake

Lijiang was partially devastated by a severe earthquake on 3 February 1996. Many of the traditional timber and mud brick buildings survived. However, repairs and rebuilding were still required. The Yunnan Provincial Government and the World Bank funded the rebuilding. The funding came with strings attached and provided a rare opportunity for the town authorities to rid the Ancient Town of modern infill and other buildings that were not constructed in the traditional style. Money was also designated as part of the earthquake effort to carry out an informed reconstruction of an ancient Han mansion in the town, the Mu Fu complex (Ebbe and Hankey, 2000).

Lijiang already had a number of laws and regulations in place to control redevelopment, but this was an opportunity to establish a set of guidelines for building redevelopment that would aid the site in passing UNESCO's unofficial 'Authenticity Test'. At the time, World Heritage inscription for historic towns involved an assessment by international experts of the integrity of historic and traditional fabric in the precincts nominated by sovereign states. The removal of modern unsympathetic elements as part of the earthquake rejuvenation gave Lijiang a major advantage over some other nominations in the evaluation process.

1997 World Heritage inscription and its impact

The town achieved its inscription not long after the earthquake, possibly to assist in channelling more international aid into its conservation[2]. Visitor management and the planning for its impacts was not at the forefront of local and international authorities' minds, as they were still trying to deal with the physical and social impacts of the earthquake. Also, the UNESCO World Heritage Committee and Centre had not yet developed the more recent and tougher guidelines on management planning at that stage. Therefore, the visitor management and planning for Lijiang was being conducted *ad hoc* by local authorities with some support from international organizations.

However, Lijiang was not alone in the region in this predicament so UNESCO and the Norwegian World Heritage Office developed the Local Effort And Preservation (LEAP) programme in 1999. Lijiang became one of the first WH Sites to be targeted for assistance. UNESCO facilitated the project, along with its Norwegian partner, with the aim of developing action plans and stakeholder involvement models to assist WH Site managers to understand and deal with tourism impacts. Overall, the main aim was to foster local community stewardship of heritage resources within the Asia-Pacific Region with the World Heritage Sites to be developed and showcased as good examples (Yang and Hou, 2002).

Part of the requirements of the programme was that study and documentation of visitor impacts be undertaken by local authorities to give an international panel of experts working with local authorities some baseline data for analysis. The local heritage authorities were given some guidelines to collect data and statistics regarding the situation. Detailed surveys were done with visitors and residents for the first time and some tentative conclusions reached about emerging problems (Duang, 2000). It was hoped that this exercise would assist the authorities to build skills in monitoring the situation in the future as well as providing data for present analysis.

The Lijiang Report to UNESCO (Duang, 2000) identified four key problems:

- tourist numbers had skyrocketed since the construction of the airport and the advent of World Heritage inscription and would likely continue to grow with the recent advent of the 'Golden Weeks' Holidays for internal tourists within China
- lack of a planning and tourism management authority solely for the Lijiang Ancient Town
- lack of an established heritage fund to make grants for ongoing conservation works and training projects etc.
- difficulties with preventing revenue leakage or collecting tourism dollars at the site. More needed to be done to benefit the host community and the heritage asset.

The conference in Bhaktapur, Nepal for LEAP in March 2000 examined these problems in detail and compiled an action plan. Its strategies included those aimed at capturing more tourist revenue (bed tax), establishing a cultural heritage conservation fund and overall management authority, relieving traffic congestion (limitations on vehicle access), and improving public amenities.

However, lurking in the background in these preliminary data were indications that problems were starting to occur with the make-up of local residents from different ethnic groups. If left to develop, these would change the social fabric of the town and, with it, much of its intangible heritage. Numerous residents were moving out in favour of people from outside the prefecture wanting to develop tourist services and retail businesses, but with no role in local culture. Locals were also leaving because of decreased local amenities and increased income from tourism that allowed them to afford larger, more comfortable modern premises for them and their extended families in the New Town (Duang 2000; du Cros, 2001). This left behind mainly those working directly in tourism and old people not wanting to leave their long-time homes.

The LEAP programme held its final conference in Lijiang in 2001. The conference reviewed progress on the implementation of the 2000 action plan and made suggestions for further improvements in stakeholder relations and services for the host community. The bed tax proposed for levying fees from tourists staying in ancient town guesthouses worked well up to a point, but was being circumvented by small illegal hoteliers setting up in New Town to attract tourists. Even so, Duang Sonting, the heritage official who wrote the original 2000 report, was happy two years later that the action plan was still working and, indeed, by 2003 the out-migration had slowed (Street, 2004). He believed the town had achieved a 'win-win' solution, with tourist money going towards job creation and the restoration of listed sites (China Daily, 2004).

However, another economic phenomenon was starting to affect the social make-up of the host community. This was one that could not be fixed easily with stakeholder relations models and heritage conservation action plans because it involved local income derived from tourism. Although the land of Lijiang's ancient town is still collectively owned and cannot be sold on the open market, the value of street facing residences for rent had dramatically risen with the advent of greater tourism. After 2000, it became apparent that as rental fees go up, fewer and fewer long-time residents would continue to stay in their old residences preferring instead to rent them out. The problem this creates had been noted in many other World Heritage historic tourist cities and towns. That is the shopping and services for the local community decrease as the dependence on tourism increases and with it the community's interest in staying in the town outside of the tourist season. The ancient walled city on Rhodes, Greece, suffers this exact problem, where after high season ends it gradually becomes a ghost town. There are no schools and very few offices or local shops to entice people to live or visit within its walls.

In Lijiang, efforts instead have gone into burying all electricity wires and cables underground and reducing the pollution in the town's famous street canals (Yang and Hou, 2002; China Daily, 2005). While these are worthy civic projects, other issues need to be dealt with too to prevent the town becoming an 'open air museum', only of interest to tourists (McKercher and du Cros, 2002). Retaining sufficient vitality and amenities for the host community to continue to stay within the bounds of these heritage sites is one of the key problems that Lijiang and other such World Heritage Sites will face in the 21st century.

Lijiang's shifting demography in response to tourism

UNESCO did not continue with this issue with Lijiang, because it has had to move onto other projects once LEAP's work was completed. Fortunately, the town had attracted much interest from anthropologists, tourism academics and others wanting to study visitor impacts. Since 2000, at least five studies have covered this topic in some way (McKann, 2001; du Cros, 2001; Yang and Hou, 2002; Yamamura, 2004; Street, 2004).

McKann (2001) noted that tensions had already arisen in 2000 between locals and the outsider population to whom they felt they were 'losing their town'. Newspaper articles and editorials devoted space to a debate about banning 'outsiders' or *waidi ren* from setting up businesses in the town (McKann, 2001: 159). Much of this relates to people with more entrepreneurial skills and capital becoming established there and out-competing locals. As the commodification of the main streets for tourism moves away from the traditional ambience of the town and its meaning for locals, some may feel alienated or inconvenienced by this new tourist development.

Yang and Hou (2002) visited not long after the UNESCO study, but still found there was a 'developer-driven' preservation ethic in place with local authorities and their partners. They estimated that along the streets in the most accessible areas for tourists, already nearly 90 per cent of the original residents had moved out. By the end of 2001, there were about 700 different stores in the historic area with 594 located along the main commercial corridors. Of these, merchants from the local area operated only around 28 per cent. Later studies by Yamamura (2004) and Street (2004) noted that the actual number could have dropped to as low as 20 per cent, half of that stated by local officials for UNESCO. In June 2004, it was observed that there were local traders in dark shadowy doorways trying to sell hand-crafted souvenirs being visibly out-competed by shops nearby rented by outsiders with air-conditioned interiors (Street, 2004). Other local merchants may just have found that the seasonality of tourism did not appeal to them and have moved out to undertake other work.

Another finding that emerged from the most recent study by Paul Street (2004) was both worrying and poignant. He discovered when distributing questionnaires 'that a significant number of people did not have a clear understanding of the significance of working in a heritage town'. He then added an additional question (that was also used in the 1999 UNESCO study) about how the person learnt about the meaning of the World Heritage status. Street (2004) found that most people learnt about it from television, elders and at religious gatherings (50 per cent) and (22 per cent) had never had it explained to them (the same number as in 1999). Inability to engage the host community in understanding the significance of World Heritage inscription is likely to have a long-term impact on maintenance of cultural values.

The same people were asked about impacts on their daily life. A few more were negative about impacts than in 1999, although 40 per cent did not admit to it having any impact on their daily life. Increases in visitor numbers, however, are causing some friction with the locals, particularly in the regard to persistent photographing and video taking. Also, they no longer use the central market square for traditional dances or catching up on gossip as the space is often overcrowded with no 'sitting out' areas. Even in a few places where there have been signs posted restricting access to tourists in favour of local residents, these spaces have been infringed (Street, 2004).

The tourists

It is not hard to understand how this situation has arisen given the huge growth in tourism since 1990. Lijiang has actually managed better than most Chinese key heritage attractions in being able to increase its carrying capacity, because of the attention it has received. In 1991, after China opened to domestic tourism, Lijiang attracted around 150 000 visitors (Yamamura, 2004). By 1995, it had jumped to around 700 000. After the airport, earthquake and WH inscription, they had jumped to 2.8 million in 2000 (Yang and Hou, 2002). The last figures available were for 2002 and numbers were still steadily rising at 3.1 million (Street, 2004). Overall, it shows an increase of a factor of twenty since it became a mass tourism destination.

Most visitors come from Yunnan, the region or elsewhere in China and are internal tourists. Travel for educational benefit is not their purpose, nor are they very experienced tourists on the whole. The main way they consume Lijiang is through photography, buying cheap souvenirs and attending the musical performances. The retail sector along the main streets answers this demand by selling music CDs and souvenirs common anywhere in China. More authentic handicrafts or deeper tourist experiences in the form of niche heritage tours are rare or poorly attended.

Figure 14.1 Shops selling traditional music CDs and other souvenirs to outsiders are now the most common on Lijiang Ancient Town's central streets

Conclusions

Lijiang is at the crossroads regarding the involvement of the local Naxi community in tourism and the involvement of the inhabitants of the town in local intangible heritage. The hardware has been well preserved, but the software still needs work to prevent the town becoming an open-air museum or theme park. More effort is needed to retain Lijiang ancient town's living culture and the Naxi community's connection to the site. This, unfortunately, is a common problem for WHS in many countries where tourism overwhelms everything else. Although, Lijiang has been open to tourism for a long time by China's standards, it is yet to reach its full potential as a mature heritage tourism area product and may start to decline when it does, if these social impacts of tourism are not addressed.

Notes

1 The Chinese character used for the word 'marketing' is often literally translated as 'propaganda'.
2 There are technically three towns included in the inscription: Dayan, Baisha and Shuhe. The latter two were satellite villages to Dayan market town that provided goods and services to the latter, but which also displayed many of the unique Naxi cultural features (du Cros, 2001).

References

China Daily (2004) Market can't rule heritage sites. www.chinadaily.com.cn/english/doc/2004-11/22/content_393530.htm (accessed 31 October 2005).

China Daily (2005) Photo on www.chinadaily.com/cn/english/doc/2005-03/30/content_429279.htm (accessed 31 october 2005).

Duang, S. (2000) A Report for UNESCO Cultural Heritage Management and Tourism Co-operation Example: Lijiang, China. Unpublished report to UNESCO.

du Cros, H. (2001) Socio-cultural analysis. *Yunnan Province Tourism Development Master Plan*. World Tourism Organisation, National Tourism Administration of the People's Republic of China and Yunnan Provincial Tourism Administration. Madrid: World Tourism Organisation.

Ebbe, K. and Hankey, D. (2000) *Case Study: Lijiang China Earthquake Reconstruction and Heritage Conservation*. Cultural Sustainable Development Series. An unpublished report by the East Asia and Pacific Urban Development Sector Unit of the World Bank.

McKann, C.F. (2001) The good, the bad and the ugly: observations and reflections on tourism development in Lijiang, China. In Tan, C.B., Cheung, C.H. and Yang, H. (eds) *Tourism, Anthropology and China*. Thailand, White Lotus Press, pp. 147–165.

McKercher, B. and du Cros, H. (2002) *Cultural Tourism: The Partnership between Tourism and Cultural Heritage Management*. Binghamton, New York: The Haworth Press.

Street, P. (2004) *A Tale of Two Towns*. Unpublished MA in Geography, Kings College, London.

Yamamura, T. (2004) Authenticity, ethnicity and social transformation at World Heritage Sites: Tourism, retailing and cultural change in Lijiang, China. In Hall, D. (ed.) *Tourism and Transition. Governance, Transformation and Development*. Oxford: CABI Publishing, pp. 185–200.

Yang, C.Y. and Hou, J. (2002) Remaking of a historical ethnic city: World Heritage Site in Lijiang as a contested space. Conference proceedings International Association for the Study of Traditional Environments, pp. 1–19. December 2002, Hong Kong.

Questions

1 What could be done to increase the amenity and convenience of Lijiang for local people?
2 What strategies could be devised to increase the local traders' capacity to compete with those from outside?
3 What incentives could be offered to feature more authentic handicrafts that would also appeal to internal tourists?

CHAPTER 15

Managing an urban World Heritage Site: the development of the Cultural Avenue project in Budapest

László Puczkó and Tamara Rátz

Aims

The aims of this case study are to:

- Discuss the challenges faced by World Heritage Site management in an urban environment
- Present an overview of the Cultural Avenue project as a management tool
- Analyse the conceptual issues and the practical difficulties in the development and the management of the project.

Introduction

The banks of the Danube and the Buda Castle Quarter in Budapest were inscribed on UNESCO's World Heritage List in 1987 under criteria C (ii) (iv). According to UNESCO's verdict, the area is one of the world's outstanding urban landscapes and illustrates the great periods in the history of the Hungarian capital. The World Heritage Site (WHS), which displays the continuity of history as an urban panorama, includes the House of Parliament, the bridges spanning the Danube, the Gellért Hill and the Buda Castle.

In 2002, the WHS was extended to Andrássy Avenue and the Millennium Underground. The extension area is a representative example of late 19th century social development and urban planning, and it reflects the latest technical achievements of the day. The buffer zone of the extension area includes the old Jewish quarter of Pest. Although the entire WHS is located in the densely populated inner core of Budapest, it also comprises a relatively sparsely inhabited region of downs. As the River Danube is also an integral part of the area, the predominantly architectural heritage is complemented by a protected landscape including the Gellért Hill and the cave system with a small dripstone cave beneath the Castle. Concerning the urban functions represented within the WHS area, the residential districts are complemented by public services, cultural and religious institutions, tourist attractions, leisure facilities and public parks.

In this case study, the discussion of the difficulties experienced in tourism and World Heritage administration is followed by the detailed assessment of the Cultural Avenue project, a complex interpretation and development tool that aims to enhance destination and visitor management in Budapest.

Tourism and World Heritage in Budapest

Both the Buda Castle Quarter and Andrássy Avenue have traditionally been the most visited districts of the city, due to their monuments and sights as well as their historic atmosphere. Practically all the international tourists to Budapest visit the key attractions of the World Heritage Site, but they are also very popular among Hungarian visitors to the capital. However, the Site's key success factor is its heritage value and its nationwide and international renown, and the concentration of visitors in the area is not directly related to its World Heritage status. Thus, the socially and politically welcomed World Heritage designation of the areas has not significantly altered visitation patterns or preferences within the city, although it may serve as a seal of approval for tourists' choice.

The role of tourism in the economy of Budapest and Hungary is generally recognized by decision-makers. The role played by architectural heritage and the built environment in influencing tourists' experiences and satisfaction is also understood. The preservation and the appropriate reuse of the Castle District and Andrássy Avenue have been a major consideration in all former and current tourism development strategies of Budapest, although very little has actually been done to realize strategic objectives. However, the World Heritage status presents an additional challenge in heritage management and conservation: the title may heighten tourists' expectations and at the same time increases the local community's associated responsibility (Rátz and Puczkó, 2003).

Although this World Heritage Site is the most visited urban destination in Hungary, the development of tourism services has been rather unsystematic in the past, and only moderate changes have been experienced to date. Compared to the more established tourism product offered by the Buda Castle Quarter, the development of Andrássy Avenue has been more spontaneous and also more dynamic following the World Heritage designation, resulting, unintentionally however, in new urban centres such as the cluster of cafés and restaurants in Liszt Ferenc Square or the theatreland (the so-called 'Pest Broadway Project') being created around Nagymező street.

The streetscape and the buildings of the Avenue have been essentially preserved in their original form since their construction at the end of the 19th century, and throughout history, most of the alterations made have respected the overall character of the place. Recently, however, the opening of the House of Terror, which commemorates the victims of Nazi and Communist terror, caused uproar in the city's heritage protection and architectural circles as its striking metal cornice is in sharp contrast with the elegant style of the surroundings.

In the case of Budapest, it is the ensemble of heritage buildings, the urban landscape and the historical-architectural development of the city that create a universal value; on their own, probably none of the buildings would deserve the World Heritage designation. Consequently, interpretation of the WHS should increase visitors' awareness of the inherent interrelationship of the site's components and create an understanding of the overall evolution of the site (Puczkó and Rátz, 2003). However, probably due to the highly complex and bureaucratic nature of urban planning and management in Budapest (described in this chapter), up to now the Cultural Avenue project is the first and only attempt of integrated WHS interpretation and management.

World Heritage management in Budapest

In order to be able to understand fully the complexity of World Heritage management in Budapest, it is necessary to provide a short overview of the protection of built heritage as well as the administrative system of the city. As this chapter indicates, decision-making concerning the WHS is generally time-consuming and rather bureaucratic, since it requires the agreement of a multitude of interrelated organizations with occasionally unclear division of labour as opposed to a single responsible body.

The local government system of Budapest is rather unique: it is based on a two-tier arrangement comprising the municipality of the City and those of the 23 districts. The City and the district governments are not subordinated to each other: the districts independently exercise the powers and rights granted to local governments within the framework of the Act on Local Governments. Although it is a fundamental principle of this dual system that the Municipality of Budapest shall perform the duties which concern the whole of the capital or more than one district, the complexity of decision-making and the uncertainty of authority on certain occasions have definitely hindered the joint management of the World Heritage area.

As a consequence, at the moment there is no accepted management plan for the entire World Heritage area of Budapest. The currently valid Protection of Cultural Heritage Act 2001 does not provide specific protection for the site either. Instead, individual monuments within the area are protected at three levels: (1) district level, (2) Budapest municipal level and (3) national level (including both territorial and individual protection).

Management of the World Heritage values is organized at the same levels as the legal protection, the result of which is a particularly complex decision-making and funding process. At national level, the main responsible bodies include the Ministry of National Cultural Heritage (NKÖM), the National Office of Cultural Heritage (KÖH), and the World Heritage Hungarian National Committee

(VOMNB). At city level, within the framework of the Municipal Government, relevant authorities include, among others, the Department for the Protection of Settlement Values, the Bureau of the Chief Architect or the Committee of City Planning and Cityscape Protection of the General Assembly of the Municipality. Moreover, to make the situation even more complicated at district level, the territory and the architectural values of the World Heritage area are managed by seven independent district municipalities. The capital's tourism authority, the Budapest Tourism Office (BTH) is responsible for marketing Budapest including the World Heritage area.

Within the WHS area, all types of property ownership are to be found: municipal as well as private property, in addition to state authority, government agencies and institutions, the church, and even international rules for foreign diplomatic representations. Public spaces within the territory of the World Heritage Site – such as roads, public transport networks, tunnels, parks – are controlled by the Budapest municipal government. District governments control certain former state-owned properties acquired in whole or in part. Buildings of mixed ownership where the resident community includes tenants, private owners and the local government are also typical in the area.

The effective management of heritage resources relies on the successful balance of conservation and visitor access. In the case of Budapest, however, the entire World Heritage Site is a densely populated urban area as well as a traditionally popular tourist destination with a metropolitan infrastructure, so the primary management challenge is to balance conservation and residential interests, including interests of inhabitants, district governments and investors. Although visitors' needs partly differ from those of the local community, the management of tourism within the World Heritage Site area is often a secondary consideration, as successful urban development is expected automatically to result in favourable visitation patterns.

At the moment, interpretation of the WHS is limited to the following tools:

- four signposts scattered throughout the city centre bearing the World Heritage logo and presenting a map of the area
- occasional city walks in the Buda Castle and along Andrássy Avenue run by an independent non-profit organization
- the Cultural Avenue initiative,

whereas tools and techniques extensively used at other sites include:

- arrows/signs directing visitors to the WHS (not only to individual buildings)
- plaques with a short description about the site at buildings which are major entry points

- special maps/brochures introducing the WHS
- official guided tours
- CD-ROMs or DVDs or other memorabilia about the WHS.

It is anticipated that the new Management Plan (due by the end of 2005) should introduce additional interpretation tools and might change the overall management approach of the Budapest WHS.

Initiation of the Cultural Avenue (CA) Project

The idea of creating a cultural route in Budapest occurred in 2000, as an outcome of a marketing plan prepared for the Museum of Fine

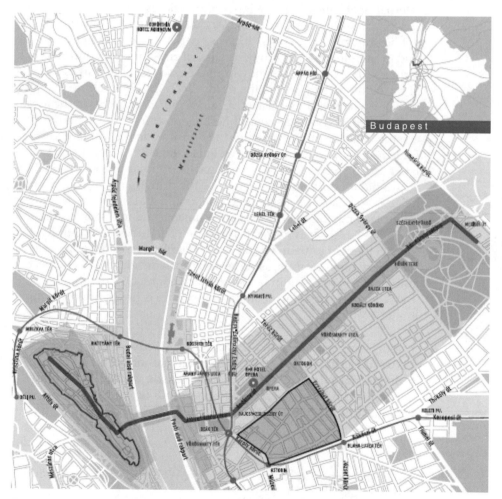

Figure 15.1 Territory of Cultural Avenue and WHS

Arts. Initially, the project was only partly related to World Heritage as the original WHS – the banks of the Danube and the Buda Castle Quarter in Budapest – was only extended to include Andrássy Avenue and the Millennium Underground in 2002, i.e. after the creation of the CA. Therefore the first versions of the brochures and the website did not carry the World Heritage logo.

Throughout the completion of the marketing plan, numerous discussions raised the problem of lack of creative initiatives in the cultural and heritage development and the marketing of Budapest. Based on international experiences, the creation of a themed route seemed to be a creative way to improve the cultural image of the city: themed itineraries are popular among visitors, they offer flexibility and efficiency in interpretation and visitor management, and their initial development requires moderate investment (Puczkó and Rátz, 2006; Rátz and Puczkó, 2002).

Looking at the topography of the city centre and locating all the main cultural and heritage attractions, the initial idea of the Cultural Avenue (CA) was born (Figure 15.1). The actual area of the WHS is indicated by shading.

It has to be noted, however, that during the development of the CA, the World Heritage status of the sites was not considered, for several reasons. First of all, at the time it was not yet certain if the proposed extension to the originally inscribed site would be accepted. Moreover, the CA was intended to incorporate contemporary as well as heritage sites and attractions along its stretch. Being a private initiative, the CA focused on the interpretation of the city rather than the interpretation of the World Heritage area. Eventually, however, the two fields have become closely linked, and the cooperation is to be accelerated as the recently accepted Tourism Development Strategy of Budapest declares the development of themed routes unquestionably important.

Unlike typical themed routes that focus on a common topic (such as the 'Renaissance Évora Historical Itinerary' in Portugal or the 'Berlin Stadt der Engel' route in Germany), the Cultural Avenue links attractions that are similar and different at the same time, their common characteristics being their location along a virtual axis of Budapest and their individual willingness to be represented in the project. In addition, similarity also lies in certain – subjectively measured – cultural and historic aspects, while differences are manifested in the variety of stops along the trail, e.g. museums, churches, cafés, historical buildings, theatres, and even a spa, that represent the history, culture and traditions of Budapest.

When selecting the stops of the CA, a wide and flexible understanding of culture, history and heritage was applied, from high culture (e.g. the Museum of Fine Arts) to common, popular or alternative culture (e.g. the Erzsébet Square Cultural Centre hosting bands and exhibitions). This approach concluded with 59 stops along the route, most of which form part of the WHS.

One of the key purposes of the route is to encourage visits to less popular or not too well-known areas, to divert traditional tourist flows and to provide an alternative itinerary. Almost all tourists visit the Castle District and Heroes' Square or the Great Synagogue, but only a very few are aware of the hidden treasures around these key attractions, e.g. the Museum of East Asia, the House of Photography or the former Jewish Ghetto. The intention of the CA project is to make tourists realize that the cultural and heritage assets of Budapest are too numerous and complex to discover in just one visit.

Implementation of the idea

The process of physical implementation started in 2002, with the help and financial support of the Cultural Tourism Department of the Ministry of National Cultural Heritage. Although every organization, site and institution approached during the preparation process supported the idea in principle, only a few contributed any useful information, such as a photo or a short description, so the project team had to compile most of the texts and photos on their own.

Selection criteria for the route's name included easy recognition and recall, international applicability and a consistency with the project's theme and position. The name 'Cultural Avenue' was selected from several options. The English and the French ('Avenue Culturel') names are literal translations; in German, however, the name is slightly different ('Allee der Kultur', i.e. Avenue/Boulevard of Culture).

Many alternatives were prepared for the logo and the visual design of the brochure. Of the various colour schemes an elegant dark red was selected, while the logo is somehow similar to an Ionic style pillar with a little arrow on the top (Figure 15.2).

The ideal brochure layout had to meet many functions, i.e. that of interpretation, information, map and souvenir. After evaluating many similar brochures from all around the world, a 14-page, single stapled, landscape layout was designed with a rear foldout map.

The route exists in two forms, in print (as a map/information leaflet) and on the Internet (www.sugarut.com). Themed signposts and plaques are to be developed along the way to help visitors identify stops.

Although themed routes are relatively easy to create, international experiences show that they quickly disappear without proper

Figure 15.2 The Cultural Avenue logo

preparation, planning and management, and most important of all, sound financial background. Routes with many stops are rarely managed by private organizations without the financial contribution of participant sites and institutions: thus, in this respect, the Cultural Avenue project is an exception.

Current situation of the project

Due to exceptional demand from visitors, the first set of 24 000 brochures ran out in a few months. Taking all requests and recommendations into consideration, a slightly modified design was created by the Spring of 2005. The following activities are planned for 2005:

- printing 130 000 copies of the redesigned brochure in three languages
- updating the website
- developing brochure stands to be placed by the entrance of members and partner hotels or catering establishments.

The total budget for 2005 is estimated at 28 000 euro. Following negotiations with the National Tourism Office and the Budapest Tourism

Office in order to identify possible ways of cooperation, and winning a tender issued by the Ministry of National Cultural Heritage, about two thirds of the budget was promised to be available by the end of February 2005.

From the very beginning, the project has been dependent on state and municipal support. During the three years of operation, no sound financial background could be established which is a major risk factor, and might be attributed to the following reasons:

- several members, especially state owned museums cannot afford any financial contribution
- commercial businesses that are in fact the main beneficiaries of the CA development show very limited willingness to become financially involved, despite the enormous publicity created by the project in printed media
- the district governments concerned either do not consider tourism development a priority or, due to the complex nature of the product and their own former experiences in a centralized system, expect to rely on state involvement and funding
- out of the 49 potential sponsors approached, only a major telecom company found the project and its target segments appealing enough to become financially involved by ordering a customized version of the brochure for their annual conference's attendees.

Conclusions

In the last few years, World Heritage management in Budapest has been rather fragmented, mostly spontaneous and often fuelled by civil initiatives. The area's metropolitan location offers both advantages and disadvantages in tourism development: on the one hand, the city's established infrastructure provides a higher carrying capacity in case of increased visitation. On the other hand, the large number of stakeholders makes it almost impossible to find an effective resource management approach that is able to satisfy all kinds of interests.

Destination marketing and destination interpretation are highly interrelated in a metropolitan environment, and the development of a comprehensive interpretation system is a particularly challenging task in the Budapest WHS, due to the Site's complexity in terms of ownership and management.

The Cultural Avenue project, which at least partially fills the gap created by the inactivity of officially responsible organizations in WHS interpretation, may lead to cooperation among the various stakeholders and may result in better coordinated World Heritage management. However, the success of the initiative depends on a sound financial background and on the active involvement of all beneficiaries.

References

Puczkó, L. and Rátz, T. (2003) Turizmus történelmi városokban. Tervezés és menedzsment. Budapest: Turisztikai Oktató és Kutató Kkt.

Puczkó, L. and Rátz, T. (2006) The Cultural Avenue of Budapest. In Richards, G. (ed.) *Cultural Tourism: Global and Local Perspectives*. Binghamton, New York: The Haworth Press.

Rátz, T. and Puczkó, L. (2002) Goethe, Humbert és Odüsszeusz avagy kulturális utak a turizmusban. Turizmus Bulletin 6 (3), 3–11.

Rátz, T. and Puczkó, L. (2003) A World Heritage Industry? Tourism at Hungarian World Heritage Sites. In Gravari-Barbas, M. and Guichard-Anguis, S. (eds) Regards Croisés sur le Patrimoine dans le Monde à l'Aube du XXIᵉ Siècle. Paris: Presses de l'Université de Paris-Sorbonne, pp. 467–481.

Questions

1 Identify the major stakeholder groups in the case study and compare their main interests.
2 How could a management plan incorporate all the contradictory interests in the most effective way?
3 What are the main threats for the further development of the Cultural Avenue project?

CHAPTER 16

Tourism development, empowerment and the Tibetan minority: Jiuzhaigou National Nature Reserve, China

Li, Fung Mei Sarah

Aims

The aims of this case study are to:

- Introduce the development of tourism in the Jiuzhaigou National Nature Reserve
- Examine the effects of tourism on the Tibetan minority residents of Jiuzhaigou Nature Reserve by utilizing the construct of empowerment as a framework for assessing how tourism has changed the economic, social and cultural environments of such communities.

Introduction

In the far north of Sichuan Province in China lies Jiuzhaigou Nature Reserve[1], a World Heritage Site (WHS) that is renowned not only for the biodiversity and geology of its mountains and valleys, calcareous lakes and glaciers, but for its rich cultural heritage based on nine ethnic Tibetan villages. Indeed, the very name Jiuzhaigou means 'Valley of nine stockaded villages'. Tibetan communities have inhabited the valleys of Jiuzhaigou for at least five hundred years and the small communities followed a traditional pastoral way of life isolated from mainstream Chinese politics and governance because of their inaccessibility and remoteness until 30 years ago. Livestock grazing – yaks, sheep, goats and horses – and some limited cropping of barley and vegetables were the major agricultural activities. In 1974 the valley first came to the attention of the Government when it was 'discovered' by state foresters.

The Reserve was opened up for tourism in 1984. As visitation increased, change gathered momentum and these hitherto very isolated communities were thrust into modernization and globalization to the point where the 1000 residents are now the object of the tourist gaze (Urry, 2002) of 1.3 million visitors each year. This case study examines the effects of tourism on the Tibetan minority residents of Jiuzhaigou Nature Reserve by utilizing the construct of empowerment as a framework for assessing how tourism has changed the economic, social and cultural environments of these communities. While Jiuzhaigou's WHS listing is based on its biodiversity values, the Tibetan communities constitute a strong attraction consistent with China's national policy of actively supporting ethnic minorities through cultural tourism (Sofield and Li, 1998a).

Jiuzhaigou: geographic location and background

Jiuzhaigou Nature Reserve is famous for 114 calcareous lakes separated by waterfalls which step down from a Y-shaped glacial valley, surrounded by thickly forested mountain slopes which rise to peaks in excess of 4000 m. This diverse environment is home to the giant panda, golden monkey, takin and more than 150 species of birds. The extraordinary scenic qualities of the area and its biodiversity resulted in the valley and surrounding mountains being gazetted as a National Nature Reserve in 1978, the borders of the park enclosing the nine Tibetan communities (Ze, 1994). The Nature Reserve was accorded World Heritage Site Listing in 1992. It was granted Global Biosphere Reserve status in 1997 under UNESCO's MAB (Man and Biosphere) Convention on significant sites for wildlife. The total area of the Reserve is 1320 km^2, or 65 000 hectares, of which only 50 km^2 of scenic area are open to the public. Access for tourists is limited to a sealed road which traverses the 114 lakes and follows them to the high alpine heads of the two valleys, and to several kilometres of boardwalk trails that circumnavigate several of the lakes and waterfalls.

The Reserve is located 400 km north of Chengdu, the capital city of Sichuan Province, in Nanping County, one of thirteen counties in the Aba Tibetan and Qiang Ethnic Minority Autonomous Prefecture. Nanping County has a population of 60 000, the great majority of whom are Tibetan (Ze, 1994). In the past five years the population living in proximity to the entrance of the Jiuzhaigou Nature Reserve/ national park has expanded from about 1000 to more than 10 000 as more than one hundred hotels with about 30 000 beds have been constructed. The nine stockaded Tibetan villages have a combined total of about 1000 people living in the park area permanently: 1007 persons were enumerated in June 2004 (Jiuzhaigou Management, personal communications).

As a component of the new nature reserve and biosphere status of the valley and surrounding mountains, in order to meet conservation and biodiversity objectives the Reserve Management gradually implemented a ban on all animal husbandry and cropping (there were small terrace holdings along the river flats and around the margins of the lakes). The Management saw grazing and farming as fundamentally inimical to conservation and in breach of the 1994 Chinese legislation for the establishment of nature reserves. The *Regulations of the People's Republic of China on Nature Reserves 1994.* Article 26 states: 'It is prohibited to carry out such activities as logging, grazing, hunting, fishing, gathering medicinal herbs, reclaiming, burning, mining, stone quarrying and sand dredging, etc.' (PRC, 1994). By 2002 all but a few ponies and yaks used for local transport had been removed from inside the park. With no economic rationale for remaining in isolated sites selected originally for their pastoral and agricultural advantages, three of the nine stockaded villages were quickly reduced to hamlets with only one or two resident families. The majority of people moved into the five communities located along the scenic routes in the park where tourism provides prospects for employment or other avenues of replacement income, and into one village located off the tourist route but relatively close to the Reserve's administrative headquarters.

In 1997, tourist visitation to the park jumped dramatically with the completion of the highway from Chengdu to Jiuzhaigou. Previously it had been less than 170 000 per annum but, in 1998, visitor numbers rose to 340 000; in 1999 to 630 000; and in 2000 to 830 000. Visitation reached one million in 2001, and increased to 1.3 million in 2002 before the sudden acute respiratory syndrome (SARS) epidemic reduced visitation to 1.1 million in 2003. The year 2004 (1.35 million visitors) was a record year with the opening of a new airfield just 40 km from the Reserve in September 2003: Boeing 737 and Airbus flights from Chengdu take 45 minutes to Nanping County, followed by a one hour drive from the airport to the Nature Reserve, drastically reducing the often dangerous 10–12 hour road journey from Chengdu. Domestic (Chinese) tourists account for 92–93 per cent of all visitation (Management Office, Jiuzhaigou Nature Reserve, personal communication, 2004).

Before progressing to a discussion of empowerment, a number of activities need to be considered in the context of economic change and the effects of tourism on the livelihoods of the Tibetan rural communities inside the park. These are listed in Table 16.1, and while the list is mainly economic, each change encompassed social and cultural impacts.

Table 16.1 Key tourism development in Jiuzhaigou Valley

Pre 1984	Tibetan communities were subsistence herders living in isolation from the monetized economy. Cash income was negligible.
Tourism	In 1984 Jiuzhaigou was opened up for tourism. Visitation grew from 60 000 in 1984 to more than 1.35 million in 2004. In 2004 entrance fees generated more than US$20 million.
Home-stays	To meet demand for accommodation, home-stays were encouraged by Management. As visitation exceeded home availability commercial lodges, often unsympathetic to traditional architecture, were built inside the villages by villagers. In 2002 Management banned home-stays because of pollution, uncontrolled construction in the villages, and social discord within the communities. Legislation gave each community member RMB 6000 annually as compensation for lost income.

(Continued)

Table 16.1 (*Continued*)

Transport	In March 1999, Management banned all private vehicles from entering the park (mainly tour buses) and set up a monopoly 'Green Bus Company' (using LPG as fuel) owned in a cooperative by the Tibetan communities. A fleet of 120 buses was purchased. Within four years the number of buses had expanded to 350, and gross turnover was more than US$12 million. In mid-year the Prefecture Government took over control of the bus company in order to disburse its earnings to impoverished communities outside the Park, and the Jiuzhaigou communities' shareholding was reduced to about 20%.
Restaurant/souvenir complex	As part compensation for the loss of the bus company, in 2003 a catering joint venture, with the communities and the Management as the holding company, was set up to provide all the catering needs inside the Reserve. A restaurant complex was constructed with seating for 5000 and each family from the villages was provided with a souvenir stall inside a central mall. This combined venture is estimated to provide the villagers with about two thirds of the income earned from the bus company.
Other ventures	With the ban on home-stays inside the villages some families invested in small accommodation units outside the Park in the new tourist township of Jiuzhaigou. Others invested in establishing cultural troupes, some with their own cultural centres, outside the Park.
Herding, cultivation banned	In 2001 all herds were removed from inside the Park, and all small terrace cropping banned, as both were considered inimical to sound environmental management. However, in 2005 Management was actively considering the reintroduction of a limited number of horses and yaks for tourist rides to a famous sacred Tibetan mountain within the Park's boundaries.

Empowerment

Of the many different ways in which the effect of tourism on the Tibetan ethnic minority of Jiuzhaigou could be examined, the concept of empowerment has been selected, since much of the tourism literature argues that without empowerment sustainable tourism development by communities is difficult to attain (D'Amore, 1983; Murphy, 1985; Butler, 1993; Sofield, 2003). Empowerment is a major component of the debate about community development and NGOs in particular have been strong advocates of the need to involve communities in meaningful ways in decisions about their futures. Because communities in many countries are left outside the decision-making process, policies and decisions are made *for* them not *by* them. One result is often an inability by governments, planners and developers to implement policy and/or to maintain the sustainability of an initiative because of community non-cooperation or even hostility.

Despite concerns about the need for community involvement in tourism planning, empowerment in any conceptual detail has often tended to remain outside considerations of tourism development. It has been more strongly explored in education literature concerning empowerment of students in an 'active learning' process; indigenous issues related to discrimination and justice where empowerment and acceptance of responsibilities is considered one way of breaking the cycle of recidivism; nursing science where the professional health worker/patient relationship has been subjected to very detailed scrutiny in terms of empowering nurses and patients; some aspects of sociology such as social exchange theory; gender studies; political science; and management practices.

In discussing empowerment, the relationship between politics and tourism must also be canvassed because politics, reduced to its fundamentals, is about power. Power is about who gets what, where, when, how and why and the politics of development are also about who gets what, where, when, how and why (Hall, 1994). The concept of empowerment applied in the analysis of the Jiuzhaigou ethnic minority situation is one advanced by Sofield (2003). It is an amalgamation of several different emphases, although two key components are the role of the state (government) without which legality of action and behavior may be challenged and sustainability of tourism developments difficult to achieve, and the decision-making model that moves beyond consultations to encompass application or implementation of decisions. Sofield's concept is derived in part also from the social exchange theory literature, especially power/dependence relations (Emerson, 1962, 1972; Blau, 1987; Molm, 1987, 1988; Ap, 1992). In this context, empowerment of communities, societal groups or organizations may be considered a strictly social phenomenon and Sofield's concept of empowerment may be considered an outcome of the social processes of social exchange where those processes result in a change of the power balance between the actors. It is particularly useful when considering the effect of tourism development on indigenous communities and has five main propositions:

i) that the exercise of traditional or legitimate empowerment by traditionally-oriented communities will of itself be an ineffectual mechanism for attempting sustainable tourism development;

ii) that such traditional empowerment must be transformed into legal empowerment if sustainable tourism development is to be achieved;

iii) that empowerment for such communities will usually require environmental or institutional change to allow a genuine re-allocation of power to ensure appropriate changes in the asymmetrical relationship of the community to the wider society;

iv) conversely, empowerment of indigenous communities cannot be 'taken' by the communities concerned drawing only upon their own traditional resources but will require support and sanction by the state, if it is to avoid being short-lived; and,

v) that without the element of empowerment tourism development at the level of community will have difficulty achieving sustainability (Sofield, 2003: 9).

The difference between legitimate and legal power in Sofield's framework needs to be explained. According to Weber (1978, cited in Sofield, 2003), legitimate power is exercised in traditional societies based on traditional forms of authority, such as a village headman or a priest. However, unless that traditional (legitimate) form of authority is supported by legislation, in a modern state it may have some attributes of moral power but it can always be challenged legally and is unlikely to be sustained in a court of law. Empowerment of ethnic minority communities, according to Sofield (2003) must have a legal underpinning if it is to lead to sustainable development.

Each of the five aspects of empowerment can be explored in the context of Jiuzhaigou.

Shortcomings of traditional or legitimate empowerment

In a centrally controlled economy such as China's, even in the present situation of a move towards market forces, the state still maintains a very strong degree of control if it wishes to exercise that authority.

In the case of the opening up of Jiuzhaigou as a national park, in order to meet the demand for accommodation the Management encouraged home-stay initiatives. As demand grew some Tibetan entrepreneurs established purpose-built accommodation units inside their village spaces and this expansion was sanctioned by their existing local traditional structures of authority. It was a classic case of demand-led supply. However, as numbers of visitors grew at an exponential rate, and as more and more structures were erected, which were 'unsympathetic' to traditional architectural design (visual pollution), traditional forms of waste disposal (especially human faecal waste and garbage with high plastics content) proved inadequate and began to result in pollution of the pristine lakes and waterways. And, as disputes within the communities over 'rights' to tourists arose – all non-traditional elements which their society was ill-equipped to handle – an external power intervened to protect the biodiversity and conservation values of the valley and restore community harmony. That external power was of course, the Reserve Management established under legislation and with the legal authority to override community actions and desires that it considered inimical to good management of the Reserve.

First of all the Reserve Management took control from the communities to reduce internal conflict. It established a central register for distributing guests to the various accommodation units around the villages. As pollution and environmental degradation increased, however, in 2002 it banned all home-stays and accommodation inside the park, enacting specific legislation for this purpose. Subsequently it demolished all non-traditional buildings in each village and began to landscape and beautify the villages according to a 'tourist benchmark' of what was considered desirable, including providing facilities for adequate parking of tour buses (previously very limited) utilizing the former terraces that had been used for cropping and animal husbandry. In other words, the home-stay industry established by the local people under exercise of legitimate power but outside a supporting legal mechanism was unsustainable. Local ownership of the land and private ownership of the buildings according to traditional Tibetan rural community social structures could not prevail against a legally sanctioned external agency.

In the same way, the traditional pursuits of the communities in terms of both pastoral activities and animal husbandry, activities which had sustained them for centuries, were barred and all domesticated animals (other than chickens) were removed from within the Reserve boundaries by the same external agency exercising its legal authority. Legislation was enacted which made it illegal to graze animals within the Park and traditional rights, exercised over centuries according to Tibetan custom, were erased. In short, the exercise of traditional or legitimate empowerment by traditionally-oriented communities was an ineffectual mechanism for sustaining traditional practices; but under a revision of the legislation some horses and yaks may be permitted inside the Park to provide a new touristic experience – transport to a new destination, a mountain that has been sacred to Tibetan Buddhists for centuries.

Traditional empowerment must be transformed into legal empowerment

With reference to the Reserve Management's intervention in home-stays inside the park, in the first instance its actions legitimized these activities. It established a central register and recognized the rights of each establishment to accommodate visitors. It coordinated each family's participation in this activity, collected the payments from guests and distributed monies according to the number of bed-nights each accommodation unit had provided. In other words it transformed 'legitimate empowerment' into 'legal empowerment' (Sofield's second proposition).

Subsequently, of course, the Reserve Management banned all overnight stays inside the park, again acting under specific legislation, which effectively disempowered the villagers from conducting hospitality operations in their own communities. However, this legislation did not disempower them completely, but recognized that they had certain rights and so a compensation factor was incorporated into the legislation. While the level of compensation bore no relationship to the loss of income in terms of past and future earnings, the compensation figure of RMB 6000 (US$750) per resident per annum on an indefinite basis is a small fortune compared with the annual pastoral income prior to advent of tourism. The wealth generated by home-stay tourism prior to the ban in 2002 was sufficient for a number of families to establish small guesthouses and hotels outside the Reserve so their involvement in the accommodation sector has continued.

The Reserve Management extended additional forms of power to the Jiuzhaigou Tibetan communities. Traffic conditions had become chaotic and so the Prefecture legislated to establish a monopoly bus service for all travel within the Park and awarded that monopoly to the Tibetan communities. The 1000 members of the Tibetan communities achieved a per capita gross income of US$11 000 while they owned the bus company. Poverty was effectively abolished, with the communities achieving economic independence through the bus company. In 2002 it was thus possible to state that empowerment had occurred through changes in the legal environment which allowed a genuine re-allocation of power, ensuring appropriate changes in the asymmetrical relationship of the communities to the wider society (Sofield's third proposition).

But, by late 2002, the situation had changed again. The Prefecture Government removed the monopoly rights over bus transport inside the Reserve from the Tibetan cooperative because it recognized the company's capacity to contribute to government programmes across the Prefecture as a whole (the 'old' CP policy of 'everybody eating rice from the same iron pot'). The Tibetan cooperative was disempowered and the associated lucrative income taken away, although individual community members were given limited shares in the new company run by the Government. Their earning capacity from the bus company operations was severely reduced.

Not surprisingly, this move created very significant dissension and tension between the communities and the Prefecture Government. In order to manage the widespread displeasure the Prefecture Government, through the Reserve Management, decided to establish a monopoly restaurant complex able to cater to 5000 visitors per day inside the Park, and invited the Tibetan community members to take up shares. Some 98 per cent of adults took up the offer, and they are now in a joint venture with the Reserve Management. Once again they have the capacity to exert some control over their lives and maintain economic independence – one could say they have been re-empowered.

In addition to providing a range of restaurant facilities, the 200 souvenir outlets installed in the central hall, one for each family, has largely centralized the existing outlets in the villages. While the restaurant complex has almost unanimous support and the socio-psychological benefits of *communitas* are welcomed, there is opposition to the idea of closing down souvenir outlets in the villages, and a number of vendors also like to sell their wares direct to visitors at different sites around the Reserve (e.g. at the 'end-of-the-line' lookout and bus park at Long Lake) where there is less competition. There are 'traditional costume' photo opportunities also dotted around the Reserve at designated places approved by the Management. These forms of small entrepreneurship are not only tolerated by the governing authorities but are supported by regulatory mechanisms of the government in contrast to hawking in many other parks in China; and this support emphasizes the point that sustainability is more likely to be achieved when legitimate power is backed up by legal power. However, a cautionary note is merited, for when communities attempt to empower themselves by direct action unsupported by a legal instrument, it raises a question over how long such activities will continue.

In this dynamic 'swings-and-roundabouts' environment it is apparent that empowerment of and for the Tibetan minority communities inside Jiuzhaigou is not a definitive concept pursued by the government authorities, and that its legal powers take precedence over legitimate power. Empowerment in its different forms has often been overtaken by a form of disempowerment before re-empowerment.

Nevertheless, there has been a change in the socio-legal environment of the communities with the advent of tourism and the gazettal of the valley as a national nature reserve in which the government has recognized, legally, the rights of the communities to share in the economic benefits generated by tourism. While the Government has removed some traditional rights (e.g. grazing and farming), it has replaced them with a range of other activities which, in fact, have provided the communities with far higher incomes than their previous subsistence. And it is not only communities that have been empowered to some extent. Individuals have also been empowered through the range of employment opportunities for which they have been accorded preference, and through the associated training and educational opportunities which have accompanied those jobs.

In socio-cultural terms, tourism on balance has empowered the Tibetan communities in the sense that it has been a contributing factor in reinforcing rather than destroying their cultural identity, even if some forms of tradition and culture have undergone significant transformation. Aspects of Tibetan culture, such as those relating to religion and place (holy sites, for example), appear to have been little affected. However, much more work needs to be carried out before any definitive comment could be made about longer-term effects of tourism on the value system and cultural mores of the Tibetan communities inside Jiuzhaigou.

Conclusions

The constant changes in community involvement in a range of tourism activities in Jiuzhaigou emphasize the necessity of adopting a longitudinal approach and the benefits of historical methodology in analysing the situation, rather than the 'snapshot' approach based on a single field trip that is common to much tourism research (Sofield and Li, 1998b). The Tibetan village home-stay business constitutes a case in point. A field trip to Jiuzhaigou in early 2000 concluded that it was an excellent example of empowerment. Another field trip in mid-2000 concluded that the 'Green Bus Cooperative' was also an excellent example of community empowerment, although the ban on home-stays was seen as disempowerment (Sofield et al., 2004). But two years later, the situation changed again and it seemed that the communities had been disempowered through the take-over of the monopoly bus service. However, a field trip in 2004 suggested that the restaurant joint venture could be viewed as an example of re-empowerment. A 'snap-shot analysis' at these three points of time showed very different pictures of community involvement in tourism development and a longitudinal perspective is needed to see the processes at work.

In examining the issue of empowerment and sustainability, particularly in the context of poverty alleviation, Jiuzhaigou provides an example of how mass tourism and the economies of scale that accompany such tourism, can be harnessed. This is in marked contrast to most of the pro-poor tourism literature which has an emphasis on small scale community based tourism that has limited visitation, often advocated as essential in order to protect and conserve both the biophysical environment and the socio-cultural environment. However, in the case of Jiuzhaigou, it is the very large scale of visitation that has provided the economic 'muscle' to underwrite the various developments that have not disenfranchised or marginalized the Tibetan communities but placed them centre stage. One may draw the conclusion that 'touristic space' has been incorporated into the social space of the Tibetan ethnic communities of Jiuzhaigou. The village communities have not been pushed to the periphery and excluded from the monetary and other benefits of tourism to the park. The sustainability of the village communities inside the park, both as economic and socio-cultural entities, seems assured, even if some of the traditions and customs have changed significantly. In the final analysis, their fundamental identity remains unchallenged: they are the Tibetans of Jiuzhaigou.

Notes

1 In China, the highest order of protected areas is 'nature reserve' which is equivalent to national park status in the Western world; so in this chapter the terms 'nature reserve' and 'national park' are used interchangeably, and Reserve Management/Park Management are interchangeable, too.

References

Ap, J. (1992) Residents' perceptions on tourism impacts. *Annals of Tourism Research*, 19, 655–690.

Blau, P. (1987) Microprocess and macrostructure. In Cook, K. (ed.) *Social Exchange Theory*. London: Sage Publications, pp. 83–100.

Butler, R.W. (1993) Tourism: an evolutionary perspective. In Nelson, G.R., Butler, R.W. and Wall, G. (eds) *Tourism and Sustainable Development: Monitoring, Planning, Management*. Waterloo: University of Waterloo Press, pp. 27–43.

D'Amore, L. (1983) Guidelines to planning in harmony with the host community. In Murphy, P. (ed.) *Tourism in Canada: Selected Issues*. Ottawa: Western Geographical Series 21, pp. 135–157.

Emerson, R. (1962) Power-dependence relations. *American Sociological Review*, 27 (1), 31–34.

Emerson, R. (1972) Exchange theory. In Berger, J., Zelditch, M. and Anderson, B. (eds) *Sociological Theories in Progress*. New York: Houghton-Mifflin, pp. 32–60.

Hall, C.M. (1994) *Tourism and Politics: Policy, Power and Place*. London: Bellhaven Press.

Molm, L.D. (1987) Linking power structure and power use. In Cook, K.S. (ed.) *Social Exchange Theory*. Newbury Park: Sage Publications, pp. 101–129.

Molm, L.D. (1988) The structure and use of power: a comparison of reward and punishment power. *Social Psychology Quarterly*, 51, 108–122.

Murphy, P. (1985) *Tourism: A Community Approach*. New York: Methuen.

PRC (1994) *Regulations of the People's Republic of China on Nature Reserves 1994*. Beijing: Information Office.

Sofield, T.H.B. (2003) *Empowerment for Sustainable Tourism Development*. London: Elsevier Science and Pergamon.

Sofield, T. and Li, F.M.S. (1998a) Tourism development and cultural policies in China. *Annals of Tourism Research*, 25 (2), 362–392.

Sofield, T.H.B. and Li, F.M.S. (1998b) Historical methodology and sustainability: an 800-year-old festival from China. *Journal of Sustainable Tourism*, 6 (4), 267–292.

Sofield, T.H.B., De Lacy, T., Lipman, G. and Daugherty, S. (2004) *Sustainable Tourism – Eliminating Poverty (ST–EP). An Overview*. Brisbane: CRC for Sustainable Tourism.

Urry, J. (2002) *The Tourist Gaze: Leisure and Travel in Contemporary Society*. London: Sage.

Weber, M. (1946, 1978) *The Theory of Social and Economic Organisation*. New York: The Free Press. Reprinted 1978.

Ze, Reh Zhu (1994) *China Jiuzhaigou Valley*. Beijing: Jiuzhaigou Administration & China Travel and Tourism Press.

Questions

1 What are the major effects of tourism on the livelihoods of the Tibetan communities inside the Jiuzhaigou Nature Reserve?

2 Explain the difference between legitimate power and legal power.

3 In your view have the Tibetan communities of Jiuzhaigou been empowered or disempowered as this WHS has been developed for mass tourism?

CHAPTER 17

World Heritage Sites in the Americas

Dallen J. Timothy and
Stephen W. Boyd

Aims

The aims of this case study are to:

- Examine the growth and distribution of World Heritage Sites in the Americas
- Describe the opportunities for World Heritage Sites in the Americas
- Describe the challenges facing World Heritage Sites in the Americas.

Introduction

Many of the world's most spectacular cultural relics and natural sites are found in the Americas, and most countries of the region are actively involved in promoting the cause of UNESCO and the World Heritage List. Many World Heritage Sites (WHS) in the Americas have gained international acclaim (e.g. Machu Picchu, Peru; Chitzen Itza, Mexico; Grand Canyon, USA) and have been a major focus of media images and national icons utilized in tourism promotional efforts and nation-building (Barnard, 1993; Kluger, 2003).

This case study aims to examine World Heritage Sites in the Americas with a focus on opportunities and challenges. For the purposes of this chapter, the Americas include North, Central and South America, as well as the islands of the Caribbean.

World Heritage Sites in the Americas

Like most parts of the world, the cultural heritage of the Americas can be roughly divided into the pre-colonial and colonial/post-colonial periods. In most of Latin and North America ancient heritage attractions reflect a pre-colonial phase of growth and development among various indigenous peoples (Lumsdon and Swift, 2001). This includes the ancient cities and temple complexes associated with the Aztecs in central Mexico, the Mayans in southern Mexico and Central America, as well as remnants of the great Incan empires of South America. There is an equally vibrant and pervasive built heritage associated with the colonial period, beginning in the 16th century until today. Most cities of Latin America are home to Spanish, Portuguese or French colonial forts, government buildings, missions, churches, plantations/haciendas, and residences which, together with the ancient structures, have become an important part of each country's cultural heritage resources.

Table 17.1 Numbers of WHS in the Americas (2005)

Country	Cultural	Natural	Mixed
Argentina	4	4	0
Belize	0	1	0
Bolivia	5	1	0
Brazil	10	7	0
Canada	5	8	0
Chile	3	0	0
Colombia	4	1	0
Costa Rica	3	0	0
Cuba	5	2	0
Dominica	0	1	0
Dominican Rep.	1	0	0
Ecuador	2	2	0
El Salvador	1	0	0
Guatemala	2	0	1
Haiti	1	0	0
Honduras	1	1	0
Mexico	22	2	0
Nicaragua	1	0	0
Panama	2	2	0
Paraguay	1	0	0
Peru	6	2	2
St Kitts & Nevis	1	0	0
St Lucia	0	1	0
Suriname	1	1	0
USA	8	12	0
Uruguay	1	0	0
Venezuela	2	1	0
Total	92	49	3

Source: UNESCO, 2005

Table 17.1 lists the countries of the Americas that have properties inscribed on the World Heritage List. From the 144 inscribed sites in the Americas, some interesting patterns can be noted. For example, there is a notable lack of WHS in the Caribbean region. Only 12 have been designated UNESCO sites in six different countries. This is a result of several factors, including a lack of indigenous culture and archaeological heritage. Few, if any, remnants of indigenous landscapes exist today, although there is a strongly cultural landscape based on Spanish, French, British and Dutch colonialism. Another factor is the small sizes of the Caribbean states, which limits the physical extent of cultural and natural resources that might be suitable as

World Heritage Sites. Likewise, many of the Caribbean islands are still European colonies and are therefore powerless to ratify the World Heritage Convention and nominate properties they might otherwise consider worthy of designation.

Another interesting pattern is the proliferation of sites in Mexico. Mexico is very serious about achieving WHS recognition and has devoted a great deal of effort in recent years to assure that its ancient and colonial locations are fit for WHS listing. There are on-going efforts to inscribe additional properties as well. Most of the country's efforts focus on pre-Hispanic cities and archaeological areas. Mexico is a large country and houses a great diversity of cultures and ecosystems that provide rich opportunities for UNESCO inscription.

All countries of Central and South America, with the exception of Guyana and French Guiana, have at least one site inscribed on the List. This is quite remarkable given the political and physical constraints that exist in many of these countries (e.g. war and other forms of political instability). These sites also represent a mix of natural and cultural areas, while the cultural sites are a blend of pre-European and colonial built heritage.

Opportunities

Several opportunities can be noted as resulting from the designation of WHS in the Americas, although owing to space constraints only a few of the main ones will be discussed here. Perhaps the most notable is the growth in cross-border cooperation, wherein national governments work together across political boundaries to plan, conserve, and operate parks and cultural areas that lie adjacent to, or across, international boundaries. Cross-border collaborative efforts require each partner country to loosen its absolute control and work together for the greater good of the entire cultural area or ecosystem. While there are some drawbacks to cross-border cooperation (e.g. differing conservation laws, varying levels of development, and policy dissimilarities), there are many benefits as well, including the upholding of the principles of sustainability (e.g. harmony, balance, and holism), achieving efficiency in infrastructure development, and saving funds through joint promotional efforts (Boyd and Timothy, 2001; Timothy, 2001). Several examples of successful cross-border cooperation in WHS exist throughout the Americas, including Waterton-Glacier International Peace Park on the USA–Canada border, Wrangell-St Elias and Glacier Bay also on the USA–Canada border, Iguazu Falls (Brazil–Argentina), and La Amistad Reserves and National Park (Costa Rica–Panama) (Timothy, 2000).

While funding for WHS is extremely limited by UNESCO's meagre budget, some sites have been successful in tapping national government and private resources for restoration and conservation, justifying their needs by using the UNESCO label. This is primarily the case in Mexico and other Latin American countries, but even in the USA it happened when the Reagan administration used the WHS designation of the Statue of Liberty to attract private-sector funding to pay for its restoration in the 1980s (Williams, 2004). The World Heritage designation also has a history of being able to bring interested stakeholders together to plan at local and regional levels and to bring about site protection and management (Williams, 2004).

WHS designation in the Americas has also resulted in a limited number of cases where indigenous peoples have been actively involved in site conservation and designation. The Taos Native Americans in New Mexico, for example, are heavily involved in operating their pueblo as a WHS and tourism destination. Others, such as the Mayans in southern Mexico, have received opportunities to work in the tourism industry generated by the existence of WHS, although their input into conservation and interpretation is limited (Evans, 2004). The inscription of cultural and natural sites throughout Central and South America has often resulted in increased employment and tourism-related training among destination residents and indigenous peoples (McGrath, 2004), although active participation in development decision-making (i.e. empowerment) is still very limited.

Challenges in the Americas

While many WHS have been developed throughout the Americas, and though there is considerable potential for listing even more, the region faces many significant challenges to the success of WHS listing. Most of these challenges are similar to those in many other developing parts of the world and will be discussed below. However, even in the context of the USA, one of the wealthiest and most developed countries, there are significant complications associated with WHS designation and management.

Human impacts

Human threats to WHS in the Americas are manifest in a variety of ways. First, in the developing countries, it is not uncommon for families and, indeed, entire villages to locate within, or adjacent to, natural and cultural sites of heritage importance. In most cases, this involves people living within nature preserves, or existing archaeological structures, or utilizing stones and other artefacts as building materials for additional homes and shelters. It is estimated that nearly 75000 people live in Natural World Heritage Sites in the Americas, with some 61849 of these being in the developing countries of the region (Thorsell and

Sigaty, 2001). In order to be designated a WHS, such situations are typically remedied by forcefully displacing people and using other means to correct the problems created by generations of use of historic artefacts. Similar issues face WHS that are integral parts of extant urban areas, such as the Historic Center of Salvador de Bahia (Brazil), City of Quito (Ecuador), and the city of Cuzco (Peru) (Barnard, 1993).

Second, and perhaps the most common, is overuse by visitors of various sorts. Every year, thousands of curious tourists climb on, or in some other way interact with, the relics of ancient empires throughout Central and South America, as well as the ruins of Native Americans and Canadians. A particular group that has raised significant controversy in recent years is spiritual-oriented tourists (e.g. New Agers), who travel to ancient WHS throughout the Americas to worship at locations they venerate as important sacred places (Timothy and Conover, 2006). In most developing countries, including those in the Americas, there is a serious lack of enforcement of laws, rules and regulations pertaining to visitor use.

The third human threat in the developing countries of Central and South America is urbanization. This form of encroachment is prevalent where cities are experiencing high growth in unofficial settlements on their peripheries, as well as the development of planned suburbs and new neighbourhoods where construction is heavy, roads are constructed through or near cultural sites, factories are built, producing high levels of toxic waste, and power lines and energy stations are erected to service new growth areas. Likewise, in smaller communities, growing prosperity puts pressure on traditional building styles and many places are beginning to experience a lack of uniform building codes. Many WHS in South America have acknowledged these problems in their management plans, although little is being done to alter the situation.

Encroaching agricultural land use is another problem in many parts of South America, where recent closures of mines have led to more people attempting to earn a living from farming (Thorsell and Sigaty, 2001). In several countries, including Brazil, for example, forest clearcutting for cattle ranching affects both natural and cultural UNESCO sites and comes dangerously close to parkland and preserve boundaries. The intensification of agriculture has also led to an increase in the use of fertilizers that drain into nature preserves, upsetting natural balances in vegetation growth and wildlife. Much of the forest clearing in Central and South America is of dubious legality, but law enforcement typically turns a blind eye to the problem.

Economic woes

In common with less-developed countries everywhere, perhaps the most endemic problem in the poorer countries of the Americas is a lack of financial ability to conserve WHS. With the exception of Canada and the USA, the countries of Latin America and the Caribbean are economically challenged and have little money to devote to heritage conservation and management. In most countries, few funds are available to sustain effective conservation and to offset the effects of weather, vandalism, and wear and tear. In most of the developing world, the conservation and interpretation of sites of historic importance is seen as a luxury that cannot be afforded in the face of illiteracy, declining health care, and food shortages (Timothy and Boyd, 2003). The colonial heritage of Old Havana (Cuba), for example, which was listed in 1982, faces many difficulties in withstanding the deteriorating effects of human use and climate, particularly in light of a lack of funds available from the Cuban government (Lumsdon and Swift, 2001; Losego, 2003).

Lack of political will

A lack of political will is perhaps the most vivid problem facing WHS throughout the Americas, both in developed and developing countries. The most lucid example of this is a lack of legislation and law enforcement – a problem endemic throughout the region. However, one of the best examples of a lack of political will has been the USA. Since UNESCO's founding in 1945, the USA has had erratic relations with the organization. The USA played a vital role in the founding of UNESCO; Americans were among the first members of the agency's governing board, the USA was a founding member, and an American wrote the preamble to its 1945 constitution. Nonetheless, the USA withdrew from UNESCO in 1984 as a result of clashes between US foreign policy and UNESCO goals. In October 2003, however, the country rejoined the organization under pressure from President Bush to affirm the USA's conviction to uphold and promote human rights, tolerance and worldwide education.

Natural wear and tear

Natural wear and tear is common to all WHS wherever they might be. However, in the context of the Americas, several serious threats occur on a regular basis. First among these is the annual occurrence of hurricanes throughout the Caribbean Basin and along the coast of Central America. Nearly every year, WHS such as the Barrier Reef Reserve System (Belize), the Colonial City of Santo Domingo (Dominican Republic), National History Park-Citadel, Sans Souci (Haiti), and the Rio Plátano Biosphere Reserve and Copan Maya Site

(Honduras) are bombarded by hurricane winds and debris. Some years this occurs several times. Flooding and landslides are another major concern, particularly at several sites in South America in areas where excessive tree felling and other changes to the vegetation have occurred in massive quantities. There are also a number of WHS in areas of high seismic and volcanic activity, which severely affect the sites, including flooding. In some remote locations (e.g. Ninstints WHS, Canada) weathering plays a significant role in site deterioration (Shackley, 1998).

The unique USA situation

Connected to the issue of political will, the USA provides an interesting example of a unique set of constraints that are different from those of the other countries of the region. Throughout the Americas, having a UNESCO WHS designation is an important achievement, as it signifies a certain status and brings about international recognition. It also often justifies budgetary requests for maintenance and infrastructure development at the national level. Perhaps the only exception to this general trend is the USA, where UNESCO designation is generally disregarded and often not well understood by the public or even by WHS management and personnel.

As Williams (2004: 412) notes, the majority of visitors to US national parks with WHS designation are completely unaware that they are visiting a World Heritage Site. Few, if any, of the USA's WHS are marked in any way or designated otherwise as UNESCO sites, and the general public is unaware of the meaning, aims and directives of the organization. Likewise, there is a dearth of knowledge among staff members as well. Williams (2004) found that park rangers at two WHS in the USA were ignorant of the WHS designation. According to observations by one of the authors of this case study, while at Independence Hall in Philadelphia in 1997, it became painfully obvious that staff were equally unaware. When asked if there was any kind of monument or marking indicating the WHS status of the site, the warden's response was 'What's a World Heritage Site?' After hearing an explanation, he responded again 'We're one of those?'

The lack of awareness likely comes from a lack of training that deals specifically with the tenets of the World Heritage Convention. The US ignorance about UNESCO WHS is reinforced by an anti-UN sentiment that pervades politics and many NGOs in the USA, as well as the growth of the American Land Sovereignty Protection Act, which was passed by Congress to protect land sovereignty in the USA and resulted in some hostility toward UNESCO. This institutional ignorance 'leads to reduced publicity which, in turn, perpetuates more ignorance' (Williams, 2004: 415).

Whereas WHS designation is of grave importance to other countries in the region, including Canada, the USA has not utilized this status to promote World Heritage the way other countries have done (Wilkinson, 1996, cited in Williams, 2004), either for public awareness or for tourism purposes. Williams (2004) suggests that this might be in part a result of the USA's mistaken fears that the World Heritage Convention is in some way an infringement on US sovereignty and private land rights. There is a common concern that the United Nations, through UNESCO, will exert an external influence over US monuments and parks. This lack of understanding and use of the UNESCO designation as a promotional tool may in fact influence the growth of tourism at many US properties. In their examination of World Heritage Sites in OECD countries, Hall and Piggin (2001) found that the overall effect of Canada's WHS designations on tourism was a positive one. In other words, with Canada's focus on WHS status in its public awareness campaigns and information dissemination, WHS designation resulted in additional tourist appeal for its heritage sites. In the USA, however, relatively few sites have experienced tourism growth that may be attributed to WHS designation. Instead, designation has resulted in neutral (and sometimes negative) overall effects on tourism in the USA. In the case of Mexico, WHS listing has overall resulted in a neutral or positive effect on visitation.

Conclusions

It is clear from this brief overview of the Americas that there are notable patterns throughout the region and different views and values placed on WHS status. In most of the Americas, with the exception of the USA, WHS status is an important achievement and one that all countries aspire to. Because the region is comprised primarily of developing countries, there is a wide range of opportunities and obstacles in the development and designation of UNESCO sites. This case study has described only a few of the major ones. Opportunities created from the designation of WHS include cross-border cooperation, increased participation by local residents in the benefits of tourism, and some (limited) funding. There are also a number of constraints, including human impacts, economic problems, lack of political will, and natural wear and tear which, although they exist in most parts of the world, have unique manifestations in the countries of the Caribbean and North, Central and South America.

References

Barnard, C. (1993) Machu Picchu: city in the sky. *National Geographic Traveler*, 10 (1), 106–113.

Boyd, S.W. and Timothy, D.J. (2001) Developing partnerships: tools for interpretation and management of World Heritage Sites. *Tourism Recreation Research*, 26 (1), 47–53.

Evans, G. (2004) Mundo Maya: from Cancún to city of culture. World heritage in post-colonial Mesoamerica. *Current Issues in Tourism*, 7 (4/5), 315–329.

Hall, C.M. and Piggin, R. (2001) Tourism and World Heritage in OECD countries. *Tourism Recreation Research*, 26 (1), 103–105.

Kluger, J. (2003) Spiritual retreat. *Time*, 24 February, 46–47.

Losego, S.V. (2003) Altstadtsanierung und Tourismus in La Habana: Vermarktung eines Stücks kulturellen Erbes. *Tourismus Journal*, 7 (2), 251–269.

Lumsdon, L. and Swift, J. (2001) *Tourism in Latin America*. London: Continuum.

McGrath, G. (2004) Including the outsiders: the contribution of guides to integrated heritage tourism management in Cusco, Southern Peru. *Current Issues in Tourism*, 7 (4/5), 426–432.

Shackley, M. (1998) Ninstints (Canada). In Shackley, M. (ed.) *Visitor Management: Case Studies from World Heritage Sites*. Oxford: Butterworth-Heinemann, pp. 182–193.

Thorsell, J. and Sigaty, T. (2001) Human use in World Heritage natural sites: a global inventory. *Tourism Recreation Research*, 26 (1), 85–101.

Timothy, D.J. (2000) Tourism and international parks. In Butler, R.W. and Boyd, S.W. (eds) *Tourism and National Parks: Issues and Implications*. Chichester: John Wiley & Sons, pp. 263–282.

Timothy, D.J. (2001) *Tourism and Political Boundaries*. London: Routledge.

Timothy, D.J. and Boyd, S.W. (2003) *Heritage Tourism*. Harlow: Prentice Hall.

Timothy, D.J. and Conover, P.J. (2006) Nature, religion, self spirituality and New Age tourism. In Timothy, D.J. and Olsen, D.H. (eds) *Tourism, Religion and Spiritual Journeys*. London: Routledge, pp. 139–155.

UNESCO (2005) Properties inscribed on the World Heritage List (whc.unesco.org)

Wilkinson, T. (1996) Global warning – the designation of Yellowstone: one of the first World Heritage sites. *National Parks*, 70 (3/4), 34–40.

Williams, K. (2004) The meanings and effectiveness of world heritage designation in the USA. *Current Issues in Tourism*, 7 (4/5), 412–416.

Questions

1 How is the USA different from other countries in the Americas when it comes to World Heritage Sites?
2 What are some of the main problems facing WHS in the developing countries of the Caribbean and Latin America?
3 What types of opportunities are created in the Americas from the inscription of WHS?

CHAPTER 18

World Heritage Listing: the case of Huangshan (Yellow Mountain), China

Li, Fung Mei Sarah and Trevor H.B. Sofield

There is no mountain as beautiful as Mt Huangshan,
No other mountain under heaven do I want to see after visiting Mt Huangshan

(Xiu Xiake, Ming dynasty geographer, 1586–1641)

Aims

The aims of this case study are to:

- Utilize the Chinese World Heritage Site (WHS) of Huangshan to scrutinize the (western) paradigms that govern WHS assessments
- Outline a Chinese world view which sees cultural and natural heritage as a single unitary construct in contrast to the differentiation espoused by a western, positivist, scientific approach to WHS inscription
- Explore the tension and dissonance generated by this world view as it affects the management of the Huangshan WHS
- Therefore reflect on the prescriptive authority of western paradigms that perhaps pays insufficient attention to culturally determined values of 'Others' (Said's Orientalism versus Westernism).

Introduction

In the south of Anhui Province lies a small mountain range that has been extolled by Chinese poets, essayists and artists for more than 2000 years. For Chinese, whether they reside in China itself or are part of the Chinese global Diaspora, its fame is perhaps greater than that of any other range. This is Huangshan or Yellow Mountain, named after the mythical/historical Huang-di, Yellow Emperor, who ruled a small kingdom about 5000 years ago. He is credited with being extremely wise, and giving the Chinese their distinctive title, the Yellow Race. According to legend he practised alchemy and produced an elixir for immortality from a purple fungus growing in Huangshan which he imbibed before ascending into heaven on a dragon.

More than 20000 poems and 200 essays have been written about Huangshan over the centuries, many of them incorporated into Chinese 'common knowledge' and known to Chinese all over the world. Ancient – and new – calligraphy adorns many rocks and cliff faces (calligraphy is more than 'writing': it is a high art form and it is believed that 'the inner man' is revealed in the way one composes calligraphy). Hundreds of paintings have also been created, and they capture for Chinese the quintessential mountain landscape – sharp peaks, deep gorges, swiftly flowing streams and waterfalls and contorted pines clinging to precipitous cliffs, with a pagoda or temple sited in the landscape accordingly to *feng shui* principles. By the Yuan Dynasty (1271–1368 AD) 64 temples and many pavilions had been constructed around the 72 peaks of this 154 km² area. More were subsequently built, e.g. Fahai Meditation Temple and Wenshu Temple in the 17th century, connected by steps cut into the mountain (PRC, 1989). Although only 20 temples now survive they form a focal point for many Chinese visitors to Huangshan.

The mountain range, isolated from other ranges by surrounding plains, encompasses several distinctive ecological niches and is rich in biodiversity with 1450 native plant species, 28 significant endemic plants, and 300 vertebrates (PRC, 1989). It is not surprising then, to find that Huangshan was accorded WHS listing based on its out-standing natural and scenic qualities as well as its cultural features. What is perhaps surprising is that in its assessment of the Chinese Government's nomination, the IUCN (International Union for the Conservation of Nature, 1990: 11) declared that Huangshan's natural values 'are predominant over its cultural heritage'; and ICOMOS (International Council on Monuments and Sites, 1990) originally deferred its recommendation for cultural heritage listing citing lack of supporting evidence. The IUCN (1990: 12) also recommended that the Chinese authorities 'should be encouraged to reduce the human influence on the mountain', a startling comment to these two authors given that the mountain has for more than 2000 years been a very rich cultural site and exemplifies the Chinese world view of 'man and nature' as a single unitary construct (this phrase accurately reflects Mandarin usage and should not be interpreted as unthinking sexist language on the part of the authors). The division between cul-tural and natural heritage is a characteristic of a western, positivist, scientific approach – reinforced by UNESCO's classification system for WHS listing – in contrast to a more holistic Chinese world view, and an examination of this binary classification system constitutes the focus of this chapter.

The cultural heritage/natural heritage divide

The Chinese world view is both anthropocentric (humans first) and anthropomorphic (attributing human characteristics to non-human features, animals, plants, etc). The Chinese word for 'nature' – *da-jiran* – may be translated literally as 'everything coming into being' and expresses the entirety of mountains, rivers, plants, animals, humans, all bound up in their five elements – metals, wood, water, fire and earth (Tellenbach and Kimura, 1989). 'Man is based on earth, earth is based on heaven, heaven is based on the Way (*Tao*) and the Way is based on *da-jiran* (nature): all modalities of being are organ-ically connected' (Tu, 1989: 67). Under Confucian values, scholars and mandarins were exhorted 'to seek ultimate wisdom in Nature' (Overmyer, 1986). Confucian thought and Daoist philosophy encom-passed the need for man and nature to bring opposing forces into a symbiotic relationship where 'harmony' rather than 'difference' or 'opposites' was dominant (Rawson and Legeza, 1973). This is an anthropocentric perspective with a sociological definition in which, because nature is imperfect, man has a responsibility to improve on nature (Chan, 1969; Elvin, 1973). It is thus distinct from a western perspective that separates nature and civilization (humans), which views nature ('wilderness') ideally as free from artificiality and human intervention.

Mountains were particularly venerated and the complementary force fields of man and nature came together most powerfully in the Daoist concept of *yin-yang*. Like a magnet with its different force fields both are needed for the magnet to function, and man is seen as indivisible from nature (Ropp, 1992; Spence, 1992). Under the religious belief system that evolved over centuries, there were nine revered sites of particular significance – five sacred *shan* or mountains and four rivers (Chinese History Museum, 1992). It was a fundamental responsibility of Chinese emperors to visit these sacred mountains on a regular basis to propitiate the spirits, gods and ancestors. Failure to do so could place the entire prosperity and well-being of the empire at risk. Grand roads were constructed for the emperor to approach the sacred mountains (the imperial way). Steps, termed 'staircases to heaven', since the emperor was revered as the son of heaven, were carved into their slopes for his ascent to the summit. Pavilions, tea houses and inns were erected at regular intervals (Sofield and Li, 2003). While Huangshan is not one of the sacred mountains, it is revered and manifests much of the pilgrimage development associated with China's five sacred mountains.

In examining how Chinese values about landscape and wilderness are translated into tourism attractions, the anthropocentric position encourages and facilitates programmes to alter the physical and bio-logical environment in order to produce desired 'improvements' (Sofield and Li, 1998). These may include landscaped gardens, artifi-cial lakes and waterfalls, facilities for recreation and tourism, roads for ease of access, observation towers, and so on. Increasing direct human use is the objective of management and the character of the 'wilderness' will be changed to reflect the desires of humans and con-temporary standards of 'comfort in nature'. Styles of recreation and tourism will be tuned to the convenience of humans, so trails will be concreted, resorts and restaurants permitted inside reserves, cable cars approved, and so forth. Huangshan exhibits all of these examples of 'man improving on nature.'

The biocentric approach that underlies the IUCN's approach to WHS assessment, by contrast emphasizes the maintenance or enhance-ment of natural systems, if necessary at the expense of recreational and other human uses (Hendee and Stankey, 1973, cited in Hendee et al., 1990). 'The goal of the biocentric philosophy is to permit natu-ral ecological processes to operate as freely as possible, because [in the western system of values] wilderness for society ultimately depends on the retention of naturalness' (Hendee et al., 1990: 18, our qualification in square brackets). It requires controlling the flow of external, especially human-made, pressures on ecosystems by restricting excessive recreational or touristic use of the bio-geophysical resources. The recreational use of wilderness is tolerated with this position only to the degree that it does not change the energy balance inordinately. A biocentric philosophy requires recreational users to take wilderness on its own terms rather than manipulate it to serve human needs. Like the anthropocentric approach, the biocentric approach also focuses on human benefits, but the important distinction between them is that, biocentrically, the benefits are viewed over a longer term and as being dependent upon retaining the naturalness of the wilderness ecosystems (Hendee et al., 1990: 19).

Huangshan as an exemplar of the indivisibility of 'man and nature'

Given the binary natural/cultural heritage approach that is integral to WHS listing, the Chinese authorities had no alternative but to seek inscription for Huangshan based on separate assessments of its qualities even if their own world view does not draw the same clear-cut distinctions between the two. Thus, a major component of the Chinese submission for WHSL (PRC, 1989) described its geological attributes and enumerated its flora and fauna, emphasizing the diversity and endemism of the site and identifying rare or endangered species in conformity with the western scientific paradigm in order for Huangshan to qualify for inscription under Natural Criteria (iii) and (iv). Its intrinsic cultural values were detailed separately under Cultural Criterion (ii).

Despite the forced separation of geological and biological features from cultural features, aspects of cultural heritage and anthropomorphic descriptors were interspersed with the scientific terminology necessary to make the case for the former. For example, in describing the vegetation of Huangshan and its endemic pine species, *Pinus huangshanensis,* the submission by the Chinese authorities to IUCN noted that: 'A number of legendary trees are celebrated on account of their age, grotesque shape, or precipitously perched position, and more than 100 bear special names' (PRC, 1989), such as 'Two Lovers Embracing' (two pines with intertwined trunks) and 'Welcoming Guests Pine' (so named because its branches open out like the arms of a host gesturing to visitors to enter his/her house). Such anthropomorphizing is regarded as inappropriate in western scientific texts but acceptable in a Chinese context. While the Huangshan pine is of intrinsic botanical interest to western science, its significance for Chinese visitors to Huangshan lies in cultural attributes, many of the trees so well known from literary references over the centuries that they form 'must-see' sights. The pine survives on precipitous cliff faces at high altitudes, its roots often twice the length of its trunk, buffeted by strong winds and heavy mantles of snow and ice in winter. It has thus been anthropomorphized as tenacious, strong, steadfast, determined, iron-willed, brave, upright – all human attributes. In this context, one of China's most famous calligraphers, Ouyang Xun, developed a style of calligraphy, subsequently named after him, that reveals these same characteristics (Ebrey, 2003: 10). Chinese visitors to Huangshan will immediately recognize the 'strong, steadfast' Ouyang Xun style of some of the engravings that may be found all over Huangshan. They will nod approval because of its appropriateness in such a setting, making the association between the calligrapher and the pine tree in a fusion of history, psychology, botany and literary art. They 'see' a profound cultural element of Huangshan in a botanical species that is invisible to non-Chinese (and was obviously invisible to the IUCN 1990 assessment panel). There is no interpretation of this phenomenon provided for visitors to Huangshan because the Ouyang Xun style is one of the three main Tang dynasty styles on which the art of Chinese calligraphy is based and, in learning how to write the characters of the Chinese language, all literate Chinese are familiar with it, so it is part of Chinese 'common knowledge'. Yet for many western visitors to Huangshan such detail, full of meaning in a cultural context, would prove of real interest.

As with the section of the WHS submission on flora, so the section on geology was also moved by its Chinese authors beyond 'western' technicalities to incorporate cultural elements that might seem inappropriate in a purely scientific document. Thus, in outlining the geology of Huangshan and noting the presence of numerous 'erratics' (a technical term for boulders which have weathered differentially and perch atop mother lodes), the Chinese submission to UNESCO added that: 'Many of these grotesquely-shaped rocks are individually named, such as "Pig-headed monk eating water melon", such names having ancient literary, historical or mythical significance' (PRC, 1989). Another isolated porphyry column with a pine tree emerging from its tip – one of the famous geological features of Huangshan – is named 'A Flower Growing from a Pen Tip in a Dream'. For Chinese visitors it is a compulsory sight, a pilgrimage to a site associated with one of China's most famous poets, Li Bai (701–762 AD), whose personal calligraphy also adorns other sites around Huangshan. Again, in learning how to read and write Mandarin, all literate Chinese will be familiar with several poets' eulogies to Huangshan. Their poems, combining descriptions of the natural with social and human emotional responses, are part of a major Chinese literary and artistic movement called 'shan shui' culture (literally, *mountain water*) that was firmly established between the 8th and 11th centuries and continues to the present day. By incorporating values that imbue nature/natural scenery with a range of human social and cultural values, such as likening mountains to benevolence and waters to wisdom (*The Analects of Confucius*, 5th century BC), *shan shui* philosophy has had a profound influence on the aesthetics of natural landscapes.

Because the Chinese world view privileges literary and cultural heritage before the sciences, Chinese tourists to national parks like Huangshan will interpret their experience through the culture of *shan shui* rather than through western paradigms of biological and geological sciences, or 'wilderness' which, in the ideal western construct, has no visible presence of humans. Their appreciation of the landscape and their motivation for visiting has a somewhat distant relationship to IUCN precepts. Many Chinese visitors follow routes established by authoritative figures over the centuries, following a preordained sequence to certain peaks, temples, pavilions and scenic sights, counting them off in much the same fashion as dedicated birdwatchers ticking off sightings from their list of rare and endangered species. Each and every step along the way will have been eulogized by poems and essays that will be familiar to most Chinese visitors and often they will recite such texts as they view the different sites. They will walk along paved trails, steps carved into the rock, bridges erected across chasms, with pavilions and kiosks conveniently located every half kilometre or so. A common reaction to Huangshan's miles of paths and stairs by western tourists is a perception of visual pollution, of a geometric, reinforced-concrete invasion of nature. But, semiotically, the Chinese will understand that such paths and flights of stairs symbolize hundreds of years of visitation by their emperors to sacred mountains to worship their ancestors and gods, and that vertical flights of steps ascending to the summit signify 'stairways to heaven' that once only their emperors would have been privileged to climb.

Management

Management of Huangshan as a WHS inevitably involves tension between the conservation ethic espoused by the western scientific paradigm for protecting natural and cultural heritage, which is embedded in WHS listing, and Chinese anthropocentrically-oriented values, which see no contradiction between major constructions for the comfort and convenience of visitors being located inside the boundaries of a designated WHS. Under the Anhui Province *Plan for the Places of Scenic and Historic Interest in Huangshan* (1987), the reserve is divided into six tourist zones and five protection zones, and while it proclaims that 'no construction will be permitted if it will impinge on the quality of the landscape', a western perspective and the Chinese understanding of 'quality landscape' differ significantly. For example, if the ideal shape is a spire, then, in terms of the Daoist need for humans to improve on nature, constructing a pagoda on the summit of a rounded hill will enhance its beauty; if the pagoda functions to provide shelter or refreshments for travellers then it will bring humans and nature into harmony; but a western perspective might see the intrusion of such a human-made construction dominating the landscape, creating visual pollution and perhaps destroying its intrinsic naturalness.

The anthropocentric Chinese approach to nature is evident in an alpine valley adjacent to the North Sea of Clouds, which now has seven hotels (three, four and five star ratings) and two hostels with a total of more than 3000 beds to facilitate travellers being able to experience the dawn rising over the peaks. There are about 70 km of concrete paths and stairs to facilitate the flow of huge crowds around Huangshan. There are three cable cars, one of them, at 7 km, the longest in China. There are two sites with large restaurant complexes and about 30 refreshment kiosks and souvenir stalls dotted around the peaks. Two alpine streams have been dammed to provide water for these facilities. They are all functional elements that enhance the experience of a visit to Huangshan for Chinese travellers. The Bureau of the WHC might recommend that management 'not permit the development of new hotels in the vicinity of popular scenic spots' (1998); but that recommendation is based on western perceptions of conservation and visual and environmental degradation and fails to take account of Chinese cultural values concerning the interaction of humans and nature. Where tourist facilities create environmental damage and water pollution through, for example, inadequate sewage treatment and waste disposal, then concerns are valid. But when assessments of what constitutes visual pollution or the quality of a landscape are based on subjective criteria – which are in fact culturally determined from both sides, whether Western or Chinese – then it is difficult to argue that one approach is right and the other is wrong. Rather they are different. And in the context of a site like Huangshan, insistence on a Western-oriented definition of what is appropriate may in fact be a denial of the very essence – the Chineseness – of the site.

Until recently there was little signage around the mountain other than directional signs devoid of interpretation but, in response to urgings from the Bureau of the WHC that the significance of Huangshan's natural heritage be communicated to visitors (e.g. 1998 report from the Kyoto meeting of the Bureau), there are now about 40 metal plaques located at key points around the reserve. However, as with the original submission seeking WHS listing, much of this signage amalgamates both Western scientific technicalities and

Chinese cultural values. As just one example, the interpretation plaque at Xihaimen (West Sea Gate) lookout has its first two sentences utilizing technical terms to describe the geological formations and processes, with the remainder of the information referencing a range of Chinese-specific myths, legends and classical tales. The Chinese characters are followed by this English language translation:

> Xihaimen is the most profound and beautiful part of the Huangshan Scenic Spot [Reserve]. A blaze of multifarious colours of medium-to-fine-grained porphyritic granite bodies, and densely distributed vertical and horizontal joints add much to the high and steep granite peaks as well as interesting and odd stones, from which countless fairy stories and sayings are handed down. The NW–SE-trending fault zone cuts into granite bodies, thus forming a quiet, deep and precipitous dreamland in the Xihai (West Sea) Canyon. Stone scenes gather together before Paiyunting (Clouds Overwhelming Temple), such as An Immortal Airing His Boots, Wu Song's Fighting Tiger, Memorial Archway Stone in the near [foreground], Immortals Walking on Stilts [a line of ascending pinnacles], Female Immortals Embroidering, Heaven Dog's Watching Moon [Rock], King Wen Pulling a Wagon, etc. in the far [distance].

As with most other signage in Huangshan, the information relies upon Chinese common knowledge to deliver understanding and Chinese visitors will automatically draw upon their knowledge of ancient poets, Confucian and Daoist philosophy and religion, imperial history, and Chinese classical literature to recognize the significance and symbolism that is captured in the scenery before them. But this information requires very lengthy interpretation if it is to be comprehensible to non-Chinese visitors. For example, the very name of the lookout is puzzling: what is this West Sea several hundreds of kilometres inland, high up in a mountain range with no lake in sight? The answer lies in classical literature when an early visitor to Huangshan climbed to its highest peaks and looked down on alpine valleys filled with surging clouds. This scene has been immortalized in numerous poems about Huangshan's West (and North) Sea of Clouds.

Other references similarly rely upon Chinese common knowledge to make sense. 'Immortals' in Chinese culture are integral to Daoist belief. They are not gods in the Western sense of that word, although they may be worshipped and shrines built for them. Nor are they angels, although they are celestial beings; they are mischievous, fun-loving, carousing creatures with superhuman strengths and skills, constantly playing tricks on each other. They dwell in mountains, and caves (the Daoist 'passage-way to Heaven') are often their abode. Evidence of the presence of immortals in mountains thus abounds and Huangshan is no exception as this example demonstrates.

The reference to Emperor Wen also links Immortals to Confucian philosophy. In the famous *Analects*, Confucius discussed the meaning of an ancient story in which Wen pulled the cart of an Immortal for 800 steps before stopping, exhausted. As a result the Immortal blessed his descendents with 800 years of unbroken rule. The reference to Wu Song fighting a tiger is taken from two of China's most famous classics, *Outlaws of the Marsh* (Shi Nai'an and Luo Guanzhong, circa 1350 AD) and *The Plum in the Golden Vase* (anonymous, circa 1618 AD). Every educated ten-year-old Chinese knows that the character Wu Song personifies manly strength because he killed an attacking tiger with his bare hands.

During a field trip to Huangshan in 2004 to prepare a new tourism master plan for the region it was noticeable that perhaps less than 5 per cent of the Chinese visitors to the mountains actually stopped to read the newly installed plaques. Questioning revealed that, on the one hand, they were on a pilgrimage to validate their knowledge of ancient cultural heritage (Petersen, 1995) and were not interested in the scientific information ('We are here on holiday, not to go back to school') and, on the other hand, the references to Chinese culture were superfluous. These observations reinforce the conclusion that, for Chinese, Huangshan is a cultural landscape before it is a natural landscape even if WHS listing favours the biological over the cultural. They are there to view the beauty of the physical features and forests, but they 'gaze' at them through cultural lenses (Urry, 2002), denying the validity of the IUCN's attempt at a scientific imprimatur.

Calligraphy may be considered a signifier of China's unbroken 4000-year-old civilization for Chinese visitors to Huangshan. It is common all over the mountains, carved into the living rock, often recently highlighted in red, yellow or blue paint, and enhances their appreciation of a site. This is in contrast to a western perception of 'seeing' graffiti that degrades the intrinsic values of mountain wilderness and imprints the dominance of *homo sapiens* over Nature. Most Western visitors will fail to understand the deep significance of calligraphy as high art and as a gift from the gods with semi-sacred connotations, or the qualities inherent in a particular style of calligraphy, the historico-cultural significance of the calligrapher and a particular text, or the fact that the colours themselves have deep symbolism for their Chinese viewers – red for happiness, blue for longevity, yellow for prosperity (Sofield and Li, 1998). On occasion, management may newly inscribe a bare site with calligraphy as a deliberate act to improve it and Chinese visitors will see this as an appropriate enrichment. In other instances, consistent with the ancient Chinese tradition of authoritative figures inscribing their thoughts for future generations, an important person may be invited to display their calligraphy skills (e.g. Mao Zedong at Huangshan, 1958). ICOMOS may recognize ancient inscriptions as significant because it places a value on antiquity, but it will frown on Dulux gloss paint being used to highlight such ancient texts and will want to prevent new additions on grounds of destroying the integrity of the historico-cultural fabric of a site. But for Chinese a newly engraved inscription may have similar authenticity as a much older inscription because they 'see' the continuity in an age-old process that should not be museumized according to some Western notion of separating out the past from the present. Authenticity is culturally defined, not a concept that can be scientifically and objectively measured and universally applied. It is one further aspect of dissonance in the management of Huangshan that resists the Western paradigms governing WHS listing.

Conclusions

Huangshan illustrates the limitations of an approach to WHS listing that is fragmented and divided along western-oriented constructs. It is suggested that there would be advantages in an increased capacity for incorporating non-western cultural values in considerations of WHS management regimes. However, this is difficult: the IUCN's experts are enjoined to focus only on natural heritage to the exclusion of other factors, and their scientific training, as per Foucault's (1980) treatise on power, dictates that they will privilege their knowledge base over other knowledge bases. ICOMOS similarly has western precepts guiding its assessments. But, without a more open, more integrated multidisciplinary approach to consideration of the merits of a place for WHS listing, we are left with a variation of Said's (1978) engagement of 'Orientalism' versus 'Westernism' – the assumption of an unquestioned 'western/modern' authority accompanying the ownership of the concept of WHS listing that subordinates Others' values to its own.

References

Anhui Province (1987) *Plan for the Places of Scenic and Historic Interest in Huangshan.* Huangshan: Anhui Province Government Press.

Bureau of the World Heritage Committee (1998) *Decisions of the Twenty-second Extraordinary Session of the Bureau of the World Heritage Committee (Kyoto, 28–29 November 1998) With Regard to the State of Conservation of Properties Inscribed on the World Heritage List.* Kyoto: World Heritage Centre.

Chan, W. (1969) *A Source Book of Chinese Philosophy.* New York: Colombia University Press.

Chinese History Museum (1992) *Illustrated History of China's 5000 Years.* Tianjin: Tianjin People's Arts Publication [in Chinese].

Ebrey, P.B. (2003) *A Visual Sourcebook of Chinese Civilization*. New York: Washington University: http://depts.washington.edu/chinaciv, (accessed 10 December 2004).

Elvin, M. (1973) *The Pattern of the Chinese Past*. Stamford: Stamford University Press.

Foucault, M. (1980) *Power-Knowledge: Selected Interviews and Other Writings, 1972–1977*, edited by Colin Gordon. Brighton: Harvester Press.

Hendee, J.C. and Stankey, G.H. (1973) Biocentricity in wilderness management. *BioScience*, 23 (9), 535–538.

Hendee, J.C., Stankey, G.H. and Lucas, R. (1990) *Wilderness Management*, 2nd edn. Golden: North America Press.

ICOMOS (1990) *World Heritage Nomination – ICOMOS Summary 547 Mount Huangshan Scenic Beauty and Historic Site (China)*. http://whc.unesco.org/archive/advisory_body_evaluation/547 (accessed 2 February 2005).

IUCN (1990) *World Heritage Nomination – IUCN Summary 547 Mount Huangshan Scenic Beauty and Historic Site (China). Summary prepared by IUCN (April 1990) based on the original nomination submitted by the People's Republic of China*. http://whc.unesco.org/archive/advisory_body_evaluation/547 (accessed 2 February 2005).

Overmyer, D.L. (1986) *Religions of China: the World as a Living System*. San Francisco: Harper and Row.

Petersen, Y.Y. (1995) The Chinese landscape as a tourist attraction: image and reality. In Lew, A.A. and Lawrence, Y. (eds) *Tourism in China: Geographical, Political and Economic Perspective*. Boulder: Westview Press, pp. 141–154.

PRC (People's Republic of China) (1989) *Submission to UNESCO for WHS Listing for Huangshan Scenic Beauty and Historic Interest Reserve*. Huangshan: Huangshan Administrative Committee in Charge of Sites of Scenic Beauty and Historic Interest.

Rawson, P. and Legeza, L. (1973) *Tao: The Chinese Philosophy of Time and Change*. London: Thames and Hudson.

Ropp, P.S. (1992) *Heritage of China: Contemporary Perspectives on China*. Berkeley: University of California Press.

Said, E. (1978) *Orientalism. Western Conceptions of the Orient*. Harmondsworth: Penguin.

Sofield, T.H.B. and Li, F.M.S. (1998) China: tourism development and cultural policies. *Annals of Tourism Research*, 25 (2), 323–353.

Sofield, T.H.B. and Li, F.M.S. (2003) *Processes in formulating an eco-tourism policy for nature reserves in Yunnan Province, China*. In Fennell, D. and Dowling, R. (eds) *Ecotourism: Policy and Strategy Issues*. London: CAB International, pp. 141–168.

Spence, J. (1992) Western perceptions of China from the late sixteenth century to the present. In Ropp, P. (ed) *Heritage of China:*

Contemporary Perspectives on China. Berkeley: University of California Press, pp. 1–14.

Tellenbach, H. and Bin Kimura (1989) The Japanese concept of 'Nature'. In Callicott, J.B. and Ames, R.T. (eds) *Nature In Asian Traditions of Thought: Essays in Environmental Philosophy*. New York: State University of New York Press, pp. 153–162.

Tu, W.M. (1989) The continuity of being: Chinese visions of nature. In Callicott, J.B. and Ames, R.T. (eds) *Nature In Asian Traditions of Thought: Essays in Environmental Philosophy*, New York: State University of New York Press, pp. 67–78.

UNESCO (1990) *Convention Concerning the Protection of the World Cultural and Natural Heritage. Report of the World Heritage Committee, Fourteenth Session, Banff, Alberta, Canada, 7–12 December 1990*. CLT-90/CONF.004/13, 12 December 1990.

Urry, J. (2002) *The Tourist Gaze: Leisure and Travel in Contemporary Societies*. London: Sage Publications.

World Heritage Centre (1990) http://whc.unesco.org/archive/advisory_body_evaluation/547 (accessed 2 February 2005).

Questions

1 What are the key points of a Chinese world view?
2 How does this world view differ from western concepts that are used to set the parameters of WHS assessments?
3 Utilizing Huangshan as an example, describe the sort of tensions and dissonance that can arise for management of a WHS for visitation when there is a clash of values between the international organizations responsible for WHS listing and the host society.

CHAPTER 19

The Megalithic Temples of Malta: towards a re-evaluation of heritage

Nadia Theuma and Reuben Grima

Aims

This case study aims to:

- Explore the impacts on local communities when inscribing sites on the World Heritage List
- Highlight the conflicting views that may exist between heritage and tourism organizations
- Discuss how WHS may be better managed and interpreted to accommodate the needs of local communities.

Introduction: the Megalithic Temples of Malta

The Republic of Malta comprises a small archipelago with a total land area of only 316 km² located around 90 km south of Sicily. Largely due to its position in the central Mediterranean and to its fine natural harbours, through the ages Malta has been frequented, exploited or coveted by many major players in Mediterranean history. This rich history is reflected in three inscriptions in the World Heritage List. The present case study focuses on one of these inscriptions, the Megalithic Temples of Malta (Figure 19.1). The megalithic temples consist of a series of sophisticated megalithic buildings, which were built by the Neolithic inhabitants between 3600 and 2500 BC. These buildings are remarkably complex and accomplished in their execution, and have been described as the world's first stone temples (Renfrew 1973).

Figure 19.1 Map of Megalithic Temples of Malta

Key themes

An important trend in the management of cultural and natural resources is the integration between global and local objectives and values. During the past two decades, this emerging trend has been witnessed across a wide variety of sectors. The Earth Summit held in Rio in 1992 recognized the important role of local communities in the sustainable management of environmental resources. The same trend may be observed in the Burra Charter (ICOMOS, 1999) and in the European Landscape Convention (Council of Europe, 2000), which recognize the importance of local communities in the care of natural and cultural resources. In the domain of conservation of cultural heritage resources, the Nara Document on Authenticity (ICOMOS, 1994) has underlined the importance of the local cultural context in determining appropriate conservation practices, as well as judgements about cultural value and authenticity.

The value of local systems of traditional knowledge has also been recognized by UNESCO. In the implementation of the UNESCO World Heritage Convention, several significant measures have been taken to ensure that traditional systems of knowledge and stewardship are recognized and safeguarded. The Operational Guidelines for the implementation of the Convention have been updated to reflect the newly-recognized importance of local stewardship (Merode et al., 2004).

A central focus in the trend outlined above is the recognition of systems of value and knowledge maintained by indigenous peoples and first nations. A more general focus has been the recognition of value systems other than western and European ones. In the implementation of the World Heritage Convention, far-reaching practical measures have been undertaken to ensure that the World Heritage List does not remain dominated by sites that were chosen according to western and European notions of value, in order to become truly representative of the cultural diversity that exists around the globe.

This case study argues that some of the important principles that have been learnt over the past two decades may also be useful and relevant within a western and European scenario. A case study from a southern European island context will be used to illustrate how, even in such contexts, divergent perceptions and value systems may result in very different attitudes towards World Heritage resources. In this particular case study, this divergence culminated in vandalism that threatened the very fabric of a prehistoric WHS. It is argued that one of the root causes of this divergence was the failure to share notions about the value of the WHS with local communities. It is further argued that this failure led to contestation between traditional local uses and the needs of a tourist destination. Archaeological interpretations and narratives as well as carefully thought out management plans have an important role to play in bridging this divide.

Case study

The Megalithic Temples are so colossal in their construction that several of them remained conspicuous features of the landscape right until the present. Successive inhabitants of the Maltese archipelago have used these monumental sites for different purposes, ranging from a Bronze Age cremation cemetery to a Phoenician and Roman sanctuary. In some cases, a large part of their building material was carried away for other uses, while in other instances temple sites were completely buried and used as agricultural land. Although we have practically no written records of what the local inhabitants in different periods thought about these strange ruins, some popular legends about their origin have been passed on orally and recorded. Several place names that have been used to refer to these sites since the Middle Ages have also been preserved. These legends and toponyms indicate that, in popular belief, the megalithic buildings were built by a race of giants that inhabited the world before the biblical deluge. What is important to note is that until the 18th century, this belief was also shared by many scholars. It was only in the 19th century that scientific interpretations began to depart from traditional interpretations, by asserting that the megalithic buildings had been built by the Phoenicians. In the early 20th century, archaeologists realized that these buildings had been created by a prehistoric culture much earlier than the Phoenicians. The accepted date of these buildings was pushed further back, first with radiocarbon dating, and then again when radiocarbon dating was recalibrated using dendrochronology. As a result of the revised dating, by the early 1970s the megalithic temples were recognized to be among the earliest known structures of such complexity. Two developments that followed were closely related. One was a progressive escalation in the promotion of the megalithic temples as a tourist attraction, as the archipelago enjoyed its first tourism boom. The other was the inscription of the first of these temples on the UNESCO World Heritage List, which took place in 1980, to be followed by the extension of the inscription in 1992 to include five other temple sites. The megalithic temples were inscribed under criterion (iv) of the Operational Guidelines, in recognition that they are outstanding examples of a type of building which illustrates a significant stage in human history.

From the 1970s onwards, the newfound reputation of the megalithic temples as the world's oldest temples was aggressively promoted by tourism organizations to attract more and more foreign visitors to the country. By then, Malta was slowly becoming a mass tourist destination. As the number of visitors rose, so did the potential for tensions and confrontations with local communities. In order to receive the growing influx of visitors, access roads, car parks and facilities had to be created, while certain traditional land uses came under threat.

This case study is focused on two of the six inscribed temple sites, namely Hagar Qim and Mnajdra, which lie within 500 m of each other, on the southwest coast of Malta. Hagar Qim stands on a ridge commanding the surrounding countryside. A massively-built protective enclosure started to be built around this site in 1970, divorcing it from the surrounding landscape. However, the wall and the steel barriers (Figure 19.2) were not completed until 1978, when access to the site became fully regulated. We suspect that the enclosure took such a long time to be built because it was highly contentious.

Figure 19.2 Hagar Qim, Malta

In 1990, around 40 hectares of land, including the Hagar Qim as well as the Mnajdra temples, were earmarked by the National Tourist Office (NTOM) to become an archaeological park and enclosed within another boundary wall. These measures were undertaken without any dialogue with communities and individuals who had an interest in this part of the landscape. The boundary wall cut across old tracks and rights-of-way, and enclosed a large area that was a favourite spot for traditional bird-trapping, as well as a popular spot for family outings and picnics. In the space of a few years, the megalithic temples were alienated even further from local communities. This alienation is evident in the number of visitors to this site.

Since the site was not as yet enclosed there are no official records of visitor numbers between 1970 and 1978. However, one of the custodians of the site at the time has stated that the number of visitors to the area was very small, averaging around 20 visitors a day, who were mostly foreign. Numbers increased over weekends, when Maltese people visited the site as part of their Sunday outing or to picnic in the area (Borg, personal communication). Another use of the area was traditional bird-trapping, a practice which is well documented at least since the 17th century, and is probably much older. The first available records for visitors are for 1978, after the completion of the boundary wall. Figures show that over 42 000 visitors came to the site. In 1979, an entry fee was introduced for adults and so the first records of fee-paying visitors are noted. Children continued to be allowed free access, while the general public could still enter free of charge on Sundays. By the early 1990s, free access to the Maltese public was restricted to one day per month. These measures progressively transformed the constituency of visitors to the sites.

Figure 19.3 clearly shows that, as paying visitors (mainly foreign tourists) increased, the proportion of visitors admitted without payment, which by 1993 accounted only for schoolchildren and pensioners, continued to decline. We have to point out that the number of tourists to Malta has increased dramatically from 12 583 visitors in 1959 to over 1.1 million visitors in 2003. A record number of 1.2 million visitors to Malta was reached in 1994.

The changes in management and admission policies had far-reaching consequences. Access to the temples, which had always been taken for granted, was transformed into a commodity that had to be paid for. The temples were now perceived as outposts of interference by meddlesome government officials, whose growing interest in transforming the temples into tourist attractions not only threatened traditional leisure uses of the surrounding landscape, but even threatened land tenure and ownership rights. The perceived threat to the practice of traditional bird-trapping within the designated park became a symbol of the nationwide debate on whether bird-trapping would be allowed at all as the country prepared to join the European Union. A reaction

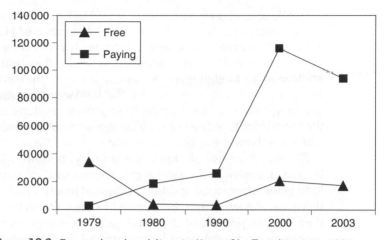

Figure 19.3 Free and paying visitors to Hagar Qim Temples 1979–2003. *Source*: Department of Museums Annual Reports, 1979–2000; Heritage Malta Annual Report, 2003–2004

was inevitable, and it came in a succession of incidents of mounting gravity. Paradoxically, the highly-publicized international importance of the megalithic temples put them at greater risk, as it made them high-profile targets for the expression of protest against the state (Grima, 1998).

During the early efforts to create an archaeological park around Hagar Qim and Mnajdra, graffiti messages threatening to blow up Hagar Qim, were painted onto the boundary wall around Hagar Qim and onto a walkway. In 1994, graffiti that made uncomplimentary references to the government of the day were sprayed over a number of cultural heritage sites across Malta, including one megalithic temple site. In 1996, graffiti were sprayed onto the façade and interior of the Mnajdra temples, making references to the environmental lobby. None of these incidents, however, prepared the authorities or the public for the violence of the vandalism that took place at Mnajdra in 2001. More than sixty megaliths were toppled out of place in the space of one night. In the preceding weeks, the Planning Authority had issued a number of enforcement notices on buildings in the vicinity that did not have the appropriate permits, and had even dismantled some of these structures. Although a connection between the enforcement action and the vandalism was never proven, it remains one of the more plausible hypotheses.

Public shock and outrage at the vandalism was immediate and widespread, both in Malta and abroad. A restoration effort was mobilized, and fortunately it was possible to reverse most of the damage sustained at Mnajdra. Security measures were also improved, with more security fences and round-the-clock surveillance. What is less clear is what circumstances led up to such vandalism, and to what extent these circumstances have changed today. One fundamental root cause appears to have been that the global value of Hagar Qim and Mnajdra was perceived to be in conflict with local values and interests. The more these sites were promoted as world-class tourist attractions and the more foreigners flocked to visit the monuments, the greater the threat to traditional uses of the landscape became. Instead of instilling a focus of local pride, the inclusion of these monuments in the World Heritage List contributed to a sense of dispossession among some members of the local community.

The direct control of the monuments by the state was reflected in the management of the landscape. The forceful expropriation of the land where they stood and the creation of fences continued to decontextualize the sites from their setting in the cultural landscape. A further, subtler process of decontextualization also took place in the narratives that were used to explain the significance of the monuments. Archaeological interpretations tended to give more attention to the issues that gave the monuments their global importance, such as their chronology and dating. Until recently, little attention was given to understanding the relationship between the megalithic buildings and their landscape setting. As a result, archaeological narratives distanced the archaeological monuments even further from the world of the present-day inhabitants of the same landscape.

Meanwhile, while tourism organizations promoted these sites as Malta's main attraction, they did not contribute to the protection or management of the sites. With a global trend of an increase in culturally motivated visitors coupled with marketing that promoted Malta's cultural heritage, tourism organizations precipitated conflicts regarding the management of cultural assets (Boissevain and Sammut, 1994; Theuma, 2002). In addition, tourism in Malta for many years has been driven by mass tourism activity and touring companies that often measure success by the increase in the numbers of visitors, rarely consulting with heritage organizations. The fact that tourism and culture fell under separate ministries did not make the task of integrating the two any easier.

Recent changes in the management of cultural assets

In recent years there have been some significant changes in the general management of cultural heritage in Malta. The first notable change was the tourism sector's increased interest in the management of cultural heritage. In 1999, the newly set up Malta Tourism Authority took over the marketing role of the NTOM but added on the management and production of cultural activities. Although there is still room for improvement, tourism organizations have taken up more responsibility towards the management and protection of Malta's cultural heritage.

Another factor is that the vandalism that took place at Mnajdra in 2001 raised public awareness and precipitated the processing through parliament of a new Cultural Heritage Act (2002), which had been evolving through a succession of drafts since 1996. The new law introduced much-needed structural changes. It updated the 1925 Antiquities Protection Act better to reflect present-day needs by making provisions for the regulation, conservation and management of cultural heritage in Malta.

Moreover, in 2004, a reorganization of ministerial portfolios brought culture and tourism within a single ministry. This change has presented an opportunity for better synergy between organizations and better management of resources. The attendant risk is the retrenchment of the perception of cultural heritage sites as primarily a resource for tourists and foreigners. If this threat is guarded against, the integration will help bridge the divide between the divergent paradigms of heritage and tourism.

Conclusions

The lessons drawn from this case study are clear. It is a short-sighted management strategy that tries to safeguard the global values of a WHS at the expense of the values of the local community. The legal, material, administrative and intellectual enclosure of the megalithic temples distanced this cultural resource from the local community, provoking a reaction. So what were the lessons learnt, and how can one better manage these sites? What is currently being done?

First, more importance is being given to consultation with all the different interest groups as key players in the development of a Management Plan for the megalithic temples. Consultation and consensus building have become integral to the development of plans for the Hagar Qim and Mnajdra Archaeological Park. A second objective is to bridge the divide between scientific knowledge and popular knowledge about the megalithic temples (Grima, 2002). The plans that are being made for the future presentation and interpretation of Hagar Qim and Mnajdra are paying more attention to themes that give the archaeological remains local relevance. The relationship of the sites to the local landscape setting and their exploitation of locally available materials are themes that are intrinsically more accessible and meaningful to the communities that inhabit the same landscape today. Third, the prehistoric sites shall be presented as part of a living cultural landscape, which has witnessed a succession of different uses. Fourth, a sustained drive has been launched to use a wider range of media to make heritage more accessible to Maltese and foreign audiences, including education programmes, TV spots, interactive media and popular publications.

The challenge that has started to be addressed is to optimize the balance between the experience of visitors and the traditional uses of the landscape. A better understanding of traditional uses of the lived cultural landscape has the potential to enrich the experience of visitors. Reciprocally, a better understanding of past uses of the landscape may help create an environment more favourable to responsible stewardship among the present day inhabitants of the same landscape.

References

Boissevain, J. and Sammut, N. (1994) *Mdina: Its Residents and Cultural Tourism. Findings and Recommendations*. Report. Med-Campus Euromed Sustainable Tourism Project, Malta.

Council of Europe (2000) European Landscape Convention. http://conventions.coe.int/Treaty/en/Treaties/Html/176.htm

Grima, R. (1998) Ritual spaces, contested places: the case of the Maltese Prehistoric Temple Sites. *Journal of Mediterranean Studies*, 8, 33–45.

Grima, R. (2002) Archaeology as encounter. *Archaeological Dialogues*, 9, 83–89.

ICOMOS (1994) The Nara Document on Authenticity. http://www.international.icomos.org/naradoc_eng.htm

ICOMOS (1999) The Burra Charter: The Australian ICOMOS Charter for Places of Cultural Significance. http://www.icomos.org/australia/images/pdf/BURRA_CHARTER.pdf

Merode, E. de, Smeets, R. and Westrik, C. (eds) (2004) Introduction. In *Linking Universal and Local Values: Managing a Sustainable Future for World Heritage. A Conference Organized by the Netherlands National Commission for UNESCO, in Collaboration With the Netherlands Ministry of Education, Culture and Science. 22–24 May 2003 (World Heritage Papers, 13)*. Paris: UNESCO World Heritage Centre, pp. 9–15.

Renfrew, C. (1973) *Before Civilization: The Radiocarbon Revolution and Prehistoric Europe*. London: Jonathan Cape.

Theuma, N. (2002) *Identifying Cultural Tourism in Malta: Marketing and Management Issues*. Unpublished PhD Thesis, University of Strathclyde.

Questions

1 Why do tourism and heritage organizations often have divergent views of culture and heritage?

2 Discuss ways in which heritage and tourism organizations can work more closely with local communities to enhance the value of cultural heritage.

3 Should the global values of WHS take precedence over local values and considerations?

CHAPTER 20

The Rainforest Ways: managing tourism in the Central Eastern Rainforest Reserves of Australia

Jo Mackellar and Ros Derrett

Aims

The aims of this case study are to describe the:

- Strategic approach taken to the development of a touring route
- Process of cooperative planning around World Heritage Sites
- Barriers and facilitators towards the development of a touring route around World Heritage Sites
- Relationships of stakeholders to the World Heritage Site.

Introduction

The World Heritage listed Central Eastern Rainforest Reserves of Australia (or CERRA) is an area of approximately 370 000 hectares, equal to the size of Switzerland. It comprises nearly 50 reserves, ranging in size from 11 hectares to approximately 100 000 hectares, which have been grouped into eight 'blocks of protected areas'. They are scattered throughout the eastern parts of two states – New South Wales and South-East Queensland. A key feature of this World Heritage Site (WHS) is the numerous adjacent land uses, with many communities living in close proximity to the sites. The potential for these land uses to impact on the area is high, with the protection of the assets resting with government resource managers such as national park managers and other government departments. Current land tenure for the reserves includes national parks, nature reserves, flora reserves, State forests and other Crown reserves.

The project described in this case study relates to three 'blocks of protected areas' in the CERRA, which receive high levels of visitation from domestic and international tourists as well as from the local communities. With visitor demand on the natural resources of the area increasing over time, a more coordinated approach to visitor management has been called for, both by local government authorities and by tourism and resource managers. The result has been the deliberate and coordinated development of a touring route with the aim to:

> ... develop and promote a primary touring route with complementary experiential loops and trails through Northern Rivers NSW and South East Queensland that will provide enhanced experiences for visitors and greater environmental, cultural, social and economic benefits for the cross border regions (Centre for Regional Tourism Research, 2001).

The intrinsic values associated with the CERRA, and its World Heritage status, were fundamental to this project. Responsible and sustainable development that respects the values of regional stakeholders

Figure 20.1 Rainforest reflection. Copyright Northern Rivers Tourism (reproduced with permission)

and communities underpinned its strategic direction. It was determined that to be successful, the project had to be market driven, realizing and facilitating the needs and wants of visitors and tourists. This case study describes the strategic approach taken by the WHS stakeholders to achieve aspirations. It highlights the issues, barriers and facilitators that occurred throughout the process. The case study is useful in identifying areas in which this process failed to deliver on expectations for some, while documenting the implications for others.

The region

The case study region includes three of the eight blocks of protected areas in the CERRA: Main Range; Focal Peak Group; and the Shield Volcano Group. These three areas are linked geographically by the ancient formations of the volcano caldera and scenic rim, as well as being linked by major roads in the region as shown in Figure 20.2. The region is also noted for its strong indigenous heritage and maintains links with several of its traditional landholder groups.

The region has a pleasant climate that allows access all year round. It is close to service and tourist centres such as the Gold Coast and Byron Bay, providing attractions for day visitors and longer stays. The region is one of the most popular tourist destinations in Australia for national and international tourists with approximately 2 million visits to the property each year (www.deh.gov.au/heritage). There are numerous tourist facilities adjacent to CERRA, notably the two lodges on private land within the boundary of Lamington National Park.

Figure 20.2 Map of the region for the Rainforest Way.
Source: Northern Rivers Tourism

Apart from tourist activity, the property also has an extremely high boundary to area ratio. This means that adjacent land uses have the potential to impact significantly on the values of the property. The land uses of adjacent properties include freehold rural grazing, State forest logging, agricultural and recreational pursuits such as off-road horse, car and trail-bike riding. Potential damage from these activities can impact upon the WHS. It is, therefore imperative to have the community involved in the protection and management of these adjacent areas for the benefit of the WHS.

Management and administration

The CERRA is administered by principal government agencies in Queensland and New South Wales in collaboration with the federal agency, Environment Australia. The management of CERRA is driven by a set of Strategic Management Objectives as determined by signature to the WHConvention. According to the Australian Department of Heritage (Commonwealth Department of Heritage, 2000):

> Australia must take measures necessary for the identification, protection, conservation, presentation and rehabilitation of its World Heritage, and, through these measures, to pass on the outstanding universal values of these places to future generations. These obligations provide the basis for the following strategic objectives for the management of CERRA:
>
> - To ensure that the World Heritage values of the property are clearly identified.
> - To ensure that the World Heritage values of CERRA are protected through appropriate long-term legislative regulatory and institutional arrangements.
> - To ensure that the World Heritage values of CERRA are conserved through both pro-active management and the control of threatening processes.
> - To ensure that degraded areas of CERRA are rehabilitated to a natural condition.
> - To ensure that the World Heritage values of CERRA are presented in the most appropriate and sustainable way to the community.
> - Through achievement of the above objectives, to transmit the outstanding universal values of CERRA to future generations.

Tourism products

The relevant CERRA area is positioned in the centre of two thriving tourism regions, being *the Northern Rivers* of New South Wales (NSW) and *the Gold Coast* of South-East Queensland (QLD). The region includes major regional tourist attractions such as Mount Warning National Park, Border Ranges National Park, Nightcap National Park (NSW), Lamington National Park and Springbrook National Park (QLD). Situated within these parks are numerous walking tracks leading to waterfalls, crystal clear streams and other panoramic landscapes.

The tracks traverse steep ranges covered in rare and endangered Australian rainforest with highly unique and sensitive flora and fauna. Their appeal is universal to both the experienced nature traveller and the casual day visitor. Their significance, however, is sometimes lost due to the geographical spread of individual sites across the State borders and through several local government areas. It is more common for tourist organizations to promote one area of the CERRA, such as Mount Warning, rather than the whole WHS. Similarly, the two State resource managers, National Parks and Wildlife Service (NPWS), and Queensland Parks (QP), promote individual sites or areas as opposed to the whole CERRA. This has resulted in a history of entrenched fragmented and parochial marketing practices. Individual efforts to promote parts of the CERRA have also contributed to the degradation of some parts of the WHS where high volumes of visitors are experienced. Overcrowding in car parks, walking tracks and camping areas has had some impact on land erosion and species protection.

In response to this, key stakeholders in the region adopted a proactive approach to planning for the sustainable development of nature based tourism and ecotourism activities. The Rainforest Way project was the first attempt at a regional collaborative approach to planning for sustainable tourism through the development of a touring route suitable to the sensitive nature of the northern part of the CERRA.

Stakeholders

The CERRA stakeholders are important to the management and marketing of the region, and to maintaining the culture, landscape and values of the area. The immediate stakeholders are those that have been given direct legislated management over the area. These include Environment Australia, NSW NPWS and QP. Other stakeholders identified include local governments, state forestry departments, tourism organizations, industry groups, state government tourism agencies, economic development groups and university research centres as well as the communities surrounding the national parks and reserves. As stated earlier, the high frequency of adjacent land use means that a large number of stakeholders needed to be included in the project.

The touring route

The creation of a touring route is not a new concept in Australia, with a number of successful predecessors including the Great Green Way in Queensland, the Alpine Way, and the Fossickers Way in NSW and Kakadu's Nature Way in the Northern Territory. The concept of a touring route or 'way' is to guide visitors through the most attractive parts of a region and to direct them to lesser known areas. A review of tourism research related to touring routes revealed six key elements constitute the development of a touring route product (Pearce, 1987; Gunn, 1988; Innskeep, 1994). These include gateways, attraction clusters, nodes, road linkages, sensitive area protection, and information.

'Gateways' are major entrances to the region that provide access to the route as well as information about the attractions and services. 'Attraction clusters' are groupings of 'things to see and do' that are attractive to the targeted visitors. They may be themed into loops and trails to provide a themed experience related to the title of the 'way'. 'Nodes' represent communities that provide services, facilities, products and attractions for visitors. Throughout the region small villages provide essential services and cultural attractions and a number of larger centres are ideally located close to rainforests and national parks.

Road linkages are an important consideration in the design of a route, providing access to attractions, linking nodes and gateways. Road quality and surfacing, signage, travel distance and travel times are all important design factors that need to be considered. The region has a good network of roads connecting the various parts of the region. It also has a variety of road types from gravel and dirt to dual-lane highways. These varying conditions provide challenging motoring for visitors, requiring careful route design.

Protecting sensitive natural environments is the fifth element. This is particularly important where World Heritage Sites and national parks form the main attraction for drive tourists. Selective promotion of some areas may enable greater protection of other important areas.

The final element is access to quality information for visitors. This is crucial. It allows tourism and resource managers to influence travelling behaviour and determine the level of visitor satisfaction. Visitor perceptions of satisfaction and safety are important and are often affected by the information provided. Information should be provided at visitor generating regions, destination regions and particularly at gateways and en route.

The strategic approach

In developing a strategic plan for the touring route two issues quickly emerged as being central to its success – cooperation between the numerous stakeholders and leadership towards the achievement of jointly agreed goals and initiatives. Failings in both of these issues later proved to be the prominent cause of the project's delayed implementation. This section describes the strategic approach taken.

The Rainforest Way has its origins in the Nature Based and Ecotourism Plan (Manides Roberts, 1994). The document set the direction for local government tourism managers to establish a project initiating a strategic plan for the design and implementation of a touring route. The process to develop the plan followed an approach similar to that of Voyer (1995), using a formal design of missions and objectives, SWOT analysis and strategy development. The SWOT analysis revealed the existence of numerous research documents describing touring patterns and tourist markets as well as current tourism and natural resource management plans. Consequently, the strategic plan was prepared within the framework of a number of other planning documents like the National Ecotourism Strategy (Commonwealth Department of Tourism, 1994) as well as State and regional government ecotourism plans.

The strategy provided an action plan for the progression of the next stages of the project's development, inviting participation and commitment from all levels of government and from other important stakeholders such as adjoining local government authorities. The plan required seed-funding for the initial management and marketing phases only – later to become a self-funded operation drawing on its beneficiaries for future marketing and management funds. The key phases of the project have been outlined as shown in Figure 20.3.

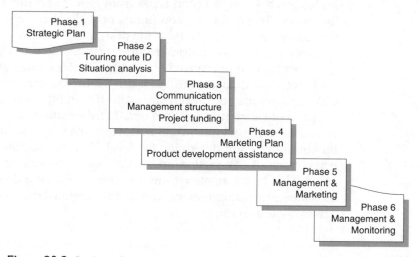

Figure 20.3 Project phases

The strategic plan provided common objectives and set the path for further cooperative action towards the development of the Rainforest Ways. The common agreement to these objectives by all stakeholders was a feat in itself. There had been little previous cooperative planning between tourism and resource managers and virtually no cooperative activity across State borders. The sign-off on the strategic plan and the commitment of so many stakeholders was a significant milestone for the project.

The project objectives were as follows:

- identify potential markets
- identify appropriate high quality products that satisfy visitor needs
- identify appropriate marketing themes that will encourage greater visitation and extended length of stay
- determine and map an appropriate primary touring route through the hinterland of Northern Rivers NSW and South-East Queensland (SEQ)
- determine and map a series of associated loops and trails that will enhance visitor experiences and provide benefits for regional operators
- develop and implement a marketing plan that will maximize the potential of the primary route and the loops and trails
- develop and implement a management committee to oversee the efficient implementation of the marketing plan and other management initiatives such as sourcing funding.

Barriers to progress

The development of the Rainforest Way slowed during Phase 4 – developing marketing and product development plans. In retrospect, this is likely to be a result of unresolved issues from Phase 3, where numerous barriers to progress emerged. The key barriers related to the management structure, project leadership and the collaborative implementation of the plan, as well as to legitimizing the touring route to its original vision. These barriers are described further below.

Management structure and leadership

The strategic plan called for the appointment of a project manager to further the project and funding was sourced from the stakeholders and from the NSW State government. The Northern Rivers Nature Tourism Taskforce (NTTF), who had guided the initial stages, handed over the project management to the regional tourism marketing body and an independently elected Rainforest Way Executive Committee (RWEC) managed the implementation of the project. The committee employed consultants as the project managers and a series of conflicts emerged. The consultants had previous experience with touring route development, but were not based in this region. Some stakeholders saw this as a weakness. They questioned the consultants' processes, recommendations, lack of consultation with the local communities and businesses and lack of understanding of local conditions. Concern was expressed about deviations from the original brief, with strategies not referred to or included in new planning initiatives. Despite these barriers, the consultants pushed forward with the development of marketing and product plans.

A major barrier to progress has been noted in the lack of individual or political leadership of the project. The consultants continue to facilitate the process of marketing and product development, however, they often receive their direction from several different stakeholders – not from one leader – be it person or organization. This can create confusion and a lack of cohesion towards previously established goals.

The consultants highlighted a lack of support for the name and branding *Rainforest Way*. It was not clear whose views were being presented. The reduction of the *Rainforest Way* to a number of smaller loops and trails became the solution to overcoming signage and product development issues. However, this met with strong opposition from several key stakeholders, again citing this as a deviation from the vision and objectives of Phase 1 of the project.

Final documents submitted by the consultants focused on NSW with reduced input from Queensland partners. This destabilized stakeholder relationships and trust diminished and frustration rose while prolonging the process.

Product design process

The challenging tourism policy environments can create barriers to success. Legislative road authorities' policies in both States have clear rules regarding the type of road that can be named a 'way'. There is not a clearly defined start and end point to the *Rainforest Way* (see Figure 20.2). In fact, most existing tourism products and services representing the themes of arts, culture, agriculture, heritage and nature based recreation are not directly accessed along the route, but by loops and trails off the Way. This means that road authorities would not construct signage along the roads legitimizing it as a 'touring route'. They expressed reluctance to adopt the title in their promotional or operational budgets or policies.

The collaborative effort to design and implement the touring route was challenged in the areas of signage for the route. Further tension points appeared with local buy-in by tourism enterprises as well as communication and consultation with stakeholders and the wider community.

Facilitators to progress

While several barriers remain to be overcome, many facilitators have emerged to provide support for the project. The efforts of some stakeholders to lobby various government agencies to include the *Rainforest Way* into higher level tourism plans has been successful, with Tourism New South Wales (TNSW) and Tourism Queensland (TQ) including the route in their five year plans. Support from resource managers such as Environment Australia, NPWS and QP have encouraged the development of the Way, including the project in their own planning documents. Continued commitment from the project's initiators maintains the theme and integrity of the whole project as they monitor its progress.

Implications

The successful implementation of the Rainforest Way will have significant implications for many stakeholders. Importantly, the function of directing, educating and assisting visitors in their visit to CERRA amenities is of high priority. As more visitors are drawn to the natural beauty, pristine landscapes and ambience of the WHS the implementation of tourist routes and their respective visitor amenities and services become increasingly important to managing the resources. Putting an effective touring route in place spreads tourism benefits to the wider regional community.

The protection of WHS within national parks and reserves makes it essential for resource managers and tourism managers to work collaboratively. Unplanned tourist development will contribute to the degradation of resources. Some high visitation areas already show signs of resource degradation which will continue if joint management of these areas is not achieved.

The implications for the success of this project go beyond the success of the Rainforest Way. Successful cooperative activity sets a precedent for further cooperative projects aimed at resource management in this region, but also as a model for other regions in Australia.

Conclusions

The development of the *Rainforest Way – the ways to the rainforests* continues. No doubt it will evolve over the next few years. This is occurring at many levels – from the ground swell of industry support, from the many small tourism operators in the region who can see the benefits of the product and collaborative marketing options, as well as from governments who have invested in the success of the project and have included the project in their long-term strategies. The WH Sites are well protected by the management policies of NPWS and QP. They have active input into the product development process.

Cooperation by resource managers with the tourism industries and local communities has proven to be essential to the protection of the WHS. It is more essential where the WHS themselves are geographically spread across a vast land area with various adjacent land uses and numerous communities living in close proximity to the sites.

The continued development of the Rainforest Way's marketing strategy requires resolution of some key issues and the removal of barriers. Paramount is the resolution of leadership and the legitimization of the product in the eyes of the road authorities. Whether an individual advocate, community champion, or effective organizational structure is best suited to progress the initiative in the best interests of stakeholders remains to be seen.

References

Centre for Regional Tourism Research (2001) *The Rainforest Way Strategic Plan*. Ballina: NR Nature Tourism Taskforce.

Commonwealth Department of Tourism (1994) *National Ecotourism Strategy*. Canberra: Australian Government Publishing Service.

Commonwealth Department of Heritage (2000) *World Heritage Central Eastern Rainforest Reserves of Australia Strategic Overview for Management*. Canberra: Department of the Environment and Heritage, Australian Government Publishing Service.

Gunn, C. (1988) *Tourism Planning*, 2nd edn. New York: Taylor & Francis.

Innskeep, E. (1994) *National and Regional Tourism Planning*. London: Routledge.

Manides Roberts (1994) *Nature-based and Ecotourism Plan*. Ballina: Northern Rivers Regional Development Board.

Pearce, P. (1987) *Tourism Today: A Geographical Analysis*. New York: Longman.

Voyer, J. (1995) Strategy design and planning. In Mintzberg, H., Quinn, J.B. and Voyer, J. (eds) *The Strategy Process*. New Jersey: Prentice Hall.

Questions

1 Who were the key stakeholders in the preparation and implementation of this WHS touring route?

2 Discuss some barriers to the effective design, management and marketing of such a product.

3 Suggest policy and planning resource management mechanisms you have read of that could be applied to such a project.

Conclusions

At the outset, the aim of this text was to combine the issues raised via academic debate and research, with the more practical and applied results from individual properties and those involved in their management. It is hoped that this has been achieved through the eleven themed chapters in Parts One to Four and the nine case studies featured in Part Five. With over 800 sites currently inscribed on the World Heritage List spread widely among States Parties, it was always going to be impossible for the text to include reference to every site. However, the text has tried to deliver a representative overview of the management issues facing the many cultural, natural and mixed sites inscribed on the WHL with a particular focus on the need to balance the two predominant activities – conservation and tourism. Although conservation, preservation and protection may have historically been the principal drivers for inscription, more recent trends suggest that the entire process is becoming more political, with motivations for nation building, national identity, and an eagerness to tap into the economic benefits to be derived from tourism at sites, becoming more prominent. However, the extent to which WHS status does in fact lead to increasing visitor levels from tourists remains somewhat vague.

As a number of chapters quite correctly stated, there remains insufficient evidence to date and a paucity of contemporary research that explains and explores this issue fully. The diversity of sites and varying resource levels, their location in developing or developed countries, expertise of staff and the local political context all contribute to making general findings inappropriate to many sites. Perhaps the biggest challenges that remain vis-à-vis the management of WHS is the need to improve the collection of data and provision of information upon which 'informed' decisions can be made. This issue was first raised in Chapter 2 where the inadequate monitoring and evaluation of visitor numbers was highlighted as a principal impediment to researchers wishing to gauge the impact of WHS status on visitor numbers. The point was made that, even in Australia, which benefits from a strong research culture and infrastructure, past data on visitor numbers and origins are generally poor with only broad trends able to be tracked. With regard to future research needs, the publication by Pedersen (2002) recommends that future research should focus on the classification of tourists according to their motivations, behaviours and desired experiences, with additional research advocated to determine the real volume and rate of growth of cultural tourism. There is also the view that tourists increasingly want 'real' experiences with other cultures and lifestyles with tourists in general seeking more active and educational holidays and visits to protected areas. Pressure on the tourism industry to take more responsibility for sustainable development is therefore substantial, with an overwhelming responsibility to protect its core asset, the environment.

Tourism aside, although the WHL has achieved significant global success and the WHS status is perceived to be a highly appreciated accolade, the future of the WHL is uncertain as discussed in Chapters 10 and 11. Chapter 10 was first to highlight the fact that a dangerous gap is increasingly evident between the goal and the evolving reality stemming from the WHL's implementation, with the national agenda tending to dominate the wider international domain. Ashworth and van der Aa rightly stated that while the rhetoric is global, the action is local, with inscription now a compromise reaction among national governments to national nominations and interests. In reality, the spatial imbalance has also grown – particularly in Europe – in that ratification of the Convention by a number of Central and Eastern European States Parties from the mid-1990s has led to many European nations being particularly proactive in seeking new opportunities.

Although gradual change in the balance of the WHL is evident via implementation of the Global Strategy (1994), worries remain over the third challenge, the potential negative consequences of its indefinite expansion. It is the view of the editors that the most likely future of the WHL is that it will continue expanding, never to be 'complete' and that more sophisticated and rigorous measures to get sites listed are needed to ensure its credibility and representativeness. To conclude this text, attention is drawn back to Chapter 11 and some of the issues identified as requiring specific attention in the years to come. These can be summarized as follows:

1 Tourism will acquire greater significance in the process of inscription with an even greater need for those managing the process to maintain the balance between heritage conservation and the development of tourism opportunities. The planning for tourism and management of visitors ought to be a central feature of future plans, with suitable visitor management techniques proposed that maintain a suitable balance between guaranteeing accessibility and preserving authenticity.

2 Those managing WHS need to understand fully what visitor groups frequent the site, their patterns of behaviour and the trends in that market that are likely to make visitation to such sites more or less popular in the years ahead. One also needs to keep

abreast of the varying, and often continuing, expansion of motivations for visiting sites.

3 For many sites, endorsement by UNESCO represents a significant
   means by which differentiation can be achieved. Tourism is a highly
   competitive phenomenon locally, regionally, nationally and internationally, so any means by which individual sites or destinations
   are able to seek additional points of differentiation are welcomed
   with open arms. Inscription brings with it a mark of externally
   recognized quality which is increasingly becoming an integral part
   of site or destination marketing campaigns.

4 If expansion of the WHL continues apace, saturation is likely to
   occur at some point in the future. Overexposure of the World
   Heritage 'brand' is likely to dilute the benefits to be derived from
   such a quality 'trademark' with the source of differentiation achieved
   through brand recognition no longer carrying influence in the
   market.

5 To date, there are too many instances of misuse and misinterpretation of World Heritage status despite operational guidelines provided by UNESCO. For consistent use of the 'brand' to be
   achieved, significant resources need to be made available – an
   unlikely event in many parts of the world.

6 There is a real need to manage stakeholders more effectively at
   sites and minimize the potential for stakeholder conflict.

7 A number of sites have yet to capture fully the economic benefits
   to be derived from tourism. Accepting that tourism is to remain a
   central component of World Heritage, more directed efforts are
   required in the future for sites to reduce leakages and improve
   economic benefits to be derived from tourism and to the local
   community.

8 Managing security and gauging the impact of security on travel
   patterns is fundamental to all attractions, but particularly WHS,
   where they are a magnet for visitors. Sites need to be fully aware
   of changing patterns of demography and leisure trends among
   their key markets and the principal sources of competition. The
   migration to 'destination' style attractions is significant in that
   those WHS that have around them a critical mass of tourist provision are likely to be those that succeed in the longer term. Clearly,
   the wider destination needs to be considered in its entirety.

9 Not only do many World Heritage Sites require more effective
   packaging but more innovative approaches to the development of
   World Heritage trails, cross-border initiatives and collaboration
   with other destination stakeholders need to be developed to maximize the benefits to be derived from tourism.

Clearly, more research – and especially the collection, analysis and
reporting of data at the micro 'Site' level – is necessary to underpin

the above issues and for sound judgements to be made and effective strategies developed and implemented. With the constant expansion of the WHL, the need for more research output becomes critical if the management of World Heritage is to move forward and make the most of the tourism potential that exists; both now and in the future.

References

Pedersen, A. (2002) *Managing Tourism at World Heritage Sites: A Practical Manual for World Heritage Site Managers*. Paris: UNESCO.

World Heritage Committee (1994) Expert meeting on the Global Strategy and thematic studies for a representative World Heritage List, UNESCO Headquarters, 20–22 June 1994. http://whc. unesco.org/archive/global94.htm (accessed 14 March 2005).

Index